OBEDIENCE AND REVOLT

Volume 22, Sage Library of Social Research

SAGE LIBRARY OF SOCIAL RESEARCH

Obedience and Revolt

French Behavior Toward Authority

WILLIAM R. SCHONFELD

Foreword by STANLEY HOFFMANN

Preface by TED ROBERT GURR

Volume 22
SAGE LIBRARY OF
SOCIAL RESEARCH

 **SAGE PUBLICATIONS**   Beverly Hills   London

For information address:

SAGE PUBLICATIONS, INC.
275 South Beverly Drive
Beverly Hills, California 90212

SAGE PUBLICATIONS LTD
St George's House / 44 Hatton Garden
London EC1N 8ER

Printed in the United States of America

Library of Congress Cataloging in Publication Data

Schonfeld, William R   1942-
        Obedience and revolt.

        (Sage library of social research ; v. 22)
        Includes index.
        1. School management and organization—France.
2. France—Politics and government.   3. Authority.
4. Socialization.   I. Title.
LB2909.S35   301.5'92   75-23616
ISBN 0-8039-0515-7
ISBN 0-8039-0516-5 pbk.

FIRST PRINTING

TABLE OF CONTENTS

for

Elena

FOREWORD

The study of political behavior, which has been the chief concern of political scientists during the last thirty years, has received new impetus from the analysis of authority relations in different societies. Why it has taken social scientists so long to discover that the way in which individuals or groups relate to one another in hierarchical situations is of considerable importance in shaping not only what can be called "the political system," but also the polity as a whole, is something of a mystery. After all, whether we deal with attitudes of voters toward their representatives or with the ways in which officials deal with the electorate, political attitudes are an expression of authority relations in a given society. In turn, these relations are shaped by the institutions of the society and particularly by the political institutions.

Both these and the authority relations which they mold reflect certain basic values which, on the whole, support the society and are the last to change when transient political institutions or socioeconomic conditions alter.

Alexis de Tocqueville, in *The Old Régime and the French Revolution*, quite systematically analyzed the complex set of relations among political institutions, classes, and attitudes toward authority. Yet these fundamental insights virtually vanished from the study of politics for almost a century thereafter. It has been only in the last ten years that new and considerable progress has been made in this field. In France, the work of Michel Crozier has given an entirely new dimension to the understanding of contemporary French society. His two books, *The Bureaucratic Phenomenon* and *The Stalled Society* have been accepted as classics with which all subsequent students of French political behavior have had to come to terms. In the United States, Professor Harry Eckstein of Princeton has examined the relation between authority patterns in society and the political system in order to explain the conditions of a stable democracy.

To this literature, Professor Schonfeld, a young specialist on France, contributes the idea of studying authority relations in one of the basic institutions of their origin: the school system. Two things are remarkable about this enterprise.

The first is that nobody has thought of it before. This is partly due to the tendency of political scientists to neglect the political significance of the educational system, despite everything that political theorists have been writing for centuries about the importance of education in shaping the citizenry. It is also due to the extreme difficulty an outsider encounters in trying to penetrate the French school system in order to study it. The fact that Professor Schonfeld succeeded in observing this fascinating and fluctuating universe not only attests to his powers of persuasion and skill, but also shows that modern social science research is at last becoming much more widely accepted in a society in which empirical investigation on contemporary and touchy subjects is a recent phenomenon.

Second, his findings are of considerable interest to any student of French affairs. Political scientists who have been writing about political attitudes either at the national level or in their discussions of local government will find Professor Schonfeld's hypotheses about the evolution and basic patterns of authority relations in French society extremely stimulating and provocative.

Moreover, Professor Schonfeld was in France at the time of the May 1968 explosion, the consideration of which is compulsory for social scientists working on contemporary France. Indeed, it can almost be said that every social scientist with a theory about France has found in those fantastic events a confirmation of a favorite thesis—but Professor Schonfeld has done far more than merely ransack the events of May for vindication. He has studied what occurred at the Ecole Nationale d'Administration, the *Grande Ecole,* which trains France's top civil servants, and is thus able to give us an excellent sketch of the importance of that school in French politics and society. This provides a way of testing his own basic hypotheses about authority relations, held up against his interpretation of the meaning of the "great explosion."

Students of French authority, many of whom are Crozier's associates, have begun to modify the master's model on various points. Professor Schonfeld's work also disagrees in some ways with Michel Crozier's model of French authority relations. How profound these disagreements are, each reader will have to judge individually. Two things are clear: One is that Crozier's work remains at the center of all these controversies; the other is that our understanding will progress and deepen as more and more students add qualifications, reservations, and generalizations to Crozier's original notions. Certainly the present book, which is rigorous and meticulous, is a major addition to this literature. It will therefore occupy an important place in the imposing body of works that study French authority relations in various institutions of society.

Stanley Hoffmann

PREFACE

William R. Schonfeld's study of authority focuses on France, and on particular French social institutions, but contributes much more than another "country study" to comparative analysis. Over the years a number of prominent political scientists have urged us to look more closely at power and authority outside the state: Sir George E.G. Catlin in the 1930s, Robert A. Dahl and Charles E. Lindblom in the 1950s, and Harry Eckstein in the 1960s and 1970s.[1] This study of authority relations in French secondary and higher education is one of the very few detailed empirical studies in this critical but neglected domain. Moreover, Professor Schonfeld has applied to it a rationale and set of concepts and methods that are applicable to the comparative analysis of authority relations in virtually any kind of social institution, and in diverse cultures.

This study does more than demonstrate the feasibility and intrinsic interest of analyzing patterns of authority outside government. One justification offered for such studies is that people's experience of authority in the family, school, workplace, and voluntary associations conditions them to their roles as citizens and rulers. There is a parallel theme in the literature on political socialization, to the effect that children's early interactions with family and school authorities set the boundaries within which adult socialization and political participation later occur. Professor Schonfeld's study is a major contribution to the limited empirical evidence for these contentions. It demonstrates the "political" nature of authority interactions in French schools and shows persuasively how the secondary school experience molds French citizens' basic orientations to authority both in higher education and in national politics.

Finally, Professor Schonfeld offers an empirical and theoretical contribution to the study of rebellion. French students evidently learn distinct modes of relating to authority. The author specifies the conditions which activate each orientation and tests the plausibility of his explanation by showing how it accounts for both the timing and sequence of events in the "revolution" of May 1968. The theory challenges many conventional interpretations of French political behavior, and, at a more general level, it provides a complement, perhaps an alternative, to theories of violence which emphasize such factors as frustration and ideological conversion.

A decade ago, a small group of us—graduate students and faculty at Princeton University—joined in the Workshop in Comparative Politics, organized by Harry Eckstein, to carry out comparative research on authority relations. Professor Schonfeld was a charter member of the Workshop, and his study exemplifies our common interests and methodological dispositions. Others more expert than I can judge the contribution of his study to the specialist's understanding of French politics. For me, it offers telling evidence of the fruitfulness of authority patterns as a renewed focus of comparative political inquiry.

Ted Robert Gurr

NOTE

1. See Harry Eckstein and Ted Robert Gurr, *Patterns of Authority: A Structural Basis for Political Inquiry* (New York: John Wiley, 1975), Chapter 1.

ACKNOWLEDGEMENTS

Without the help and support of numerous people, I could have never researched or written this book. My greatest practical debt is to the students, teachers, and administrators in the secondary schools and the National School of Administration. They gave generously of their time, were extraordinarily tolerant of my probings into their everyday lives, and provided a great deal of intellectual stimulation. Perhaps most importantly, they made fieldwork enjoyable.

Academics on both sides of the Atlantic have made sizable contributions to my work. Access to a random sample of secondary schools was only obtained as a result of the tireless efforts of François Bourricaud. I discussed my ideas for research with Michel Crozier and also benefited from his comments on a draft version of this book. Stanley Hoffmann provided valuable criticism and valued support. W. Lance Bennett, more than anyone else, played a key role during the final stage of writing; his suggestions and friendship were crucial. I would also like to thank Lewis A. Froman, Jr.; Serge Hurtig; Viviane Isambert-Jamati; Marcel Merle; Marie-France Toinet; Gordon Wright; Laurence Wylie; and Jacques Zwirn.

This book began as a doctoral dissertation at Princeton University, where I was very fortunate to be a "charter member" of the Workshop in Comparative Politics. Organized and directed by Harry Eckstein, the Workshop was an intellectual community of graduate students and faculty members intrigued by the nature of authority relations and democratic stability. I benefited enormously from my participation in this collective body, drawing upon its general facilities and project design and receiving constant, valuable and supportive criticism of my ideas during the first major stage of research and writing.[1]

At Princeton, I found three intellectual mentors: Harry Eckstein, Ted Robert Gurr, and A. Nicholas Wahl. Since the planning stages of my research through the completion of this book, they have provided support and encouragement. In addition, their constructive and detailed critiques of many drafts of these chapters are largely responsible for whatever merit and rigor my research may have. Their help and friendship has been of enormous value. Within this group, my greatest intellectual debt is to Harry Eckstein. From him, more than from anyone else, I learned what political science is (or perhaps should be) all about, but, even more crucially, he taught me how to cogently disagree with his ideas.

The School of Social Sciences at the University of California (Irvine) has offered a cooperative, congenial, and stimulating intellectual environment for completing this book. The staff, including Mary Rezich, Pat Montgomery and in particular Gayle Hill (who typed the bulk of the manuscript), have helped me in an endless number of ways.

My research in France was chiefly financed by a graduate fellowship from the Danforth Foundation. Supplementary support came from the Workshop in Comparative Politics.

Sara McCune and Rhoda Blecker have been the perfect publisher and editor; they have permitted me to do what I thought best.

Last, but certainly not least, I want to thank my wife, Elena Beortegui Schonfeld. Her pragmatism, common sense, and constant support carried me over innumerable intellectual and practical obstacles which were encountered in doing this study. In addition, her willingness to directly participate in the field research by doing classroom observation and helping to administer questionnaires in the secondary schools, and the insights which she gained from this experience and passed on to me, were of inestimable value. I dedicate this book to her.

W.R.S.

NOTE

1. The members of the Workshop were: Gurston Dacks, Harry Eckstein, Francisco Ferraz, Robert Friedman, Philip Goldman, Ted Gurr, Norman Jacknis, Richard Johnston, Stein Larsen, Robert Laurenty, Muriel McClelland, Craig MacLean, Martha Mendelsohn, Donald Newman, Joel Prager, Rafael Rivas, Ronald Rogowski, Susanne Mueller Tufte, Lois Wasserspring, Susan and the late Peter Woodward, Alan Zuckerman, and Ronald Zuckerman. I particularly gained many insights from discussions with my friend Philip Goldman.

INTRODUCTION

This book seeks to create an understanding of how the French *behave* toward authority. Attitudes, beliefs, conceptions, and opinions are not the focal points of inquiry. Rather, I have directed my efforts toward describing what people actually do when control is exercised over them and toward locating the conditions responsible for changes from one form of interaction with superordinates to another. On the basis of empirical case studies conducted in two distinct types of social units—an agency of general, mass socialization (secondary schools) and an agency of elite training and recruitment (the Ecole Nationale d'Administration)—I develop a set of interrelated hypotheses capable of describing and explaining subordinate behavior toward authority. Then this "model"[1] is used to illuminate corresponding aspects of French citizens' behavior toward the national government.

Hence, my main research goals are: (1) to increase understanding of the way in which authority is dealt with by those over whom control is exercised, and (2) to provide insights into a specific nation's political behavior on the basis of a study of its social authority relations. In this context, what is the rationale behind the decisions to study France, secondary schools, and the E.N.A.?

France

Given a prime interest in how people behave toward authority, France is an apt choice for analysis. While, for example, Britain is known for deference, Germany for regimentation and authoritarianism, and the United States for acceptance of self-chosen authority, France is not normally perceived as fitting neatly into any single category of authority relations. To some, the French are individualists opposed to all forms of authority; but to others, the French are seekers of authority and even authoritarianism. Surely, if one were seeking to develop theoretical insights into the way in which people live with authority on the basis of a case study conducted in a single society, it seems wiser to select a nation whose citizens have been viewed as exhibiting diverse and even contradictory tendencies along this dimension than to choose a polity in which there seems to be a coherent pattern (even if that pattern is only vaguely understood).

France was also selected because, despite much study of its political behavior, little understanding of that behavior seems to exist. Observers of French politics and society have usually been struck by the existence of numerous contrasts. This has led to the view of France as a particularly complex society defying generalized explanations.

Even a cursory review of the literature suggests France is a nation of antitheses. The country which invented and sought to put meaning into the phrase *liberté, égalité et fraternité* also gave rise to Napoléon and provided the intellectual basis for "totalitarian democracy" and "fascism." Although long regarded as an ideal-type of political instability, France has one of the most stable administrative systems in existence. Neither the combination of an omnipotent executive and a weak parliament nor that of an impotent executive and a powerful parliament is foreign to France. It has been claimed that the French are inherently opposed to government, and also that they are very dependent upon it. They are "anarchists," and also "authoritarian." They are a people who systematically refuse to cooperate with one another, and yet, during World War II, they had one of the most effective resistance organizations of any nation under German control. France, a nation of small shopkeepers, invented the department store. The French have been regarded as revolutionary and reactionary, progressive and conservative, dynamic and stagnant.

No wonder that so many people have been "in search of France." Nor is it surprising that so many of the scholars who have turned their attention toward this country have warned their readers to beware of the complexity of the phenomenon about to be studied and its resistance to any sort of generalization.[2] The student of government who looks at France, even more than his colleagues, has been prone to bemoan his fate. These lamentations have been stimulated by the large quantities of "data" which he must attempt to assimilate—i.e., the number of political parties, former cabinet holders, elections, constitutional changes, and incidences of civil strife.

The investigator (struck by the complexity of the phenomenon which he seeks to examine) tends to consider his analysis completed once he has described or categorized his special focus of study. Furthermore, when he does attempt to "explain" something, this explanation is usually couched in such specific and concrete terms as to illuminate only a particular event or set of events without increasing comprehension of other phenomena which fall within the same general category. Thus, many scholars have sought to explain why there was a crisis in France in May 1968, but few have generated explanations which are applicable to other incidences of civil strife in France, and, to all intents and purposes, no one has developed an argument which could be placed within the context of a general theory of the occurrence of civil strife. Likewise, much has been written on why a particular cabinet under the Third or Fourth Republic was overthrown, and some scholars have even tried to explain French cabinet instability during a specified historical period, but arguments which might help to explain cabinet instability per se are rare. Finally, when explanations are presented, there is a tendency to use as independent variables ill- or undefined concepts which cannot be readily operationalized—e.g., class consciousness, the actualization of the revolutionary spirit, or the fear of a powerful executive.

Thus, the view of France as a very complex society has affected the style of scholarly research done on the country. But one may wonder whether the caveats about the complexity of French society and its polity provide more information about the frames of mind of scholars attracted to France, about the manner in which this nation has usually been studied, or about the nature of the polity itself. In any case, the assumption that the existence of a large number of antitheses within a politically event-filled society makes it inherently more difficult to understand that society or its politics has no logical foundation.

Of course, all human behavior is complex, and, therefore, any attempt to locate the motor forces behind such behavior is bound to be difficult. Descriptions of uniform and consistent patterns of conduct and thought are probably less intellectually intimidating than descriptions of heterogeneous and contradictory patterns, but the task of the social scientist who seeks to explain why people behave in a uniform way is no less arduous than that of his colleague who seeks to explain inconsistent patterns of behavior.

In fact, the often-noted "complexity" of French life provides the student interested in the bases of French politics with important cues. This advance warning gives him an advantage over unwary colleagues examining more "simple" and "easily understood" societies. In addition, it highlights the need for extreme judiciousness in the selection of phenomena to be examined.

Social Authority Relations

A wise policy would be to select a single variable for intensive study. This variable should logically have the potential to *explain* in large part why political behavior in France has taken the form it has. Harry Eckstein has argued:

Institutions other than governments have political characteristics, at least in one sense: in that they involve authority relations, or patterns of subordination and superordination, among actors. In that sense, families have political characteristics, as do schools, economic structures, voluntary associations, parties, bureaucracies, and military establishments. Strangely enough, no concerted attempts have been made systematically to link non-governmental and governmental authority patterns, except perhaps only in the realm of family sociology. . . . [This] is all the stranger because many well-established types of social theory point to a linkage between different kinds and levels of authority patterns. . . . Besides, to search for such a linkage seemed to be simple common sense. Surely one may expect, even without the support of sophisticated theories, that men's experience with authority in other contexts will, in important ways, condition their attitudes toward and behavior in the national political system.[3]

Hence, for someone seeking a better understanding of the bases of French politics, an empirical investigation into the nature of social authority patterns in that society seemed a potentially valuable means for achieving his goal. And even if in-depth research were to cast doubt on the value of Eckstein's argument, the effort would not be wasted. Failure would have the value of eliminating one plausible explanatory variable from further inquiries. Even if unable to aid in explaining much of French politics, it might prove to be useful for understanding certain important features of French social and/or political life. And a study of social authority patterns, even if found devoid of explanatory power for national politics, would provide a description of a phenomenon significant in and of itself which has not received much intensive study.[4]

However, in the French case, strong evidence already existed to suggest that Eckstein's argument was anything but implausible, chiefly due to the research carried out by Michel Crozier and published in *The Bureaucratic Phenomenon* (Chicago: University of Chicago Press, 1964). Crozier studied two government-owned and -operated organizations. Much of his effort was concentrated on trying to understand the style of human relations, especially authority relations, that were prevalent in these social units. Among other things, he developed a potent tool for explaining why French politics have taken the form they have. His work has opened up a series of new horizons for those interested in French society and politics, and has stimulated numerous scholars by providing them with a series of sharpened insights into the functioning of this "complex" nation.

It might well be asked: If Crozier's work is so valuable, does a need exist for doing more research along similar lines? There is indeed such a need. First, Crozier had no special interest in French political behavior. Rather, he sought to understand the transnational phenomenon of "bureaucracy." As a result, only a small portion of his work was concerned with the French style of politics, leaving many questions unanswered. Second, the social units he examined are not sufficiently representative of the types of organizations within which French citizens function; nor are they crucial in the process of developing an individual's behavior toward authority. Hence, they do not provide the soundest bases for generalizations about the nature of French social authority. Finally, the fact that Crozier's work has been of value should be a stimulant, rather than an obstacle, to further research along similar lines. He has given us a foundation to work with, but a foundation which must be carefully tested so that the defective elements can be removed and strengthened enough 'to support a tall superstructure. Moreover, once the foundation is completed, the edifice upon it must still be constructed. This book is an attempt to further develop and strengthen that foundation.

Secondary Schools and E.N.A.

If social authority relations are to be used to increase understanding of political behavior, more than an impressionistic grasp of the nature of these relationships is necessary. Hence, it was decided to select specific social units on which in-depth empirical research would be carried out.

Research could have been conducted in any number of social units, where subordinates perceive and live with authority on an everyday basis—in schools, in the family, and on the job. However, since the model to be derived from the case studies was to be employed in an attempt to make sense of the general nature of French political behavior, the core case study should have been done in an environment with which virtually all French citizens have had prolonged contact—i.e., an agency of general, mass socialization. Of the three possible choices—family, primary schools, and secondary schools—the last was chosen because, given the desire to use the micro-level to increase understanding of the macro-level, it presented two very important advantages.

Within the family and primary school, authority relations are concentrated and highly "personal," but the modal type of authority relationship between adults in modern societies is dispersed and "impersonal."[5] During early socialization experiences, children are under the supervision of individuals whom they know very well. In the primary school, they function under the control of a single teacher all day long, having no respite from this person's presence and authority. Within the family, the situation is much the same: Although there are, simultaneously, at least two superordinates, the behavior of the child toward one is not without concern to the other—e.g., if the child fails to follow the directives of the mother, it is likely that the father will interfere to support the mother. As a result, pre-secondary school-age children tend to have authority interactions only with superordinates whom they personally know well and with whom they tend to have or may develop affective ties. But, as an adult, an individual plays the role of a subordinate in many social units, and, in most of these, the process of directive-issuing is not concentrated in the hands of one individual or a very limited group of individuals with whom the subordinates have close personal relations. The secondary school experience seems to represent the individual's first encounter with a series of superordinates who directly give orders to subordinates, but who are not, to a large extent because of their number, in an affective relationship with the subordinate.[6]

A second reason for choosing secondary schools over family and primary schools is that the secondary school represents the last point at which all members of French society can be observed in a common institution. If the goal were to study the socialization process—e.g., how people acquire and/or learn appropriate social behavior and attitudes—then it might have been more valuable to study the family or primary schools, since they may play a stronger—and certainly do play a more fundamental—role in the formative process. However, since I sought to locate the already basically formed social individual in his most general shape, the simple fact that contact with institutions of secondary education occurs after the early family and primary school experiences dictated the choice of secondary schools.

To obtain an empirical basis upon which the core findings of the secondary school study could be supplemented, broadened, and tested, I examined the way in which people deal with authority in a distinct type of social unit, an elite recruitment and training agency. The National School of Administration (Ecole Nationale d'Administration—E.N.A.) was selected. The school, in principle, will train virtually all French high-level civil servants; in practice, its alumni already dominate the upper echelons of the administrative sector of the government, even though E.N.A. was only created in the aftermath of World War II.

Two factors suggest that this case study should provide a meaningful test of the secondary school findings. First, E.N.A. explicitly and consciously seeks to prepare its young civil servants for occupying key positions of command and responsibility in the society; the secondary schools are, de facto, oriented toward training individuals how to play subordinate roles, to be the ordinary citizen. On a priori grounds, important leaders may be expected to deal with authority differently than the ordinary person does. Consequently, those being trained for high superordinate positions are not likely to live with authority in the same way as those who effectively are being trained to play subordinate roles. Second, E.N.A. tends to recruit almost exclusively from the upper echelons of the French social hierarchy;[7] in contrast, the social class composition of secondary schools is heterogenous. Both because attitudes and behavior toward authority among members of the upper class have typically been found to differ from those among the members of the lower and middle classes (who are numerically predominant in the secondary schools), and because one environment is relatively homogeneous while the other clearly is not, we may logically expect to find distinct ways of dealing with authority in these two social units.

If, despite these two factors, a single set of interrelated dependent and independent variables can describe and explain the way in which people live with authority, this model should have broader application within French society.

This book is composed of three main sections. Part I focuses on French secondary schools. The behavior of students toward teachers is described in Chapter 1. Then, in Chapter 2, the factors responsible for the development of these behavioral patterns, as well as the conditions which cause a change from one mode of interaction with teachers to another, are analyzed; finally, the pupils' normative orientation toward authority is discussed. (In order to place this analysis in context, readers should be acquainted with the overall structure of French education, and, more specifically, with the secondary school system. Those who are not, should read Appendix A before Part I.)

Part II examines the nature of authority relations between young civil servants being trained at the National School of Administration and their superordinates. Chapter 3 begins with a description of the E.N.A.s' normal behavior toward authority figures. Then the factors responsible for the development of the crisis at the school in May-July 1968, the style of authority relations existing during the crisis, and the factors leading to a resolution of the crisis are examined. Throughout this chapter, I attempt to determine if the descriptive and explanatory concepts developed in the secondary school study might be used to understand what had been observed at the Ecole Nationale d'Administration. (Appendix B fully presents the sources upon which the analysis of E.N.A. is based. In addition, the school's role in French society, its structure, and its program of studies are described.)

Part III synthesizes the case studies and analyzes French politics in these terms. In Chapter 4, the findings presented in Parts I and II are incorporated into a theoretical summary. In other words, the model is explicitly defined in its cross-social-unit sense. Then, in Chapter 5, the model's capacity to illuminate politically relevant phenomena is examined. After a synthetic review of the literature, the model is used to both describe and explain a relatively prolonged sequence of events—the overall nature of behavior toward national political authority since the beginning of the Fourth Republic—and a very short, dense sequence of events—the May crisis of 1968. Finally, in Chapter 6, I consider how my findings develop and modify the view of authority in France developed by Michel Crozier and operationalize a test of the model, specifying data which would refute my argument.

In addition to the three main sections, there is an epilogue in which I speculate on the implications of the research reported in this volume for our general understanding of the nature of authority.

Three Notes on Method

(1) The model of authority relations presented in this book was derived from the secondary school context, tested and further developed in light of the behavior observed at E.N.A., and applied to political authority relations. Before beginning research, I had no idea of what my conclusions would be; I set out lacking both preconceived notions and a well-developed set of hypotheses for testing. The organizational scheme adopted in this book reflects the way in which I worked.

(2) Throughout the forthcoming analysis, *modal* forms of behavior toward authority are described and explained. Deviant individuals as well as variations between subgroups are not subjects of basic concern. Naturally, an examination of such differences is a worthwhile project, but my inquiry is focused at a somewhat more general and abstract level; I have sought to identify what is common to rather heterogeneous groupings and not what distinguishes them.

(3) Each of the defined modes of behavior toward authority and explanatory variables is not only applicable to the specific cases studied, but also potentially locatable in other societies and social units—i.e., none of the model's elements is considered idiosyncratic to France. What seems distinctive is not the presence of particular kinds of behavior toward authority or specific explanatory variables, but rather a special normative structure *combined* with a distinct and limited number of interrelated behavioral patterns linked to specific variables which explain when one or the other of these behavioral modes will occur. In other words, I do not treat France as an "extraterrestrial polity"; my goal is to come to grips with France, not with any purely unique "Frenchness."

W.R.S.

NOTES

1. The term "model" refers to the set of interconnected hypotheses derived from the case studies.

2. One of the earliest "warnings" came from J.E.C. Bodley, who referred to France as "the most complex product of civilization on the face of the globe" (p. 5) and "the last country in the world about which it is possible to generalize" (pp. 3-4). (*France* [London: Macmillan and Co., 1907])

3. Harry Eckstein, "Proposal for a 'Workshop' on the Social Bases of Stable Rule," mimeo, 1965, pp. 10-11. See also Harry Eckstein, "Authority Patterns: A Structural

Basis for Political Inquiry," *American Political Science Review* 67 (December 1973), pp. 1142-1161.

4. Many scholars use the word "authority." Attitudes and opinions about authority in social settings are studied, but behavior is, to all intents and purposes, ignored. Some examples of the work which has been done in the French context are: François Bourricaud, *Esquisse d'une théorie de l'autorité* (Paris: Plon, 1969); Robert Gloton, *L'autorité à la dérive*... (Paris: Casterman, 1974); Annick Percheron, "La conception de l'autorité chez les enfants," *Revue française de science politique* 21 (February 1971), pp. 103-128; and Gérard Vincent, *Le peuple lycéen: Enquête sur les élèves de l'enseignement secondaire* (Paris: Gallimard, 1974), esp. Chapters II-IV in Part Two, pp. 111-175.

5. This point is made in a somewhat different form by Richard E. Dawson and Kenneth Prewitt in *Political Socialization* (Boston: Little, Brown, 1969), p. 90.

6. A study of the family would have presented a second disadvantage, besides the "personalism" of its relationships. Work on this social unit would have been entirely dependent on questionnaires and/or interviews, because it is not possible to "observe" over prolonged periods of time the authority relations in a series of families. Thus, the analysis would have to be based solely on the participants' perceptions, and the researcher would have no way of judging the degree of distortion between the actual and the perceived practices. Obviously, this is not meant to suggest anything more than a cautionary note if a study of family patterns were to be undertaken.

7. See: Jean-François Kesler, "Les anciens élèves de L'Ecole Nationale d'Administration," *Revue française de science politique* 14, no. 2 (April 1964), pp. 250-252; and Ezra N. Suleiman, *Politics, Power, and Bureaucracy in France* (Princeton: Princeton University Press, 1974), pp. 52-63.

PART I

AUTHORITY IN FRENCH SECONDARY SCHOOLS

The educational system of a given society reflects that society's social system, and at the same time it is the main force perpetuating it. It may be perceived as the most powerful means of social control to which the individual must submit, and as one of the most universal models of social relationships to which they refer later [p. 238].

The secondary schools... still remain the backbone of the French educational system [pp. 241-242].

Michel Crozier, *The Bureaucratic Phenomenon*

The Empirical Basis of the Case Study

A stratified sample of secondary schools, with the particular institutions in each stratum being randomly chosen, forms the basis of this case study. Thirteen schools were examined, all of them being part of the public educational system and all of them being either a *lycée* (the elite educational institution), *collége d'enseignement général*–C.E.G.–(a form of postgraduate primary school education), or *collége d'enseignement secondaire*–C.E.S.– (an institution comparable to the British comprehensive schools). Lycées have tended to offer a full secondary education–i.e., the first *cycle* of four years as well as the second (three-year) cycle. Many lycées are presently only offering a second-cycle program. The C.E.G. and C.E.S. only offer the first cycle. Since all the teachers, students, and classes in the thirteen schools could not be studied, research was limited to pupils in two grades in the first cycle (cinquiéme–the second year of secondary education with mostly twelve- and thirteen-year-old students–and troisiéme–the fourth year of secondary education with mostly fourteen- and fifteen-year-old students) and two grades in the second cycle (seconde–the fifth year of secondary education with mostly fifteen- and sixteen-year-old students–and terminale–the seventh and last year of secondary education with mostly seventeen- and eighteen-year-old students.)[1]

My goal was to develop a model of behavior toward authority applicable to all major segments of French society. Consequently, the sample had to be as diverse as possible, for only then could I reasonably expect that hypotheses supported in the distinct settings which were visited would also be tenable in general. The thirteen schools are located in three different regions: Paris and its suburbs, one department in northern France, and two in southern France. One of the non-Parisian regions is highly industrialized;

the other is oriented toward agriculture. One tends to be politically to the right; the other, to the left. Beyond the geographical, political, and urban-rural variations, the institutional sample is extremely heterogeneous, including schools dispensing a very high quality of secondary education and those transmitting only elementals to their pupils. Certain teaching staffs are extremely competent; others leave much to be desired. Many of the institutions are traditional; others are more progressive; one is experimental. Included are Parisian schools and institutions in towns with a population of less than 5,000. Some schools cater to students coming from the wealthiest segments of French society; others deal with the sons of workers or farmers; still others have a rather heterogeneous student body. Some of the institutions are restricted to boys, others to girls, and still others are coeducational. Some have long histories; others are newly established. Some are housed in dilapidated or ancient structures; others have all the modern conveniences an industrialized society can offer.[2]

Within each school, data were gathered through casual conversation with pupils, teachers, and administrators, extensive classroom observation (approximately 200 hours), structured interviews with teachers (82), and student questionnaires (1,901 filled out by pupils in 69 different classes). In the following analysis of authority relations in French secondary schools, I draw most extensively on observation to capture pupils' behavioral patterns.[3] Questionnaire results are employed to get at norms and perceptions.[4]

Research was carried out from January through May 1968.

NOTES

1. For a description of the complex system of French secondary education, see Appendix A.

2. For a complete description of the sampling procedure, see Appendix A.

3. For a more extensive statistical analysis of the questionnaire findings, see William R. Schonfeld, "Youth and Authority in France: A Study of Secondary Schools" (Sage Professional Papers in Comparative Politics, 1971).

4. Given my research goals, the attitudes, opinions, and "world views" of secondary school students have been largely ignored. There is, however, an extensive literature dealing with these phenomena. See, for example: Jacques Duquesne, *Les 13-16 ans* (Paris: Bernard Grasset, 1973); Georges Fouchard and Maurice Davranche, *Enquête sur*

la jeunesse (Paris: Gallimard, 1968); Pierre and Marguerite Lambert, *Des jeunes parlent* . . . : *Une enquête de "Clair Foyer" sur les relations filles-garçons* (Paris: Les éditions ouvrières, 1968); Annick Percheron, *L'univers politique des enfants* (Paris: Armand Colin, Travaux et Recherches de Science Politique, Fondation Nationale des Sciences Politique, 1974); Annick Percheron and Françoise Subileau, "Mode de transmission des valeurs politiques et sociales chez les pré-adolescents," *Revue Française de Science Politique* 24 (February 1974 and April 1974), pp. 33-51 and 189-213; Charles Roig and Françoise Billon-Grand, *La socialisation politique des enfants: Contribution à l'étude de la formation des attitudes politiques en France* (Paris: Armand Colin, Cahiers de la Fondation National des Sciences Politiques, 1968); Gérard Vincent, *Les lycéens* (Paris: Armand Colin, Cahiers de la Fondation Nationale des Sciences Politiques, 1971); and Gérard Vincent, *Le peuple lycéen: Enquête sur les élèves de l'enseignement secondaire* (Paris: Gallimard, 1974).

Chapter 1

BEHAVIOR TOWARD AUTHORITY IN FRENCH SECONDARY SCHOOLS: A DESCRIPTION

The French secondary school student lives in a world where ambiguity and uncertainty seem minimal. What to do, how to do it, and how to behave in the classroom are questions for which there are well-defined responses. These responses, however, are not internally derived but rather are imposed or are perceived of as being imposed upon oneself by others. Thus, avoidance of the anxiety which stems from inhabiting an uncertain universe appears to be "paid for" in terms of a rather consistent feeling of being constrained. Like the proverbial bureaucrat or the modern worker in an assembly-line factory, pupils possess finely delimited models of what should be done and how they should do it. These models have been transmitted to them by outside authorities, who will also provide the appropriate cues to activate the relevant repertoire of behaviors for any given concrete situation.

I am not suggesting that there is a single, modal type of authority relationship between pupils and teachers. Quite to the contrary, there are three distinct, but associated, styles of interaction, but all involve constraint and avoid uncertainty.

During the early years of French secondary education, two modes of interaction exist. The usual relationship is rather "authoritarian." Teachers issue numerous precise and detailed directives defining what should be done and how it should be done. Consequently, students know *exactly* what is expected of them before undertaking any task. The pupils respond to this very high level of explicit directiveness with total compliance. This mode of student-teacher relationship will be labeled *authority-laden.*[1] With between twenty and twenty-five percent of their teachers, the pupils establish a very different kind of relationship; they are totally insubordinate, at least part of the time. Under peer direction, students pay little attention to their teachers' instructions; in fact, they systematically take a stance of opposition. The French word employed to describe this mode of organized classroom insubordination is *chahut.*

As the pupils grow older and go into the upper grades, the authority-laden and chahut modes continue to persist, but they are no longer either the dominant or the exclusive pattern of student-teacher interaction. Rather, in most classrooms, the behavior of the pupils is as regimented as it was under the authority-laden mode, but, in contradistinction, the number of specific and detailed directives issued by teachers is minimal. Students obey a set of directives which are, in fact, internal to them (which they have learned from their previous teachers), but which they perceive, nevertheless, to be directives—the prescriptions of their actual teachers—rather than their own norms. To be more concrete, the older pupils normally tend to act as if their behavior were being precisely circumscribed by their teachers and perceive their teachers as giving them numerous precise and detailed directives, even though the teachers rarely tell the students what to do. This form of compliant behavior is analytically and concretely distinct from habit, custom, or simple internalization.

The Younger Pupils

THE AUTHORITY-LADEN MODE

The authority-laden mode seems to be the one most usually associated with the French educational system, even though its component elements have never been precisely defined. This form of interaction is defined in terms of the behavior of teachers and students on four basic dimensions of authority: directiveness (directive-issuing tendencies of teachers), compliance (extent to which students obey teachers), participation (students' tendencies to attempt to influence teachers), and deportment (ways in which students and teachers observably treat each other).[2]

Within this mode, the students' activities are very heavily "covered."[3] Theoretically, coverage can be applied to four distinct domains. "Task coverage" refers to prescriptions defining the activities which are to be undertaken by subordinates. In the school context, this would include determination of curricula, books to be used, sections to be studied, and homework to be done. "Instrumental coverage" refers to directives on how to do the tasks which have already been defined. Orders to pupils on the type of paper, writing instruments, and format to be used in their written work, as well as directives on how to study or give a classroom presentation, are examples. "Comportmental coverage" refers to prescriptions, beyond those which form part of the task, about how to behave within the unit. Directives regarding entering the classroom, talking with one's neighbors, or smoking in school fall within this category. Finally, "ideological coverage" refers to directives attempting to control the ideas and attitudes held by the members of the unit. Such control may be exerted over unit-based attitudes—e.g., toward other members of the unit or the unit itself—or general philosophical, religious, or political opinions. A concrete example of ideological coverage would be a teacher's directives specifying the interpretation a student should make of a historical event upon which divergent defensible views exist.

Authority-laden pupil-teacher interactions are in the first place characterized by a great deal of explicit behavioral coverage (i.e., task, instrumental, and comportmental coverage). As a result of the unit's demands on the children's time, this high level of attempted coverage has a great deal of significance. The actual time French students spend in class is comparable to that spent by American pupils. Approximately twenty-seven hours each week are taken up by courses.[4] But a series of other factors combine to make the unit demands on the time of the pupils much greater than in American high schools. The existence of a two-hour lunch break stretches out the school day and contributes to the fact that classes tend to begin at 8:00 a.m. and yet are not finished until 4:00 or 5:00 p.m. In addition, class time is reserved almost exclusively for academic subjects with, for example, only two hours per week set aside for physical education. In some cases, school lasts six days per week, but even for those who have classes just five days each week, the impact of these rest days is sometimes reduced, since they are not consecutive—i.e., Thursday and Sunday. Finally, and most importantly, the homework load borne by the French student is much greater than that of his or her American counterpart. As a result, the study halls which he may have during the school day, as well as a large part of his evening, are spent doing homework assignments. In many cases, this work seems to have been designed with the idea of keeping the youngsters occupied: The ordinary student spends many hours recopying notes taken in class or reproducing maps from his textbook.

The pupils' course of study is largely determined by detailed curricula drawn up by the Ministry of Education and implemented by the teachers. Whatever latitude is left in the ministerial instructions is removed in each school by decisions of either the school administration, the senior teachers of the subject, or the particular instructor. As a result, the pupils play no role in determining what they shall study.

While the very nature of an educational institution militates against the possibility, in any society, of students playing a key role in defining the content of their work, such is not the case for questions of classroom behavior and methods of working. Although some limitations are virtually universally imposed,[5] these tend to leave the child a large margin of acceptable behavior. In France, the tendency is to issue highly specific directives to *define exactly and positively* what the pupil is supposed to do, rather than simply to prohibit certain types of activity.

French students are given extremely precise instructions on how to write their homework assignments. The teacher tells them to use a specified type of paper and color of ink. Usually a fountain pen is required, even for homework and examinations in mathematics. Pupils are asked to make an additional margin of two or three centimeters and leave a prescribed amount of space between each paragraph. The title of the work is to be written at the top of the paper and underlined in a particular color of ink; then so many spaces are to be skipped before beginning the first paragraph. In addition, certain types of key phrases are to be underlined in a specified color. Demands for neatness are so exacting that most pupils must recopy their work several times in order to be sure that their teacher will accept it. In sum, when students set out to do written work, they already possess a detailed image of how the finished product should look.

An interesting illustrative example of the extent to which students are habituated to this sort of procedure occurred during the periods when we were handing out and explaining our questionnaire to the younger pupils. In the great majority of cases, the first question posed was: "What sort of writing instrument should we use for filling out the questionnaire?" When told they could use anything they they wished—i.e., pencil, fountain or ball-point pen—and in any color, many students showed signs of puzzlement and hesitation for fifteen or twenty seconds before deciding what to do.

The pupils' style of behavior in the classroom is specified with a somewhat smaller, yet high degree of precision. In most schools, they must wait at the door of the room until the teacher tells them to enter and sit down. During the class tiself, if some adult enters the room, everyone rises and does not sit again until told to do so. Talking to one's neighbor, doing other work, or not appearing to be attentive are prohibited. In many schools, if the teacher asks a question, the pupil must stand up when giving his response. Finally, since the option of leaving the class for even a few moments does not exist, one must, for instance, be sure to use the lavatory before coming to the course.

Accompanying this very high level of behavioral control, there is very little attempted control over the ideas which pupils should express. In fact, an integral part of the system is an overt attempt not to restrict or influence the ideological options open to the individual. Thus, teachers in the humanities and social sciences present their subject matter in as objective a manner as possible, trying to keep their own religious, philosophical, and political opinions out of the discussion. (Such attempted objectivity is particularly meaningful in a society such as France where most educated adults seem to have strongly entrenched sympathies and/or antipathies for highly divergent ideologies.) In addition, teachers try to inculcate within their students a critical bent of mind. These tendencies are clearly illustrated in the French school exercise called an *explication de texte,* in which the pupils must analyze in depth and criticize a given passage in a work selected by the teacher—what to do and how to do it are precisely defined, but the student is given total freedom of expression. The attempt not to restrict the philosophical options open to the child is apparently successful, since the belief systems of the pupils gradually become dispersed all along the ideological spectrum.[6] Nonetheless, when it comes to writing an interpretative essay or making a verbal classroom presentation, the students try to write or say what they think comes closest to the view held by the teacher. In addition, even during the rare informal discussions between students and their teachers, pupils hesitate to state their opinions freely. They tend to be silent unless they feel the teacher either might agree with them or is a particularly tolerant individual. These two types of inhibition, written and verbal, result from overspills of other kinds of coverage. In the former case, as a consequence of the very high level of behavioral control, pupils assume that they should, in the process of fulfilling their tasks, present ideas which conform to those they believe are held by their teachers. In other words, they are unable to completely segregate the different types of control. In the latter case, this same phenomenon arises and is joined by the inability to play different roles with a particular superordinate according to whether one is inside or outside the unit.

To ensure compliance in the school, pupils are continually being supervised. They are rarely left unattended; even when going from one class to another there are *surveillants* (proctors)[7] or teachers in the halls to make sure that everyone behaves properly. The teachers check up on their students in a number of ways. Homework is always collected and graded. Periodically, the teacher goes around the class to examine the pupils' notebooks to make sure they have been doing the work they are supposed to do. From time to time, teachers verbally "interrogate" their students on what they have been studying and grade them on their individual performances. And, of course, there are written exams.

French parents have tended to support the action of their children's teachers.[8] By means of a *carnet de correspondance* (the French equivalent of the American report card, except that it is a much more detailed record with weekly evaluations of the child's school work) which must be signed every week, the parents are kept informed of the work and behavioral imperfections of their child.[9] In many French families, punishments and/or rewards will be used as incentives for the child to perform well in school. Sometimes parents come to school to speak with their child's teachers, but during these conversations the parents rarely defend their own child; rather, the tendency is to search for ways in which the parents can back up the teacher through their behavior toward the child at home.

Despite this extensive supervision, there are infractions of "the law." However, in most cases, the simple pointing out by the teacher that a violation has occurred serves to eliminate the transgression. Sometimes more severe sanctions—e.g., requiring a student to do a supplementary homework assignment, noting his form of misconduct in his carnet de correspondance or his *carte de conduite* (which often exists as a supplement to the carnet de correspondance and in which the teacher notes each occasion on which the child misbehaves; in other cases, the carnet is used for this purpose), or sending him to the detention hall for a couple of hours on Thursday or Saturday, days on which he normally does not have to come to school—are meted out, but usually only after a pupil has repeatedly violated a rule. Finally, for certain grave transgressions—e.g., cheating on an examination—pupils may be sanctioned by a two- or three-day suspension or, if the violation is repeated, by permanent exclusion from the school.

In sum, the pupils live within a highly directive environment. Their response to this, within the authority-laden mode, is a very high level of actual compliance. Virtually all cases of noncompliance can be attributed to a failure to correctly understand the original directive or a mental or physical inadequacy which prevents compliance. A simple reminder and explanation from the teacher is normally sufficient to obtain future compliance.

As might be expected within an atmosphere of this sort, student participation tends to be minimal. Not only do they virtually never attempt directly to exert influence on a teacher to get him to change the way in which the class functions, but even participation in the form of raising questions on the subject matter being treated is quite rare. Most teachers behave in a manner which tends to suppress potential participatory behavior. The majority of courses are conducted in the form of a lecture, even though there may only be a small number of students in the class. When a teacher "forces" his students to participate, it is usually in the form of responding to a question he poses or writing their homework on the blackboard. In both cases, the teacher corrects the pupil's work and judges him. Sometimes the form of the teacher's correction seems to belittle the work and/or intelligence of the child. Obviously this tends to teach the students not to participate unless required to do so, because, for the large majority of them, participation can bring no rewards but only the possibility of sanctions.

It is true that some teachers overtly attempt to stimulate individualistic forms of classroom participation. But most of them complain that, even after numerous attempts to get the pupils to raise questions, only one or two, if any, will actually do so. In addition, those questions which are posed invariably seek additional information, while questions that are veiled criticisms or suggestions are, for all intents and purposes, nonexistent.

While students, in fact, rarely attempt to exert influence on their teachers, the large majority (seventy percent) seem to have relatively strong personal opinions about the ways in which their class units should function.[10] There is obviously a potential dissonance here, which becomes actualized when the pupils' views conflict with those of their teachers. This dissonance could be resolved through more active participation. And the great majority of pupils do normatively value more participation than actually exists: In fact, more than fifty percent think that students should express their opinions much more often to teachers and that there should be many more opportunities for pupils to express their views.[11] But, participation is not seen as a practicable option: Between sixty percent and seventy percent of the pupils have a low estimation of their "competence" (in Almond and Verba's sense) to affect the functioning of the system and also perceive their teachers as being rather nonresponsive.[12] Thus, students do not actually participate, not because they would not like to but because participation does not appear viable.

Two practices prevalent in the lower grades of French schools may provide an explanation for the development of the view that participation is not a realistic option. In the primary schools and in the first years of the C.E.G., there is a tendency for classroom participation to take the form of all students responding in unison to a question posed by the teacher. As a result, no individual is singled out from the group. This guarantees everyone the ability to respond without anyone taking the risk of giving an incorrect answer and being sanctioned for this. A second practice suggests why there is a prevalent fear of being sanctioned for giving an incorrect answer. The French functional equivalent of the American school "quiz" is a short verbal *interrogation* of the pupil by the teacher. Normally, the student is called up to the front of the class, and then the teacher poses a series of questions. When the pupil is unable to respond, the teacher seeks the correct answer from another member of the class or gives it himself. At the end of this questioning period, the teacher publicly gives the student his grade and may make a critique. Due to this technique, combined with the earlier experiences children have had in the primary school, where their mistakes are often publicly ridiculed,[13] it is quite natural that they should not only prefer the group style of classroom participation, but that they should simultaneously also seek to avoid any form of individual participation because it is likely to have negative consequences for them.

The final component of the authority-laden mode is a series of deportment practices in which teachers tend toward observably treating their students as quite inferior to themselves while students respond "correspondingly"—i.e., as if the teachers were clearly superior to them. Many overt signs of this style of deportment exist. Teachers call their students by their last or first name alone, while the students address their teachers as "sir" or "madame." Teachers are often impolite to their students, but the pupils always show great respect for them. Some teachers will ridicule or belittle their students, who seem passively to accept this. The pupils stand up when their teacher enters the classroom. Many teachers use the familiar form (tu) with their students, but, of course, the pupils respond in the formal form (vous). There are certain structural supports for this sort of behavior, the most visible of which is the existence of a raised platform on which the teacher's desk and chair is placed. In an important sense, this symbolizes the "higher level" of the teacher who can, thus, easily "look down" on his pupils (who are normally given desks for two or more people rather than individually).

In sum, the dominant mode of interaction during the early years of secondary school is authority-laden: Teachers tend to be very directive and nonresponsive, while pupils are totally compliant and do not try to participate. In addition, teachers tend to treat their students arrogantly—i.e., almost as if they were lower forms of humanity—and the students tend to respond appropriately—i.e., obsequiously. These behavioral aspects are consonant with each other. There is no tension or conflict between them. But this behavioral consonance in no way suggests consonance between norms and practices.[14]

THE CHAHUT

The chahut, which occurs in twenty to twenty-five percent of the younger pupils' classes, represents a sharp departure from the authority-laden mode. Teachers have no effective authority; students disregard their directives. The pupils "participate" in the sense of deciding what shall be done during the class time spent with the teacher who is unable to channel or control their behavior. Deportment practices approach arrogance, but on the part of the students toward the teacher.

To clarify what is meant by the chahut, some concrete examples of this form of behavior should be provided. Students might constantly talk with one another, get up and walk around the room whenever they feel like it, and if the teacher should call on them to respond to a question, they would answer disrespectfully—e.g., Teacher: "When you mix two atoms of hydrogen with one atom of oxygen, what do you get?" Pupil: "It rains," or *"Merde!"* Or the students might jeer at the teacher in unison, call him nasty names—e.g., idiot—and run around the classroom. In certain classes, wet wads of paper will be thrown across the room, landing and then sticking on the wall behind the teacher's desk. Or there might be a fist fight, with the winner ejecting the loser from the room, while the other pupils stand around cheering for one or the other of the pugilists. With some teachers, the students might bring small glass sulphur bombs into class which would be simultaneously broken, creating such a stench that the teacher is usually driven into the hall while the pupils stay in class, happily suffering the odor. Finally, students might bring a tent, camping equipment, and food into their class and, during the lesson, set up the tent, prepare lunch for each other, and then eat it—the teacher being powerless to stop them.[15]

A key facet of the pupils' behavior during a chahut is the existence of a small group of students who initiate the chahut and then direct the actions of their classmates.[16] Therefore, following contemporary sociological usage, chahut participants do not form a true peer group. Rather, they are part of what might be called a transient gang—i.e., a nondurable group composed of nominal equals in which certain members occupy leadership roles vis-à-vis the others. In a sense, the relationship between chahut leaders and their followers approximates the one existing between teachers and students in the authority-laden mode. Of course, there are fundamental differences: (1) the chahut leader does not have nominal authority over the other pupils and (2) the control of the leader is less effective than that of a teacher in an authority-laden relationship, partly because he has no sanctioning power and partly because the chahut per se is by no means a rigidly defined activity. Nevertheless, if the leader can initiate the chahut,[17] he will have a great deal of control over the behavior of the other students and will be able to determine the general form and development of the chahut. It is the existence of these leaders and the controlling role they play vis-à-vis the other students which distinguishes the chahut from forms of anarchic, individualistic rebellion.[18]

This description defines a phenomenon which is narrower than that which the French sometimes call a chahut. Often this term is applied to any classroom situation in which the behavior of the students is not as precisely circumscribed as in the "ideal" authority-laden interaction—e.g., to a class where students whisper occasionally to their neighbors without effective action by the teacher to stop this. For analytical purposes, the term chahut will denote only those cases where the teacher has basically lost control of the class. Those situations where the teacher maintains tight, but not total, control will be considered authority-laden, because, in reality, the divergence from the ideal form is quite minimal. However, these cases of slight divergence might also be regarded as *potential* transitional stages toward establishing a chahut relationship with a particular teacher. For once a teacher deviates from the ideal authority-laden relationship, even if he stops the students' growing area of permissible behavior very rapidly, the pupils remain tense and on the lookout for signs of weakness on the teacher's part, which would allow them to augment the limits of permissible behavior to such an extent as to turn the relationship into a chahut.

To most Americans, chahuting would evoke thoughts of schools peopled with juvenile delinquents and depicted in such films as "Blackboard Jungle." However, this sort of behavior can be found not only in the worst but also in the best schools in France—i.e., those which cater to the intellectually gifted and to the children of the members of the upper echelons of society. The chahut is significant precisely because it exists in *all* secondary schools, in all grades, and in virtually all sections and subsections in each school.

Thus, from an authority-centered perspective, the chahut is a form of organized classroom insubordination initiated and guided by a small group of leaders and occurring in *all* French secondary schools. This purely empirical view overlooks what may well be a crucial aspect of the chahut: It is a lot of fun! Students, when participating in a chahut, enjoy themselves thoroughly. Afterwards they talk about what happened as a way of reliving the experience, just as they might discuss a wild party at a friend's house. In addition, it appears that the memory of the pleasure of chahuting does not fade with time. When talking casually with French adults and asking them to discuss their own high school experiences, invariably they would begin by referring to the "oppression" and then quickly add "But, there was the chahut!" They would go on to recall with rather great precision specific teachers whom they had chahuted. They spoke of the "terrible" things they had done and, with at least feigned guilt feelings, how much fun they had. At times, it was hard to believe that, for instance, a sixty-year-old man could remember with such accuracy his behavior and that of his school mates of forty-five years ago. In discussing these chahuts, the adults frequently seemed to relive the incidents—a gleam would appear in their eyes, and they would become visibly excited.

Yet it is not altogether surprising that high school students, as well as their elders, should literally revel in their memories of chahuts. The stifling authority-laden atmosphere must certainly be difficult to bear. And, as many students pointed out, the chahut is a way to relax. It is a holiday, a festival, which breaks the monotony of normal, oppressive, authority relations. That the chahut serves this function is even evident from the origins of the term: It originally referred to a wild, joyous dance in the streets.[19] Dancing in the streets is fun and is long remembered because it sharply clashes with the drudgery and routine of everyday life. The chahut in secondary school classes is fun and long remembered for the same reasons.

THE ALTERNATION BETWEEN THE AUTHORITY-LADEN AND CHAHUT MODES OF INTERACTION

In all the classes of the lower grades which were studied, both modes of student-teacher interaction existed. Consistently, one found the same group of pupils establishing an authority-laden relationship with some, usually most, of their teachers, and chahuting the others. The amount of "forcefulness" attributed by the students to a particular teacher seemed to determine what type of relationship would be established.

The young students only appear to comply with the directives issued by teachers they perceive to be forceful. But what does it mean for a teacher to be forceful? Observation suggests that, first, he must avoid appeasing his students. When he makes demands which are viewed as unreasonable or as in conflict with student desires or needs, he does not seek to compromise with his pupils, but rather steadfastly insists that they comply. Second, under no conditions should the teacher vacillate. Once a directive has been given, he must stick to it and not change his mind and withdraw it. Third, the forceful teacher must exhibit self-control. He cannot lose his temper in front of the students and yell at them. Even when goaded, he should remain "calm, cool, and collected." Finally, he radiates self-confidence. He is sure of himself and his decisions, or at least must appear to be. Such are the major defining characteristics of a forceful teacher, one who will be given "legitimacy"[20] by the students.

Chahuted teachers typically lack these qualities. In fact, their attempts to stifle the chahut, given the bases for evoking legitimacy, serve the opposite effect. Thus, the chahuted teacher may try to halt insubordination by telling a particularly rebellious pupil that he will have to serve two hours in the detention hall. The magnitude of the chahut increases. Then the teacher may hand out more harsh sanctions only to be confronted with even more insubordination. Finally, in a last ditch attempt to restore order, the teacher may promise the students that they will not be punished if they will just stop. But, the chahut continues. To cite another example to support the same point, chahuted teachers will scream and yell at their students. They may even beg the pupils to be good. Or they may physically threaten them. For instance, one teacher who had long been *chahuté* started to take karate lessons, in the hope that if he could demonstrate his physical strength, the chahut would stop. One day, having been pushed so hard he could no longer stand it, the teacher announced his expertise and proceeded with a demonstration. He gave his desk a karate chop which split the desk in half. The result, unfortunately from his perspective, was only to increase the merriment of his students. While the karate example is atypical and extreme, numerous chahuted teachers will grab coat hangers and twist them or bang them against the wall, irrationally hoping, thereby, to "scare" their students into submission. But, all these tactics are to no avail.

Obedience is not a function of force.[2][1] Even chahuted teachers who hand out sanctions and do not change their minds find the strategy counterproductive. When the *chahuteur* returns to class, after having been kicked out or sent to the detention hall, he comes with a taste of vengeance, and his peers join him in making the teacher's life even more miserable than it had been. Thus, it is the teachers who are chahuté who seem to give the largest number of severe sanctions. This, however, does not mean that forcefulness and force are totally antithetical phenomena. Rather, if the students perceive a certain teacher as being forceful, that means they believe he *could,* if necessary, effectively force them to do what he wants them to do, even if, in fact, he has never used force on them. In a sense, not having to use force signifies that one is capable of using it effectively.

This conception of the teacher's authority being based on

perceived forcefulness is quite similar to one of Emile Durkheim's arguments. In responding to the question, "What conditions must the teacher fulfill in order to radiate authority?" he points out:

> Certain personal qualities are necessary. Notably, the teacher should be decisive, have some will power. Since the imperative character of the rule derives from the fact that it silences all doubts and hesitations, the rule cannot appear obligatory to the child if applied indecisively—if those charged with teaching it to him do not seem always certain of what it should be.[22]

In addition, Durkheim clearly suggests that the teacher's authority is not based on force:

> The fear of punishment is something altogether different from respect for authority. It has a moral character and moral value only if the penalty is regarded as just by those subjected to it, which implies that the authority which punishes is itself recognized as legitimate. However, this is what is in question. It is not from the outside, from the fear he inspires, that the teacher should gain his authority; it is from himself . . . from his innermost being.[23]

Since the chahut is a form of systematic noncompliance and since a defining aspect of the authority-laden mode is total compliance with the orders of highly directive teachers, the most crucial aspect of the pupils' normative structure required for the alternation to occur would be indifference toward compliance —i.e., compliance per se being neither positively nor negatively valued.[24]

One of the questionnaire items sought to tap the pupils' valuation of compliance. They were asked to select from among the following three points of view, the one which came closest to representing their personal opinion:

(1) All the rules and order should always be followed by the students.

(2) The students should obey the rules and orders of their teachers only when the benefit derived from obedience is superior to the inconveniences caused by disobedience.

(3) The students should try to evade or resist the rules and orders of their teachers as much as possible.

TABLE 1.1: Students' Normative Valuation of Compliance:
Students in the First Cycle

	Cinquième		Troisième		TOTAL	
	%	N	%	N	%	N
(1) Commitment	33	173	21	137	26	310
(2) Indifference	47	246	62	409	55	655
(3) Defiance	20	108	17	109	18	217
TOTAL:	100	527	100	655	100	1,182
Mean Response:	1.8766		1.9572		1.9213	

The first point of view represents commitment to comply, the second indifference, and the third defiance. An examination of the responses from the students in the first phase of their secondary education reveals a strong preference for the indifferent point of view in cinquième and an even stronger preference in troisième (see Table 1.1). As a result, as the younger pupils rise in grade level, it becomes increasingly easy to submit themselves totally to forceful teachers while concomitantly being completely insubordinate and chahuting the weak teachers. It should be noted that for those who either positively or negatively value compliance, participation in both the authority-laden *and* the chahut modes of interaction causes significant cognitive stress.[25]

INTERSCHOOL VARIATIONS IN BEHAVIOR TOWARD AUTHORITY

Up to this point, the general pattern of authority relations prevailing in the early years of French secondary education has been discussed. However, given the heterogeneity of the sample, is it not possible that the general pattern is violated in many, or at least some, of the important subgroups into which the population might be divided? Analysis of the data showed that more significant variations occurred between the C.E.G. section and the lycée sections[26] than between any of the other subgroups into which the general sample had been divided—i.e., distinguishing between students according to their sex, religious practices, and social class background, as well as distinguishing between schools according to their geographical location and sexual composition (all male, all female, and coeducational). Since the purpose of this study is not to analyze subgroup variations but rather to describe and explain the general nature of authority relations, only this most serious variation will be examined.

It is not surprising that lycée-C.E.G. differences should be most significant. This categorization encompasses a set of other variables which on a priori grounds might well result in distinct types of authority relationships. Probably most important among the differences is the fact that pupils in the lycée sections tend to come from much higher echelons of French society and to be more intellectually gifted than the students in the C.E.G. section. In addition, the pedagogical styles characteristic of the two subgroups are quite dissimilar. Teaching in the lycée sections approaches what occurs in universities, but in the C.E.G. section it is reminiscent of primary school educational methods. Furthermore, students following the lycée programs tend to have a different teacher for each subject they study, but pupils in the C.E.G. section will typically have two major teachers, one for "literary" and one for "scientific" subjects.

Despite the numerous objective differences between the subsamples, both conform to the general pattern of authority interactions characteristic of the early years of French secondary education. In other words, pupils in the C.E.G. section as well as those in the lycée sections participate alternatively in both the authority-laden and the chahut modes depending on whether they perceive their teacher as being forceful or not. However, below this level of general similarity, there are noteworthy differences.

While throughout the first cycle there is a very high level of coverage, within the C.E.G. section the level of attempted coverage is noticeably greater than in the lycée sections. For example, teachers in the short-modern program tend to dictate the lessons to the pupils. The teacher will speak very slowly and the students will copy down his remarks verbatim in their notebooks. Sometimes the entire course will be presented in this manner; in other cases, the teacher may "dialogue" with the pupils about a problem—i.e., explain a certain number of points and ask students short, relevant questions—and then dictate a summary and conclusion. This practice is rather widespread in the C.E.G. section, but it is totally absent in the lycée sections. In general, teachers who dictate all or part of their classes will check the pupils' notebooks each day or periodically to make sure that everyone is taking down the dictated remarks.

That dictation occurs only in the C.E.G. section is not surprising. Most of these teachers formerly taught in primary schools where it had been a commonly accepted practice for the teacher to dictate his course to the pupils. More recently this practice has been officially repudiated and strongly frowned upon, but, at least in the C.E.G.s, it remains rather widespread.

Dictation is a form of increased task coverage. Similarly, there seems to be more instrumental and comportmental coverage in the short-modern section than in the lycée sections. Instrumental coverage is equally high in both sections, but in the C.E.G. section there is a much more exclusive reliance on continually issuing directives covering how the pupils are supposed to do their assigned tasks. This is not meant to suggest that teachers in the lycée sections issue few directives of this type, but rather that there is some assumption of learned behavior in the lycée sections which is almost totally absent in the short-modern program. Similarly, within the C.E.G. section, teachers try to cover their pupils' comportment more directly—i.e., by issuing more specific directives and relying less on learned behavior. In addition, there is less reliance on non-teachers to look over and control the students between classes. There are rarely surveillants in the C.E.G.s. Rather, after a particular class is over, the teacher will, if the students are to stay in the same room, wait with them until the next teacher arrives, and, if they are to go to another room, the teacher will normally accompany them there. Such a procedure is absent in the lycées, and even though there are surveillants in the halls to watch over the pupils, the surveillance between classes is not nearly as tight, because they must control many more pupils.

The differences between the lycées and C.E.G.s on ideological coverage are much more subtle. Although all French secondary school teachers are rhetorically committed to keeping their personal religious, philosophical, and political opinions out of the classroom and although most of them are rather successful in being "objective," the C.E.G. teachers carry these tendencies much further than those in the lycée do. For example, we have observed violently anti-Gaullist history teachers in C.E.G.s give lectures on the Fifth Republic which in no way suggested what their real political preferences were. Similarly, in a C.E.G. located in a Communist stronghold, we saw the principal, a member of the

Party, call the police to remove demonstrators who were carrying pro-North Vietnamese signs within a hundred yards of the school, because such an expression of partisan political preferences could not legally be done so near the school. Finally, in teachers' lounges in the C.E.G.s there was a total absence of any political posters, while in every lycée we studied the lounges were normally filled with conflicting types of political propaganda. In sum, within C.E.G.s, but not in the lycées, there seems to be a total, effective prohibition on the expression of partisan views.

A question now arises: What effect do these two different atmospheres have on the pupil? Paradoxically, it seems that there is more attempted ideological coverage within the C.E.G. than within the lycée. C.E.G. pupils are expected to express nonpartisan views, and any view which does not correspond to the teacher's notion of "objectivity" is likely to be rejected. On the other hand, the lycée teachers seem more prepared to accept partisan views even if they strongly conflict with those espoused by the teacher. The basic empirical support for this argument is the fact that C.E.G. pupils are much less likely than lycée students to state views differing from those held by their teachers. However, it must be noted that, rather than being a function of greater ideological coverage, the decreased tendency to express opinions which contradict the teacher's point of view may be related to the greater amount of behavioral control in the C.E.G.s and the concomitant increase in overspills of authority. Another explanation might be related to the varying intellectual capabilities of C.E.G. and lycée students. The short-modern pupils tend to be less intelligent than those in the lycée sections, and there is certainly some relationship between intelligence and the ability to express opinions in the presence of an important authority figure who disagrees with them.

Besides variations in attempted coverage practices, the deportment practices characteristic of the two subsamples differ. In the C.E.G. section, students normally spend more time with each of their teachers and have fewer teachers than pupils in the lycée sections. Given this, plus the fact that most teachers in the short-modern section have previously had experience in elementary schools, student-teacher relations in the C.E.G. section tend to be more "family-like," in some sense. Teachers are much more likely to use the familiar tu form when addressing their pupils and to conceive of themselves as surrogate fathers or mothers.

Despite these factors, or possibly because of them, teacher deportment practices toward pupils in the short-modern section tend more toward the pole of arrogance than in the lycée sections. This arrogance is reflected in certain participation practices. Within the lycée sections, students will, at least occasionally, pose information questions to their teachers or ask them to give additional examples to illustrate a point which has been made. But in the short-modern section, even this innocuous form of classroom participation is almost totally absent. Students functioning within the authority-laden mode very rarely, if ever, play any role in determining what is to be done during class. To all intents and purposes, the teacher is the sole initiator of activity. Thus, if he feels all of the pupils have not understood a point, he will ask a question, the correct answer to which is dependent on having comprehended what has been said. In many C.E.G.s, the pupils will respond to such questions in unison. This practice of group response is, in principle, frowned upon, but in many schools it remains modal in practice. In sum, short-modern pupils have no influence on the functioning of their classes.

As a counterpart to the more regimented, authority-laden mode in the C.E.G. section, there is an augmentation of the role played by the chahut, both in the sense of the number of teachers chahuté and in the frequency with which chahuts occur. In the classes studied, pupils in the short-modern section had approximately seven or eight different teachers while those in the lycée sections had about nine or ten. Since the students in the short-modern section work with fewer teachers than do those in the lycée sections, if both groups chahut the same proportion of their teachers, those in the short-modern section would be chahuting fewer teachers than those in the classical or modern sections. Our questionnaire results suggest that both sections chahut approximately the same number of teachers—i.e., on the average between two and three teachers; hence, pupils in the C.E.G. section tend to chahut proportionately more teachers— about twenty-five percent compared to approximately twenty percent in the lycées. Similarly, they seem to chahut more frequently.[27]

To summarize: During the early years of French secondary education, the general pattern of student-teacher authority relations is characterized by a process of alternation between an authority-laden mode and the chahut. The content and relative importance of these two forms of interaction varies somewhat between subsamples of the whole population. For example, students in the C.E.G. section tend to chahut more frequently than the other pupils, but when they do participate in the authority-laden mode their activities are even more controlled and regimented than in the authority-laden mode within the lycée sections.[28]

The Older Students

As the students grow older and move into the upper grades, the pattern of alternation between authority-laden and chahut relationships continues to exist but ceases to be the dominant mode of pupil-teacher interaction. There is no precisely definable time at which this change occurs. Rather, the modes of interaction characteristic of the early years of secondary education gradually lose predominance to a new pattern in which the behavior of the students is as regimented as it was with authority-laden teachers, but, in contradistinction, only a minimal number of specific or special directives are issued to the pupils. This new pattern starts becoming dominant in seconde and is modal by the time the students reach their last year of high school. However, it is never the exclusive form of pupil-teacher interaction in the upper grades, for, the authority-laden and chahut modes continue to exist under specific conditions (to be defined in the next chapter).

The behavior of older pupils is as regimented as under the authority-laden mode, but directives are only given infrequently and are not very specific (both from the perspective of the outside observer and according to teachers who simultaneously give instruction in the upper and the lower grades). This in and of itself is, of course, neither surprising nor apparently unusual. It seems reasonable to assume that teachers in any educational system would find it bothersome to have to continuously tell students in the senior high school grades what to do. Likewise, it seems "natural" that, after going through eight or nine years of formal

TABLE 1.2: Students' Perceptions of Coverage: The Mean Responses at Each Grade Level

	Cinquième		Troisième		Seconde		Terminale		TOTAL	
	$\bar{X}$	N	$\bar{X}$	N	$\bar{X}$	N	$\bar{X}$	N	$\bar{X}$	N
(a) Task Coverage	3.75	(522)	4.02	(660)	4.03	(299)	4.01	(403)	3.94	(1884)
(b) Instrumental Coverage	3.02	(524)	2.99	(658)	2.74	(303)	2.91	(404)	2.94	(1889)
(c) Comportmental Coverage	3.53	(529)	3.62	(657)	3.32	(303)	3.55	(404)	3.53	(1893)
Average Mean Perceived Coverage	3.44	—	3.55	—	3.36	—	3.49	—	3.47	—

NOTE: A mean of 1.00 signifies a very low level of coverage, and a mean of 5.00 signifies a very high level of coverage.

education, a child would have internalized his teacher's expectations and do what he is supposed to do without receiving directives. However, at least in the French case, this commonsense notion seems, at best, misleading. For, although the students in the upper grades are typically not issued numerous directives, their *perceptions* of the extent to which their in-school behavior is controlled explicitly by teachers are indistinguishable from the perceptions of the younger pupils.

To tap perceived coverage, three separate questions were asked:

(a) To what extent are you able to determine by yourself the content of your schoolwork—i.e., what to study? [task coverage]

(b) To what extent are you able to determine by yourself the form of your schoolwork—i.e., how to do it (for instance, how to present your homework?) [instrumental coverage]

(c) To what extent are you able to determine by yourself how to behave—deport yourself—in class and in school? [comportmental coverage]

In each case, the pupils could choose among five responses, from "to a very large extent" to "to a very small extent." These responses were coded from "1" to "5," the former representing a very low level of perceived coverage and the latter a very high level of perceived coverage. Then, to obtain a combined score for each grade level, the means for the responses in each grade to each of the three questions were averaged. Table 1.2 presents these mean responses; there is no tendency as students go into the higher grades to perceive lower degrees of coverage. (Figure 1.1 exhibits these results in the form of a bar graph.)

The older pupils, therefore, regard their environment as being just as directive-ridden as the authority-laden mode, even though objectively this is far from being the case. They inhabit a world of *assumed coverage*.

This new pattern is based on "remembered" socialization. In contradistinction to "normal" socialization, the students follow prescribed patterns of behavior, actually internalized as a consequence of past incidents of precise and detailed directive-issuing, but still *perceived as externally imposed.* By definition (i.e., being internalized), it must be effective. But, such is not so with *direct*

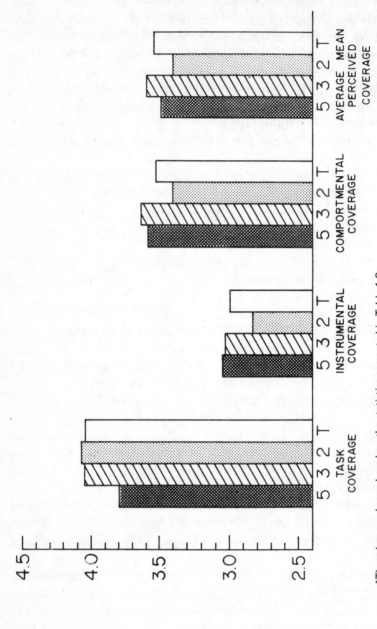

*These bar graphs are based on the statistics presented in Table 1.2.

FIGURE 1.1: Students' Perceptions of Coverage (Mean Responses): Pupils in Cinguième (5), Troisième (3), Seconde (2), and Terminale (T)*

coverage—the issuing of directives to prescribe an ongoing activity. In this case, there is a very close temporal association between the directives and the activity; the directive is linked to a particular directive giver; and the effectiveness or ineffectiveness of control cannot be predetermined but rather depends on the type of relationship established between the superordinate and the subordinate.

The notion of remembered socialization should not be confused with the various types of internalized behavior usually cited in the literature.[29] For example, because the prescribed, internalized pattern of behavior is *perceived* as being externally imposed even though, in fact, directives are not being issued, remembered socialization is quite different from Urie Bronfenbrenner's "internalized obedience—fulfilling the wishes of adults not as commands from without but as internally motivated desires."[30] Furthermore, it would be erroneous to identify remembered socialization with "authority avoidance," because even though authority contact between superordinates and subordinates is reduced from the objective observer's viewpoint, it is perceived by subordinates as being virtually identical to the authority-laden mode.

NOTES

1. I have developed the term "authority-laden" rather than using the term "authoritarian" for two reasons: (1) to avoid the pejorative connotation associated with "authoritarian," and (2) because authoritarianism may be defined as a high level of behavioral and ideological control exercised by superordinates over their subordinates, but by authority-laden, as discussion below will show, I am only referring to behavioral control.

2. For a more complete discussion of these concepts, see William R. Schonfeld, "Authority in France: A Model of Political Behavior Drawn From Case Studies in Education," Ph.D. dissertation, Princeton University, 1970, and Harry Eckstein and Ted Robert Gurr, *Patterns of Authority: A Structural Basis for Political Inquiry* (New York: John Wiley, 1975).

3. The term "coverage" refers to the extent to which superordinates seek to control and direct the activities of their subordinates.

4. This figure may vary according to the grade or section, but it never exceeds more than about thirty-two hours nor is it ever less than twenty-four hours.

5. For instance, "Don't disrupt the class!" or "Write your homework neatly so that I can read it."

6. To argue that the ideological heterogeneity of French high school students is a

result of cross-cutting attempts at indoctrination by teachers with highly divergent belief systems, is erroneous. While many university professors, as well as some lycée teachers of philosophy in the terminal class, have a tendency to present and justify their own political and philosophical opinions in class, such is hardly the case with the overwhelming majority of French secondary school teachers.

7. French surveillants are not the same thing as American monitors. They are, in general, university students who take this job as a means of earning money for their education. As a result of their age and position, they do not identify with the secondary school pupils. Such, of course, is not the case with a monitor.

8. For a description of this sort of behavior in the context of a primary school unit in a small town, see Laurence Wylie, *Village in the Vaucluse* (Cambridge, Mass.: Harvard University Press, 1974), pp. 82-83.

9. It should be noted that French teachers do not hesitate to give their students poor marks in conduct, and the pupil who consistently receives good grades for his classroom behavior is the exception rather than the rule. This is rather significant because, from the perspective of the outside (American) observer, the students' conduct within classrooms adhering to the authority-laden mode of interaction is usually irreproachable.

10. For a full data display including the question used to tap the existence of personal opinions, see Schonfeld, "Youth and Authority in France," Table I, p. 20. Eloquent testimony to the presence of strongly entrenched opinions, at least among lycée students, is presented by Gérard Vincent (*Les lycéens* and *Le peuple lycéen*).

11. For data displays, see Schonfeld, ibid., p. 23, Tables 4 and 5.

12. For further discussion of these points and for full data displays, see ibid., pp. 20-22, Tables 2 and 3.

13. See Wylie, *Village in the Vaucluse,* pp. 84-87.

14. This type of consonance will be discussed in Chapter 2.

15. The examples cited, as well as, of course, many more, were observed during our research in the secondary schools. One exception to this rule is the tent chahut. In this case, the students told us about the chahut, which we had been unable to observe, because the teacher would not, quite understandably, admit us to his class.

16. An examination of the questionnaire results from the first cycle reveals that in eighty-eight percent of the classes studied (thirty-seven of forty-two), all or almost all the pupils said there were chahut leaders.

17. The students tend to follow the initiatory action of the leader unless they feel chahuting with the particular teacher at this time is too risky.

18. The French have a specific word to label an anarchistic revolt–*pagaille*–which is clearly distinguished from a chahut.

19. According to the *Robert* dictionary, the word chahut was derived from the hyphenated term chat-huant (howling cat).

20. In other words, there will be voluntary compliance with the directives.

21. Questionnaire results provide additional support for the notion that the alternation between the authority-laden and chahut modes is based on a legitimacy notion (perceived forcefulness) rather than coercion. Within the responses to a question which presented a long list of qualities and asked the students to select the three or four qualities which together best described a teacher subject to the chahut, as many of respondents in the first cycle chose being "severe" (seventeen percent, N = 208) as chose being "liberal" (seventeen percent, N = 197) in terms of sanctioning practices. On the other hand, the most frequently chosen quality was having a "weak personality" (thirty-nine percent, N = 468), while having a "strong personality" was one of the qualities least chosen (three percent, N = 35).

22. Emile Durkheim, *Moral Education: A Study in the Theory and Application of the Sociology of Education,* trans. Everett K. Wilson and Herman Schnurer (New York: Free Press, 1969), p. 154.

23. Ibid., pp. 154-155.

24. Amitai Etzioni refers to this type of compliance as being based on "calculative involvement" which is characteristic among subordinates in "utilitarian organizations." (See his *A Comparative Analysis of Complex Organizations: On Power, Involvement, and Their Correlates* [New York: Free Press, 1961], passim.)

25. See Schonfeld, *Youth and Authority in France,* pp. 29-30 for a demonstration that the valuation of compliance is a general norm and not teacher-specific. That is to say, pupils do *not* positively value compliance with teachers to whom they attribute legitimacy and negatively value compliance with teachers who chahut.

26. Pupils in the C.E.G. section are those following a short-modern program of study. Most of them are in Colleges of General Education and the rest are in C.E.S.s. In all cases, they follow the same courses, taught by the same type of teacher, utilizing similar pedagogical methods. By students in the lycée sections, I am referring to those following a classical or a modern course of study. The majority of them are in lycées, but there are some in the C.E.S.s and the C.E.G.s. As in the C.E.G. section, there is a homogeneity within the lycée sections as to the courses studied, types of teachers, and pedagogical methods. (The differences between these programs are discussed in Appendix A.)

27. For questionnaire items and data displays on the number of teachers chahuté and chahut frequency, see Schonfeld, *Youth and Authority in France,* p. 35, Tables 10 and 11.

28. For an explanation of the variation between sections, see ibid., pp. 41-45.

29. For an overview of the meaning of "internalization," see Justin Aronfreed, *Conduct and Conscience: The Socialization of Internalized Control Over Behavior* (New York: Academic Press, 1968), esp. Chapter 3, "The Concept of Internalization."

30. Urie Bronfenbrenner with the assistance of John C. Condry, Jr., *Two Worlds of Childhood: U.S. and U.S.S.R.* (New York: Russell Sage Foundation, 1970), p. 10.

Chapter 2

BEHAVIOR TOWARD AUTHORITY IN FRENCH SECONDARY SCHOOLS: AN EXPLANATION

The first years of secondary school are characterized by an alternation between two very directive and personal modes of authority interaction (the chahut and authority-ladenness), but in the upper grades, although this patterned alternation continues to exist, assumed coverage is dominant. This summary statement raises three crucial questions: How did the alternation between the authority-laden and chahut modes develop? Why does it cease to be dominant in the upper grades? What conditions determine when the older students will follow the alternating pattern or the assumed-coverage mode of interaction?

The Development of the Alternation Between the Chahut and Authority-Ladenness

Young French secondary school students seem to follow a pattern of testing to determine whether each of their teachers should be considered legitimate—i.e., authorities to be obeyed. The first few days or weeks of class are often analogous to the relationship established between a lion trainer and the lion. The pupils search to see how far they can go with each of their teachers.[1] The process is one of determining the permissible limits of behavior.[2] If the teacher cannot enforce a narrowly defined area of authorized behavior, then the students will "eat him up"—i.e., inflict the chahut.

To avoid being chahuté, it is not necessary for the teacher to be "totalitarian." For example, some teachers permit a certain amount of talking during class but do not permit pupils to leave their desks. Others demand silence but not immobility—e.g., students will often get up during the class to throw paper into the wastebasket. These sorts of divergences from the ideal-typical authority-laden mode are acceptable: While pupils are permitted to do certain things they are not normally allowed to do, their behavior is still very precisely defined by the teacher. Only if definition is vague or changeable will the chahut become operative.

The pupils' attempt to find out exactly what they can and cannot do grows out of their earlier life experiences in the family and the primary school.[3] At that age, when the phenomenon of noncompliance seems rather unusual, they are confronted by a group of superordinates who carefully prescribe for them a "correct" behavioral pattern. They are consistently told what to do and how to do it. Concomitantly, little effort is made to teach them to set self-limitations on their own behavior. Both family and primary school seem to operate in the manner which I have described as authority-laden.[4]

It is of fundamental importance that both these agencies of socialization—i.e., family and primary school—seem to have the same sort of authority pattern. If either or both of these social units did not have modal patterns, or if there were conflicting modal types of authority patterns in the two social units, the children would probably have a great deal of difficulty in coping with the various roles they are expected to play. But, in France, the great majority of children seem to face different superordinates who act toward them in virtually identical ways and have very similar expectations about how the young should behave.[5] As a result of these parallel authority patterns, children internalize a legitimacy notion based on perceived forcefulness.

When the pupil passes from the primary to the secondary school, he brings with him these dispositions. But now the child is faced with a series of teachers, rather than with a single one, as had previously been the case. Given this situation, it is very difficult for each of these superordinates to play successfully the role of surrogate father or mother, as the primary school teacher could. The removal of the paternalistic element has the effect of narrowing the boundaries of the type of behavior, on the part of the teacher, which the child will accept as demonstrating strength and forcefulness. In the case of the parents and primary school teachers, the personal and affective component of the child's dispositions toward them result in a greater willingness to overlook—i.e., not perceive—divergences from the ideal form of forceful behavior. But, with secondary school teachers, this personal and affective element is no longer operative to the same extent, and, thus, for the child to perceive his secondary school teacher as being forceful—as he perceived his parents and most of his primary school teachers—the secondary school teacher must *in fact* be "stronger" than certain of the weaker primary school teachers were. In other words, some primary school teachers were probably given legitimacy by their students because of an affective and personal element which helped to compensate for their comparative weakness, but this advantage no longer works in favor of secondary school teachers.

It is on the axis of forcefulness that the alternation between authority-laden and chahut interactions rotates. But the question arises as to why the chahut mode of insubordination has developed, rather than some other behavioral reaction toward weak teachers.[6] This is explicable on the basis of two interrelated factors. On the one hand, when pupils enter secondary school and confront for the first time superordinates who fail to conform to their model of expected forceful behavior, they are "uncertain" how to respond—i.e., their expectations as to how a superordinate will act do not correspond with the actual behavior of certain of their teachers, and, therefore, they enter an "anomic" state. On the other hand, any means developed to avoid this "anomie" must take into account the lack of training students have had in taking initiatives or acting independently. At first, the pupils entering secondary school may try different ways to resolve their "uncertainty" when confronted by a weak teacher, but eventually (probably before the end of sixième) the chahut becomes the institutionalized response to this type of teacher, thereby eliminating "uncertainty" and "anomie." The major advantages of the chahut over other behavioral responses to nonforceful teachers are: (1) the pupils' behavior is externally imposed by a group of leaders who play a guiding role vis-à-vis the rest of the class, (2) the chahut may, theoretically, have functional consequences (e.g., it may force certain teachers to be stronger or else drive them away so that they might be replaced by more forceful ones), and (3) the pupils find chahuting to be an enjoyable form of activity which, among other things, helps to reduce the tension and boredom of school days.[7]

The Development of Assumed Coverage

During the early years of secondary school, pupils seem predisposed toward chahuting. But with a teacher who is chahuté the educational process is made more difficult. Students become dependent on their textbooks as the only source of information. Class time is not available for explaining difficulties or clearing up confusions. As a result, the individual student is in an inferior position when competing with other pupils who have studied the same subject matter with directive teachers. More precisely, he has an important disadvantage on the competitive national examinations, the passing of which is the culmination of one's education.

If passing these examinations were only slightly important for the child, the chahut would not necessarily be dysfunctional. However, passing the exams is the only way to complete one's education, and this goal is very highly valued. Eighty-three percent of the pupils in the first cycle view it as either having fundamental importance or being very important.[8]

Thus, the student finds himself on the horns of a dilemma. He chahuts those teachers whom he considers nonlegitimate, but this makes the accomplishment of a highly valued goal—successfully completing his education—more difficult. Since the pupils were not taught how to set self-limitations on their own behavior, control, to exist at all, must be externally imposed. But certain teachers will be unable to do this and thus be chahuté, even if the students consider the subject matters taught to be important. The problem, therefore, is to find a method by which control can be externally imposed regardless of the forcefulness of a given teacher.

Assumed coverage is a solution. Within this mode of interaction, a student obeys directives which are internal to him, but which he perceives, nonetheless, to be directives (i.e., the prescriptions of others) rather than norms. Along with putting an end to the importance of direct coverage, remembered socialization bypasses the question of legitimacy. Within the new authority relationship, the real directive givers are superordinates of the past to whom the pupils attributed legitimacy. Hence, students do not need to judge the forcefulness of their actual teachers, because neither a positive nor a negative judgment would have any effect on the pupils' behavior.

But why, in fact, is assumed coverage adopted rather than some other basis for behavior? In part, this is explained by the double fact that: (1) rational needs militate against the continued, exclusive usage of authority-laden and chahut modes of inter-action and (2) the development of assumed coverage resolves the dilemma posed by the conflict between the highly valued goal of successfully finishing one's education and the continued use of the chahut with any teacher who lacks forcefulness. However, to complete the explanation, we must bear in mind the tendency which exists in all societies for teachers to give fewer directives to older students than to younger ones. Teachers expect older pupils to be more independent and find it onerous to constantly give them directives.[9] As a result, the rational needs which push French secondary school students away from continued exclusive reliance on the alternating pattern are directed and channeled toward developing a new pattern of relationships which is based on teachers issuing relatively few directives. Gradually, as pupils are receiving less overt direction from teachers, they adopt a basis for behavior which requires neither setting self-limitations on their own in-unit behavior (something they have never been taught to do) nor directives, and which avoids posing the legitimacy question. The result is assumed coverage based on remembered socialization.

TABLE 2.1: Chahut Frequency: Students in the First and Second Cycles

Q. How often are there chahuts in your class?

	Cinquième		Troisième		Seconde		Terminale		First Cycle Total		Second Cycle Total		TOTAL	
	%	N	%	N	%	N	%	N	%	N	%	N	%	N
(1) Never	2	(8)	3	(16)	7	(18)	9	(28)	2	(24)	8	(46)	4	(70)
(2) Almost Never	8	(39)	6	(36)	15	(41)	17	(56)	7	(75)	16	(97)	11	(172)
(3) Rarely	8	(40)	10	(54)	19	(52)	23	(74)	9	(94)	21	(126)	13	(220)
(4) Sometimes	33	(152)	31	(176)	39	(106)	36	(117)	32	(328)	37	(223)	34	(551)
(5) Often	31	(143)	34	(191)	17	(46)	11	(38)	33	(334)	14	(84)	26	(418)
(6) Very Often	18	(84)	16	(87)	3	(9)	4	(13)	17	(171)	4	(22)	12	(193)
TOTAL	100	(466)	100	(560)	100	(272)	100	(362)	100	(1026)	100	(593)	100	(1624)
Mean:	4.3624		4.3411		3.5441		3.3681		4.3509		3.4482		4.0185	

The development of assumed coverage also serves to reduce a tension in the authority-laden mode between students' distance perceptions and their deportment practices. The large majority of pupils (seventy-four percent) consider their innate worth to be equal to or superior to that of their teachers.[10] This normative posture is sharply contradicted by the "arrogant" deportment practices of teachers during authority-laden interactions. Such a sharp contradiction between distance perceptions and deportment practices is bound to induce cognitive dissonance in the student. We may speculate that one of the ways to reduce this dissonance would be to limit the amount of authority-based personal interaction between the pupils and their teachers. This is certainly one of the basic effects of assumed coverage. Within this pattern, the present teachers, in a sense, are not part of the authority relationship which, nevertheless, remains highly directive.

The Acquired Secondary School Authority Pattern: Assumed Coverage and the Alternating Pattern

The development of remembered socialization is not accompanied by a termination of the alternation between the authority-laden and the chahut modes. Rather, there is a significant deemphasis of the earlier pattern and a transformation of the conditions under which it becomes operative.

Students in the upper grades follow the alternating pattern less often than the younger pupils.[11] This is shown clearly in Table 2.1, where, for example, it can be seen that forty-nine percent of the pupils in cinquième and fifty percent of those in troisième said chahuts often occur in their classes while only twenty percent of those in seconde and fifteen percent of those in terminale gave a similar response. The older pupils also chahut a smaller number of teachers. This was clearly reflected in observation: In the upper grades, we rarely saw a chahut. Table 2.2 also supports this point: Students in the first cycle chahut, on the average, 2.3 teachers while those in the second cycle chahut, on the average, only 1.7 teachers. (Figure 2.1 graphically portrays the decreasing tendency to chahut, both in the sense of frequency and number of teachers chahuté, as the students move into the upper grades.)

This decreased tendency to chahut in the upper grades

TABLE 2.2: Number of Teachers Chahuté: Students in the First and Second Cycles

Q. How many of your teachers are chahuté?

	Cinquième		Troisième		Seconde		Terminale		First Cycle Total		Second Cycle Total		TOTAL	
	%	N	%	N	%	N	%	N	%	N	%	N	%	N
(0) 0 Teachers	0	2	3	18	8	21	12	34	2	20	10	55	5	75
(1) 1 Teacher	30	132	21	116	36	94	40	119	25	248	38	213	30	461
(2) 2 Teachers	36	158	37	201	36	92	32	96	36	359	34	188	35	547
(3) 3 Teachers	22	98	22	118	12	31	11	33	22	216	11	64	18	280
(4) 4 Teachers	7	32	12	66	6	14	2	7	10	98	4	21	7	119
(5) 5 Teachers	3	15	3	19	1	3	1	2	3	34	1	5	3	39
(6) 6 Teachers	1	3	1	7	1	2	1	2	1	10	1	4	1	14
(7) 7 Teachers	0	1	0	1	0	1	0	0	0	2	0	1	0	3
(8) 8 or more Teachers	1	3	0	1	0	0	1	4	0	4	1	4	1	8
TOTAL:	100	444	100[a]	547	100	258	100	297	100[a]	991	100	555	100	1546
Mean Response:	2.2387		2.3547		1.7868		1.6566		2.3027		1.7171		2.0925	

a. The sum of the percentages in this column adds up to 99% because each represents a rounded-off figure.

conceivably could occur simply because the most chahut-prone students dropped out or were excluded from school before they completed their secondary educations. However, as Table 2.3 clearly indicates, there is no empirical support for this explanation. In fact, although the percentage is virtually identical from one grade level to the next, if anything, a slightly higher percentage of the older pupils are chahuters!

Rather, the reduced frequency of the alternating pattern seems to occur because, while the younger students tend to chahut solely on the basis of the forcefulness they attribute to a given teacher, the older pupils bring into consideration other criteria which strongly modify and limit the scope of their chahut behavior. To be specific, the older students are especially likely to follow the alternating pattern with teachers whom they consider incompetent or who give too many directives, as well as with those who teach subjects perceived as having little importance.

This argument is largely based on questionnaire results. One of the questions asked the pupils to select from a list of twenty-two qualities, three or four which *when clustered* would define a teacher who is chahuté. Table 2.4 presents a list of the eight qualities chosen by at least twenty-five percent of the pupils in the first or second cycles. Among the five qualities chosen by at least twenty-five percent of the younger pupils, four are associated with a lack of forcefulness—"weak personality," "newcomer," "substitute teacher," and "women." Thus, for students in the first cycle, it seems as if any teacher who is insufficiently strong will be chahuté. Such is not the case for the older pupils. Within the cluster of qualities they tend to associate with a chahuted teacher there is one quality of lack of forcefulness—"weak personality"—but also three other qualities—"insufficient competence," "giving too many orders," and "teaching an unimportant subject"—which cannot be considered as suggesting a lack of strength. Therefore, it seems that, for the older students, the lack of forcefulness of a particular teacher is not a *sufficient* condition for chahuting. Rather, teachers who lack forcefulness will only be chahuté if they are not very competent, if they give too many directives, or if they teach an unimportant subject.[12]

This is a rational, logically explicable development. Since the major motivating force for eliminating the alternating pattern was

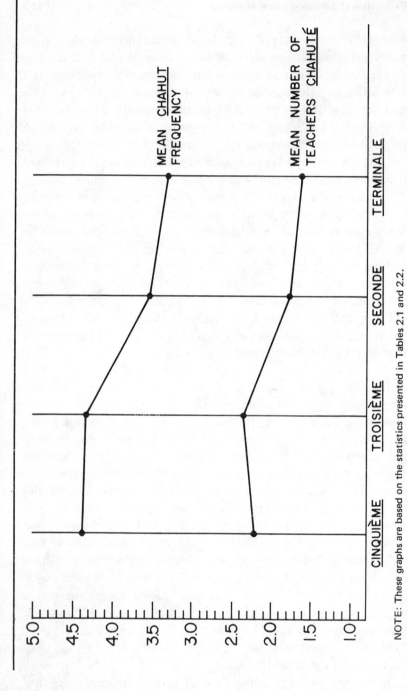

NOTE: These graphs are based on the statistics presented in Tables 2.1 and 2.2.

FIGURE 2.1: Mean Chahut Frequency and Mean Number of Teachers Chahuté: Students in Cinquième, Troisième, Seconde, and Terminale

the conflict between the high value attributed to education (i.e., passing the competitive national examinations) and the chahut, there is no incentive to stop chahuting teachers who are not contributing to the fulfillment of this valued goal—i.e., incompetent teachers and those who teach an unimportant subject. On the other hand, there is a strong rationale, during the time when assumed coverage is dominant, to chahut teachers who give too many orders, since they are acting in a manner which is incompatible with the basic element of assumed coverage.

In sum, students in the upper grades (since they highly value completing their education) will interact with most of their teachers on the basis of assumed coverage. But, with incompetent teachers or with those whose subject matter is not perceived as important (i.e., with teachers who are not contributing to the achievement of their valued goals), as well as with teachers who give too many orders, they will follow the alternating pattern, chahuting those who lack forcefulness while establishing an authority-laden relationship with the others. This is the authority pattern acquired in French secondary schools.

The Pupils' Normative Structure

A large percentage of French secondary school pupils have norms that are in sharp conflict with the type of authority behavior required of them. For example, as was pointed out, the younger students participate little in practice but highly value participation. Although the older pupils tend to participate at least as much as, if not more than, the younger ones, they have an even stronger normative desire for more participation. Similarly, students at all levels have a high valuation of responsiveness but do not perceive their teachers as being responsive. Likewise, a large majority of the students in both the upper and the lower grades believe their activities are too heavily controlled. Finally, the pupils have a strong negative valuation of their teachers' arrogant deportment practices.[13]

What is the meaning of this conflict between the expressed norms and the actual behavior of students? The two most plausible interpretations are unfortunately not empirically tenable. First, it might be argued that French secondary school pupils

TABLE 2.3: Personal Chahuting Practices: Students in the First and Second Cycles

Q. With what frequency do you tend to participate in chahuts?

	Cinquième %	N	Troisième %	N	Seconde %	N	Terminale %	N	First Cycle Total %	N	Second Cycle Total %	N	TOTAL %	N
(1) Always or almost almost all the time	10	53	13	82	13	37	13	51	12	135	13	88	12	223
(2) Often	15	79	27	175	27	78	29	114	22	254	28	192	24	446
(3) Sometimes	31	160	33	210	33	94	31	123	32	370	32	217	32	587
(4) Rarely	29	148	22	144	18	52	21	83	25	292	20	135	23	427
(5) Never	15	75	5	35	10	28	6	24	9	110	8	52	9	162
TOTAL:	100	515	100	646	100[a]	289	100	395	100	1161	100[a]	684	100	1846
Mean Response:	3.2194		2.8065		2.8478		2.7848		2.9896		2.8114		2.9219	

a. The sum of the percentages in this column adds up to 101%, because each represents a rounded-off figure.

normatively reject any form of pupil-teacher interaction which approaches the authority-laden mode.[14] If this were the case, the chahut would represent the students' protest against authority-laden relationships. But it has already been pointed out that, among teachers subject to the alternating pattern, those who fail to control closely the activities of their pupils are most prone to be chahuté.

In addition, among this group of teachers, those who in other ways alter their behavior toward students away from the authority-laden mode—e.g., by being increasingly responsive or "familiar" in their deportment practices—are also liable to be suddenly chahuté. Thus, in fact, within the subset of teachers subject to the alternating pattern, those who come closest to acting in a manner consonant with the students' norms seem to be chahuté.

This first plausible interpretation would be tenable if the pupils "fear authority" but even more strongly value the chahut. Then, pupils' high valuation of the chahut would lead them to chahut those teachers who were insufficiently forceful while being totally compliant with others, even though this would contradict their norms which reject authority-laden relationships. The result of these conflicting norms would be strain. While such an argument seems logical, it is not empirically tenable, because the students do not highly value the chahut.[15]

The second plausible interpretation of the apparent conflict between actual behavior and expressed norms suggests that the latter are simply "official peer group norms." The major characteristic of "official" norms is that, while being rhetorically expressed by the members of the unit, they seem to have no effect on the way in which members behave. At least partially, the responses given by the secondary school pupils are official peer group norms; they coincide with critiques of the actual school system's structure, functioning, rules, regulations, and/or leaders frequently made by the students to individuals who are not superordinates in their school.

These norms, however, are not simply "official," for they may be actualized in behavioral efforts to change the social unit. These attempts at transformation do not occur within the unit itself—for instance, in the form of noncompliance. Rather, they may come to fruition by membership in or support of another unit which has

TABLE 2.4: The Characteristics of Chahuted Teachers: Students in the First and Second Cycles

Q. Here is a list of characteristics of teachers. Choose at a maximum 2, 3, or 4 qualities which when clustered together define a teacher who is chahuté. The qualities are: a newcomer to the school, insufficient competence, strong personality, very old, impolite, man, woman, liberal (against punishing), those who give their classes at the beginning of the day, those who do not give much homework, very young, too friendly with the students, very competent, those who have taught at the school for a long time, weak personality, those who give their courses at the end of the day, those who give a great deal of homework, substitute teacher, those who give too many orders, those who teach an unimportant subject, and those who give disagreeable orders.

	Cinquième		Troisième		Seconde		Terminale		First Cycle Total		Second Cycle Total		TOTAL	
	%	N	%	N	%	N	%	N	%	N	%	N	%	N
Newcomer to school	28	150	29	192	28	84	10	39	29	342	17	123	24	435
Insufficient competence	11	59	28	185	40	122	68	274	20	244	56	396	34	640
Women	33	177	20	134	9	27	9	35	26	311	9	62	20	373
Weak personality	26	140	50	328	66	202	75	302	39	468	71	504	51	972
Substitute teacher	25	135	28	188	27	81	15	62	27	323	20	143	25	466
Too many orders	17	90	27	176	31	93	35	143	22	266	33	236	26	502
Unimportant subject	7	37	20	135	23	69	33	132	14	172	28	201	20	373
Disagreeable orders	28	147	27	180	25	77	28	114	27	327	27	191	27	518

NOTE: I have only listed in this table those qualities which have been chosen by at least 25% of the pupils in either the first or the second cycle.

at least as one of its goals the transformation of the core unit—e.g., the older students may join the youth section of a political party.

In sum, it would be equally inaccurate to interpret the expressed norms (which challenge the ongoing pattern of authority behavior) as either an expression of "fear" for authority or *simply* rhetorical, "official" peer group norms. Rather, they seem to signify a desire for serious modifications in the nature of the unit, which has behavioral implications. By returning to the types of activities typically controlled in the French educational system, the conditions responsible for generating these norms can be inferred. Within the authority-laden mode, there is a very high level of attempted and effective control over what to do, how to do it, and how to behave in class, but a very low level of idea control. In fact, teachers actively seek to inculcate within their pupils a critical bent of mind. This attempt is highly successful and bears fruit in the form of students adopting widely divergent philosophical orientations and in the growth of critiques of the way in which the unit actually functions. But the pupils readily express their opinions only when out of the presence of a potentially disapproving authority figure. Since teachers and students virtually never discuss the way in which the school functions, the pupils are accustomed to give free rein to their critiques of the system. This constant verbal expression of discontent leads to desires for modifications in the nature of the unit, which may be behaviorally actualized through joining or strongly supporting the activities of another social unit which has, at least as one of its goals, the transformation of the educational system.

If these norms had unit-centered behavioral implications, the students would only behave in an authority-laden manner when forced to do so. Yet, it has already been suggested that the use of force is irrelevant to obtaining compliance. Furthermore, if forcefulness were understood as the constant implication that force might be used, through the continual issuance of specific directives, then the older students, given the fact that they have the same basic normative stance as the younger ones, would not act as they do within the remembered socialization pattern.

Simultaneous with and segregated from these rhetorical, non-unit-centered behavioral norms, there exists a series of guides to action consonant with the way in which things are actually done in the unit. The alternation between the authority-laden and the chahut modes of interaction, as well as the development of assumed coverage, is built on the triple normative basis of attributing legitimacy to those who are perceived as forceful, indifference toward compliance, and a high valuation of the major function performed by the unit. The alternating pattern is based on perceived forcefulness which leads the pupils to conduct themselves in an authority-laden manner with some of their teachers, while they chahut others. To behave in these contradictory ways would cause severe cognitive strain were it not for the fact that students tend to value compliance indifferently. The high value pupils place on education conflicts with their legitimacy notion which results in chahuting certain competent teachers of important subject matters; this conflict is resolved by assumed coverage.

Thus, French secondary school pupils tend to have a dualistic normative structure. This permits those who desire serious modifications in the nature of the unit to remain behaviorally within the bounds of the actual system without suffering from cognitive strain, while simultaneously providing them with an escape hatch for their normative desires for a transformed system. Such dual guides to action seem to have a particular value in a regimented social unit, the function of which is highly valued and in which the subordinates have developed a strong critical spirit. Without dual guides to action, the normative desire for serious modifications would simply result in systematic rebellion; but this would militate against the smooth functioning of the unit, which is also normatively repugnant. The individuals holding both sets of norms would find themselves between Scylla and Charybdis. Since satisfying both norms simultaneously is impossible, the only way to bypass the dilemma is through dual and segregated guides to action. This is exactly what happens with those French secondary school pupils who are most critical of their educational system.

Conclusion

The description and explanation of pupil-teacher authority relationships in secondary schools which has been presented is essentially developmental. On the basis of their experiences in authority-laden families and primary schools, French children seem to develop a legitimacy notion based on forcefulness and fail to learn how to set self-limitations on their own behavior. Upon entering the secondary school, they are, for the first time in their lives, placed simultaneously under the authority of a sizable group of superordinates with whom they cannot, because of their number, develop strong affective ties. These superordinates act toward the pupils in different ways: Some do not behave in an authority-laden manner. The pupils, confronted by such a pattern of superordinate conduct, for which their earlier socialization experiences did not prepare them, enter an anomic state. This anomie gives birth to the institutionalization of the chahut.

Thus, the alternating pattern becomes modal during the early years of secondary school. Special norms are required if an individual is to cope with such highly divergent forms of conduct, without suffering from severe cognitive strain. Strain is avoided because pupils tend to be indifferent toward compliance; this is the only posture which allows them simultaneously to be very submissive with certain superordinates and completely insubordinate with others.

While functioning within the alternating pattern, students develop a series of norms that are in sharp contradiction with the type of behavior required of them within authority-laden interactions. However, this potential dissonance is avoided through the development of dual guides to action: A legitimacy notion based on forcefulness and indifference toward compliance support the students' in-unit pattern of behavior and are segregated from a set of critical norms which lead to strong rhetorical denunciations of the unit's practices and, sometimes, to joining or supporting other social units which have as one of their goals the revamping of the French educational system.

Although these threats to the continued dominance of the alternating pattern are successfully met without forcing a change in pattern, this situation does not endure. Conflict arises between chahuting any teacher who is not perceived of as forceful and the very high value given to the goal sought by membership in the unit—i.e., education and passing exams. Rational, goal-oriented behavior plays the chief role in eliminating the dominance of the alternating pattern. The problem is solved through the development of assumed coverage, utilized with all competent teachers of important subjects who do not issue too many orders to their pupils. With less "valuable" teachers, however, the students continue to participate in the alternating pattern.

By the time the pupils terminate their secondary school education, they have learned to function under two different types of authority patterns: (1) the alternating pattern and (2) the assumed coverage pattern. Whether one or the other pattern will be followed in any given case is determined by two independent variables: (1) the value attributed to education (the goal to be achieved by membership in the unit) and (2) the pupils' perception of how effectively the unit and its superordinates are functioning to achieve this goal. If the goal sought by membership in the unit is valued *and* if the unit and its superordinates are perceived as acting in a way that seems effectively to achieve this goal for the subordinates, assumed coverage will dominate. The alternating pattern will occur when either or both of these two conditions are absent.

NOTES

1. There is, however, one very significant difference between these analogous relationships: The domination of the animal by the man is grounded on the use of force, while the teacher's domination is contingent on forcefulness.

2. For a discussion of the interpretations of the French conception of limits, see Viviane Isambert-Jamati, "L'autorité dans l'education française," *Archives européenness de sociologie* 6 (1965), pp. 154-155. See also Laurence Wylie, "Youth in France and the United States," *Daedalus* 91, no. 1 (Winter 1962), pp. 198-215.

3. The following discussion is, by necessity, speculative and impressionistic. A reliable explanation would have as its basis a systematic analysis of behavior toward authority in French families and primary schools, including a longitudinal study of a group of students as they pass from the last year of primary school to the first year of secondary school. Unfortunately, such analyses do not presently exist. Even information on attitudes toward familial and elementary school authority is scarce, although some new data should be available in the near future. (I am referring to research conducted in Great Britain, France, and the United States by Fred Greenstein and Sidney Tarrow. Using elementary school pupils as their respondents, they are examining the socialization process in these three Western democracies.)

4. For a discussion of the authority-laden nature of the French family, see Rhoda Metraux and Margaret Mead, *Themes in French Culture* (Stanford, Ca.: Stanford University Press, 1954), pp. 1-88. The authority-laden nature of the primary school is described, along with some references to the family, by Wylie in *Village in the Vaucluse*,

pp. 55-97. In addition, Wylie suggests that there is an expectation in France that the same type of authority relations will exist in the primary school as in the family.

5. In all societies there will be some families and some primary school teachers who fail to conform to the modal type. Children who come from these sorts of homes or who come into contact with these types of teachers may be expected to have problems in segregating the different roles they are expected to play.

6. That some form of rebellion should develop alongside the authority-laden mode (given that French children are frequently punished by shaming) is in some sense predicted by psychoanalytical theory. As Eric H. Erikson points out: "Too much shaming does not lead to genuine propriety but to a secret determination to try to get away with things, unseen—if, indeed, it does not result in defiant shameless-ness. . . . There is a limit to a child's and an adult's endurance in the face of demands to consider himself, his body, and his wishes as evil and dirty, and to his belief in the infallibility of those who pass such judgment. He may be apt to turn things around, and to consider as evil only the fact that they exist" (*Childhood and Society,* [New York: W. W. Norton, 1963] , p. 253).

7. Quite a few interpretations of the meaning and/or function of the chahut exist. Rose-Marie Mossé-Bastide (*L'autorité du maître* [Neuchatel, Switzerland: Delachaus and Niestlé, 1966] , passim) simply views the chahuted teacher as one who lacks authority. For Gérard Vincent, the chahut is a "collective manifestation of aggressiveness" (*Les professeurs du second degré: Contribution á l'etude du corps enseignant,* Cahiers de la Fondation National des Sciences Politiques [Paris: Librairie Armand Colin, 1967] , p. 87). According to Jesse Pitts ("Change in Bourgeois France," pp. 254-259), the chahut would be a particular manifestation of the "delinquent peer group community." (See also "The Family and Peer Group," Chapter 21 in *A Modern Introduction to the Family,* ed. Norman W. Bell and Ezra F. Vogel [New York: Free Press, 1960] , passim.) An interpretation of the chahut which relates it to anomie is presented by Jacques Testanière ("Chahut traditionnel et chahut anomique dans l'enseignement du second degré," *Revue française de sociologie* 8, special issue [1967] , pp. 17-33). He argues that the "traditional chahut," which was an expression of the integrated school community as well as a form of recreation (p. 23), has been replaced in most schools by the anomic chahut in which there are no chahut leaders and there is "generalized disorder" (p. 25). My argument strongly conflicts with Testanière's: (1) I have interpreted the chahut as originally developing from anomie rather than as a symbol or sign of anomie; and (2) on empirical grounds, I disagree with Testanière's assertion that the modern chahut is characterized by an absence of leaders.

My own interpretation of the origin and meaning of the chahut seems to make more empirical sense than any of these conceptions, but other arguments with more or less equal tenability could have been advanced. For instance, the chahut might be conceived of as a surrogate rebellion against "authoritarian" teachers, or, simply, as a protest against ambivalence.

8. For a full data display, see Schonfeld, *Youth and Authority in France,* Table 8, p. 47.

9. For some relevant data, see ibid., pp. 48-49.

10. For a full data display and discussion, see ibid., pp. 49-51, Table 20.

11. Throughout this discussion, I operationally define the extensiveness of the alternating pattern by the amount of chahuting which occurs. This procedure is totally justified because, in practice, the authority-laden mode is linked with the chahut; it had to be adopted, because pupils cannot clearly distinguish between the authority-laden and the assumed-coverage modes and, therefore, cannot estimate how often they participate in one or the other of these behavioral patterns.

12. After consulting Table 2.4, some readers might question this interpretation because a higher percentage of students in the upper grades chose "weak personality" (seventy-one percent) than those in the lower grades (thirty-nine percent). However, when it is remembered that pupils were asked to select a few qualities which *when clustered together* define a chahuted teacher, this objection should disappear. For the older students "weak personality" is the deciding factor for chahuting "incompetent teachers," those who teach an "unimportant subject" and "those who give too many orders." In other words, within a limited segment of teachers, having a "weak personality" alone will virtually always bring about a chahut. But, for the younger pupils, the only type of quality which plays an important role in deciding if *any* teacher will be chahuté is a lack of forcefulness, which is not simply seen abstractly (i.e., "weak personality") but also concretely (i.e., "substitute teacher," "women," and "newcomer to the school").

13. For the relevant questionnaire items and full data displays, see Schonfeld, *Youth and Authority in France,* pp. 58-63, Tables 24-33.

14. Such an interpretation would be in conformity with a widely adopted conception of French dispositions toward authority which argues that within each individual there are two different (and usually diametrically opposed) attitudes toward authority, one of which is hostile toward or fearful of authority. An early exponent of this view was Robert Dell, who argued that the French had a "natural dislike for authority" (*My Second Country (France)* [New York: John Lane, 1920], p. 32). More recently, Michel Crozier has spoken of the French desire to avoid "face-to-face dependency relationships" (*The Bureaucratic Phenomenon,* p. 222). In a similar vein, Stanley Hoffmann has argued that the Frenchman has both a "need for and fear of authority" ("Paradoxes of the French Political Community," in *In Search of France,* ed. Stanley Hoffmann et al., p. 9). Finally, Roy Macridis suggested that the French "political culture" exhibits a dualism between "the search for authority" and "the deep distrust of it" ("France," in *Modern Political Systems: Europe,* ed. Roy C. Macridis and Robert E. Ward [Englewood Cliffs, N.J.: Prentice-Hall, 1968], p. 158).

15. For a full data display, see Schonfeld, *Youth and Authority in France,* p. 64, Table 34. Dissonance reduction theory could have predicted this result, at least for the pupils in the second cycle. Since chahuting is dysfunctional for the achievement of a highly valued goal—i.e., successfully completing one's education—to attribute a high value to chahuting would create a great deal of dissonance. There would be a natural tendency to try to reduce this dissonance, and one way of accomplishing this would be to reduce the value attributed to the chahut.

PART II

AUTHORITY IN THE NATIONAL SCHOOL OF ADMINISTRATION (E.N.A.)

Even though E.N.A. is just reaching the age of adulthood, it is already an institution. For France is first and foremost an administration, and Enarques [the graduates of E.N.A.] are in the process of conquering the high command posts within it. Henceforth, each year that passes is a year in which they win embassies, préfectures, and directions [major divisions of the ministries]. Thus, it is the Enarque who now represents in our country the daily face of state power.

Jacques Mandrin, *L'Enarchie*, p. 10.

The Empirical Basis of the Case Study

The Ecole Nationale d'Administration (National School of Administration—E.N.A.) is an agency of administrative elite recruitment par excellence. Although only established in the aftermath of World War II, its graduates already dominate the upper echelons of the French civil service, and within a decade or two, E.N.A. alumni will virtually monopolize such positions. In addition, the school's graduates are obtaining important positions in the political world; currently both the President of the Republic and the Prime Minister are E.N.A.s.

Each year approximately 100 students are admitted to the school through two distinct but parallel channels:[1] one open to university students with a *license* (approximately equivalent to an M.A.) and one open to practicing civil servants with at least five years of experience. Admission is determined by performance on two examinations, one written and one oral. (The examinations in the civil service channel are easier to pass than those for the students.) Competition is fierce, especially for the student admittees, who tend not only to be an intellectual elite, but also to be largely drawn from the Parisian region, former students at Paris' prestigious Institute of Political Studies (Sciences Po) and upper class. The successful civil servant candidates have these characteristics to a lesser degree.

The school's program of studies begins in February with a year-long on-the-job training period (stage) in an important administrative agency, usually in a *préfecture* to assist the *préfet* who represents the central government in the provinces and implements its decisions. After the "stage" is completed, the *promotion* (i.e., class) begins a seventeen-month period of course work in Paris divided into four trimesters. Small seminars are the exclusive form of instruction. Just prior to the beginning of classes, the students elect a *délégation* (composed of almost ten percent of the promotion) to serve as a transmission belt between the students and the school's administrators.

Throughout the program of studies, the E.N.A.s are being graded. These grades are of fundamental importance. In April-May of the last year at E.N.A., the school administration, using a weighted average of the grades received by each student, makes a rank-ordering (classement) of the promotion. This serves as the base on which the various posts offered by the ministries and public agencies are distributed—i.e., among the available jobs, the students choose whichever position they want with the first person having first choice, the second person second choice, etc. The status and career possibilities vary significantly from post to post. The first fifteen students normally go to one of the three *Grands Corps—Inspection des Finances, Conseil d'Etat,* and *Cour des Comptes*—and thereby have an excellent chance to become an administrative head of one of the ministries in ten or fifteen years. The possibility for one of the lower-ranked students to obtain such a future post is to all intents and purposes nonexistent.

The major portion of my research at E.N.A. took place from May to July 1968. Besides observation of the students' activities during the period of crisis at the school, fifty percent of the members of the 1967 promotion (the only class in attendance at the time) were randomly selected for nondirective interviews. These tended to last for between thirty-five minutes and an hour and centered on behavior toward superordinates during the "stage," teachers at E.N.A., members of the school administration and classmates.

Since May through July 1968 was quite an exceptional period in the history of the school, I returned to E.N.A. for a few weeks in February-March 1969. This visit permitted observation during a routine period and enabled me to locate differences and similarities between normal and crisis times. I randomly chose forty percent of those students who had been interviewed in 1968 and gave them another nondirective interview, going over the same terrain which had previously been covered. In addition, the classes followed by the 1967 promotion as well as those followed by the 1968 promotion (the new cohort of students who had recently completed their "stages") were observed. Finally, both promotions were asked to respond to a written questionnaire. (Appendix B provides a detailed view of the school's importance, its structure and organization, and the sources upon which the following analysis is based.)

NOTE

1. In the rest of this section, as well as in Appendix B, I describe the E.N.A. system as it was during the time of my case study. The system of admissions and program of studies has since been reformed. (For details, see *Rapport sur la reforme de l'Ecole Nationale d'Administration,* January 1970, written by Pierre Racine, the actual Director of the School and a forthcoming thesis being prepared by Rey Reimer for Johns Hopkins University.) The first group of students to which the reform will fully apply are those who will leave E.N.A. in 1976.

Chapter 3

BEHAVIOR TOWARD AUTHORITY AT THE
ECOLE NATIONALE D'ADMINISTRATION

The National School of Administration was created explicitly to train high-level civil servants. Serious questions have been and may be raised in regard to the utility of the knowledge acquired at E.N.A. But, from the perspective of behavioral formation, the school appears to be performing its assigned task very well—that is to say, students seem to learn a pattern of behavior toward authority and a method for determining what is expected of them which fit perfectly with the bureaucratic roles they will be called upon to play.

To be more concrete, without either face-to-face directives or extensive written instructions, subordinates follow a rather rigidly defined pattern of behavior which seeks to conform with their hierarchical superiors' (unexpressed) expectations. They live in a world of assumed coverage. However, especially during the stage, remembered socialization is not the basic source of behavioral direction, since relevant past incidents of direct coverage are not readily available. Rather, largely through observation of how others behave and overt solicitations of advice, the young E.N.A.s seek to divine what is expected of them, and then act accordingly.

The grading system, culminating in the final *classement*, theoretically helps to prepare the student for his future professional lot—i.e., to reduce uncertainty by providing feedback on how well one is living up to expectations. However, since the grades received for exercises performed at the very end of the program of studies play a major role in determining one's *classement*, the system rather tends to generate simultaneously feelings of constraint and uncertainty.

In this context, it is not surprising that many E.N.A.s desire a fundamental reform or even an abolition of the school. Acting under the guidelines of a dualistic normative structure, they conform to the expected patterns of behavior during the *stage* and in the classroom, while, at the same time, strongly criticizing the system and possibly joining or supporting outside groups which have as one of their goals a thorough transformation or even an elimination of the school. The general, societywide crisis of May 1968, combined with special events occurring within E.N.A., provided a virtually unique conjunction which led the students to break out of their normal pattern of behavior and participate in a serious attempt at reform—centered, as might be expected, on a suppression of the system of *classement* along with the inequity between beginning civil service positions which results in highly unequal career potentials. If the reform proposals had been adopted (which they were not) both uncertainty and feelings of constraint would have been reduced for future students at the National School of Administration.

In this chapter, the crisis authority relations will be described and the development as well as the resolution of this severe departure from the routine will be explained. However, before directing attention toward understanding the unusual and atypical, we must analyze the normal situation—the classroom style of behavior toward authority will be discussed, then the more complex interactions which characterize the *stage* will be examined, and finally the dualistic normative structure of E.N.A.s will be described.

Classroom Authority

Instruction at E.N.A. is carried out in small seminars (having ten to twelve students) led by a *maître de conférence* (usually a civil servant recently graduated from the school). Each weekly session is centered on the reports prepared by one or more students. The substantive and stylistic aspects of these reports, as well as the general organization of the seminar meeting, provide an important key to understanding authority at E.N.A.

The maître de conférence issues only directives which delineate the problem to be examined in class. Yet the students' presentations systematically seek to adhere to a single, well-defined model, having four major characteristics. First, the reports are all organized according to a detailed outline. The argument is divided into two or three equal parts with a brief introduction and conclusion. Facts are presented in an orderly fashion to support each point made in the presentation. Second, a good report avoids polemics and attempts to balance carefully the pros and cons on every issue. The student refrains from making an overt personal commitment to a particular interpretation; he presents himself as a detached, if not aloof, observer and commentator. Third, the presentation must regard the problem with a critical eye. Defects are to be pointed out and remedies suggested, but these should not challenge the fundamentals of the system. Finally, students normally express opinions which they believe coincide with those of their teacher.

A presentation usually lasts at least thirty minutes and sometimes as much as three-quarters of an hour. Once finished, there is "discussion" and/or a critique of the report by the teacher. Discussion takes a rather curious form. The maître will ask if any other members of the class have remarks to make. Typically, one or two students will raise their hands and then politely and briefly seek to undermine the presentation, either by pointing out a lack of logical consistency or by noting a certain number of "important" (and often obscure) facts which have been overlooked and which tend to place some discredit on the report's argument. Most of the other students will either remain silent, add a brief point, or ask for further clarification. Throughout the "discussion," there is no real dialogue or attempt to build on the presentation. Classroom participation either solicits additional information or seeks to demolish the argument which has been presented.

After the discussion (but occasionally before), the professor gives an alternative presentation on the problem covered in the student's report. Sometimes he uses the same general outline, but at other times he employs an alternative organizational plan. His presentation serves as the class' model of a good report on the given problem.

The role the professor plays vis-à-vis the students is clearly indicated in the following extract from one of the interviews:

> The role of the maître de conférence is very directive, because he is not simply the dispenser of knowledge, but more importantly he is a social model on which the students must pattern themselves. The maître de conférence is, generally, an alumnus [of the school] who has succeeded; the alumnus of E.N.A. who is Inspector of Finances or subdirector of a ministry. He is the social model on which everyone patterns himself. This mimicry is unbelievable; it goes far beyond the intellectual domain, almost to the affective domain—it includes questions as to how to dress and the structure of the language—in the sense that the vocabulary, sentences, and patterns of thought closely imitate those of the maître de conférence.

Or as another interviewee commented:

> With five out of the six maîtres de conférence that I have had, I did not feel very free. Rather, I felt obliged to conform to the maître's ideas because of his grading power. . . . You are in the seminar, you make a presentation, you intervene orally; well, none of that is gratuitous. You are going to be graded on what you do. You cannot say what you want to say or what you think, you must say what you think is going to please your maître de conférence.

Thus, E.N.A.s view themselves as living in a highly directive classroom environment: They must follow the tenets of what they perceive to be a detailed and externally imposed behavioral model. But the instructors actually tend to issue only task-centered directives—i.e., those which define what work is to be done. This suggests that there is a high level of *assumed* instrumental, comportmental, and ideological coverage—i.e., control over how to do one's tasks, how to behave in the seminar and what ideas should be expressed, respectively.[1]

Since students rarely overtly challenge the opinions and ideas advanced by the maître, how can they demonstrate their intellectual skills? The most general method is by means of very well organized and researched presentations and by careful refutation of the arguments and views of one's classmates. In addition, to stand out (to shine), students may exhaustively research and become expert on relatively minor points. Then, at the proper moment in the seminar, when such information can be introduced to the advantage of the student, he raises a question the answer to which depends on having the information he has assiduously acquired. Or else he directly introduces his obscure points in an attempt to demonstrate his breadth of knowledge. Of course, to succeed in this method requires a great deal of skill in deciding which points to research and when to produce one's information in the seminar.

The modal style of classroom presentation and discussion which characterizes the National School of Administration can be called the "Sciences Po" model, for as every student at E.N.A. is quick to point out, one in fact acquires this behavioral pattern at Paris' Institute of Political Studies.[2] But not all of the E.N.A. students have studied at Sciences Po: While seventy percent of those who passed the 1967 entrance examinations reserved for students had a diploma from the Institute, only fifteen percent (five of thirty-three) of the former civil servants did.[3] As a result, we might expect the former civil servant to have difficulties in coping with E.N.A.'s seminar system. The interviews clearly reveal this to be the case: The large majority of former civil servants (as compared to only a small percentage of the "former students") could verbally describe the general outlines of the model of expected seminar behavior but had a great many problems in following the model in practice. For example, some noted their difficulties in creating a precise and detailed logical order for the presentation; others were unsuccessful in their attempts to balance the pros and cons on every issue; others did not know how to select and research a minor point which could be used in class to help them stand out; and still others were incapable or unwilling to divine and imitate the ideas of their teachers. These deviations from the seminar model were considered by the former civil servants as having an important negative influence on their grades, but, certain of the interviewees complained, the maîtres de conférence did not give them specific suggestions for improving their style of presentation or classroom participation.

From the evidence presented, the modal authority behavior of students toward teachers at E.N.A. appears to be based on remembered socialization. Few overt directives are issued by the superordinates, and these directives are largely task-oriented (because, of the four types of coverage, control over what to do alone cannot be learned in a social unit where subordinates are constantly expected to do different types of work; nor can task coverage in one unit performing a particular function be used to determine what to do in another unit performing a different task). Second, there are prescribed styles of instrumental, comportmental, and ideological behavior, but these basically follow the tenets earlier instilled in Sciences Po. Finally, this prescribed pattern of behavior, which is not defined by explicit directives from the students' actual superordinates, is perceived by the students as being externally imposed. Interviews reveal that among those who follow the Sciences Po model, many do so consciously and with the feeling that they must act thus even though they may not consider it a natural or desirable seminar style.

Authority During the Stage

Since everyone admitted to E.N.A. is very familiar with the French classroom environment, the employment of remembered socialization techniques in teacher-student authority interactions should be easier than applying these techniques to the stage in préfecture,[4] for which their background has not prepared them. The student, sent to a region of France with which he is not acquainted, is to work with the decision makers of an important governmental agency, but either he has never worked before or he has never been associated with a high-level decision-making process. Few of the *stagiaires* have ever even met a préfet, and none have reliable knowledge of the daily functioning of a préfecture. Prior to his arrival in the field, the student may ask himself: What am I supposed to do? How should I do it? And how should I behave toward the people with whom I will be working? Answers to these questions are derived from directives issued to the stagiaire by the préfet and his collaborators, written instructions given to the student by the school administration, and observation of the actual functioning of the préfecture by the stagiaire. In addition, for about ten percent of the students, partial answers are provided by their familial experiences. (These are the individuals who come from the very highest levels of French society or whose fathers are high-level civil servants. The normal pattern of behavior which they learned from their home environment is eminently suited for leading a successful stage.) Finally, the large majority of former civil servants drew upon their past experiences in the public service to provide guidelines for their stage behavior. However, given their impression, before receiving grades, that they had done very well, combined with the relatively mediocre evaluations they actually received for the stage, the former civil servants' past experiences seem to have been an inappropriate model on which to base stage behavior.

Questionnaire results, supported by the interview responses, are my primary source of information on coverage of the stagiaire's behavior. The questions used to tap coverage sought to determine the frequency with which the superordinates during the stage issued directives regarding tasks, instrumentalities and comportment. The results suggest that attempted task coverage was moderate, instrumental coverage was slightly less, and comportmental coverage was even lower. Furthermore, in each of these domains, the préfet seemed to issue fewer directives to the stagiaire than the other member of the decision-making body of the préfecture with whom the student worked most closely (in the majority of cases this was the Directeur de cabinet). Since I could not observe the relationships between the stagiaire and the members of the préfecture, it is very difficult to determine the degree of correlation between actual directive-issuing practices and students' perceptions of these practices as revealed in the questionnaires. However, if we assume that the relationship between actual and perceived directive-issuing practices is the same during the stage as during the course work, then—since I have observed student-teacher relations at E.N.A. and since the same questions on coverage were asked for these relations as well as for those that prevailed during the stage—we have an acceptable indicator of the actual directive-issuing tendencies of the préfet and his collaborator. The responses given to the perceived coverage questions clearly reveal that, in reference to tasks, instrumentalities, and comportment, the préfet and the maîtres are seen as being virtually equally directive. In fact, the average mean responses are identical (see Table 3.1 for a complete data display).

Thus the préfets (like the maîtres de conferénce) seem to issue some directives to cover the stagiaires' tasks, but do not attempt to explicitly control how they perform these tasks or their general behavior in the préfecture. However, within each of these three domains, the collaborator of the préfet with whom the student worked the most appeared more directive.

What accounts for this difference? The interviews provide some insights. The stagiaires tended to develop one of two very different kinds of relationships with this other member of the préfet's

TABLE 3.1: E.N.A. Students' Perceptions of Coverage: The Mean Responses[a]

	Maîtres		Préfet		Préfet's Collaborator	
	$\bar{X}$	N	$\bar{X}$	N	$\bar{X}$	N
Task Coverage[b]	3.06	134	3.05	164[c]	3.39	140[c]
Instrumental Coverage[b]	2.62	129	2.48	162[c]	3.08	137[c]
Comportmental Coverage[b]	1.96	131	1.90	164[c]	2.44	140[c]
Average Mean Perceived Coverage	2.55	—	2.55	—	3.00	—

a. A mean of 1.00 signifies no coverage, and a mean of 5.00 signifies total coverage.

b. The questions used to tap perceptions of coverage presented the respondents with an incomplete phrase. The respondent decided how to complete this phrase by placing an "X" on a continuum whose end-points had been defined. With each phrase, a series of continua were presented: one to define his "relations" with the préfet, another for the maîtres de conférence, and another for the collaborator of the préfet with whom he worked the most. Thus, the complete question to measure task coverage was:

To define my tasks and obligations, (my préfet, the collaborator of the préfet with whom I worked the most, my teachers at E.N.A.) *issued directives to me*

PREFET   = NEVER :_____:_____: _____ :_____ :_____ : ALWAYS
                          1   2   3   4   5

PREFET'S
COLLABORATOR = NEVER :_____:_____: _____ :_____ :_____ : ALWAYS
                          1   2   3   4   5

TEACHERS   = NEVER :_____:_____: _____ :_____ :_____ : ALWAYS
                          1   2   3   4   5

The basic phrase used to measure instrumental coverage was: *To determine how to fulfill my tasks and obligations,* (. . . . .) *gave me directives: Never . . . . . Always.* And, the basic phrase used to measure comportmental coverage was: *To determine how to behave in the institution,* (. . . . .) *gave me directives: Never . . . . . Always.*

c. While only 145 students filled out the questionnaires, 22 of these respondents worked with two préfets: this explains the very large "Ns" for préfet and préfet's collaborator.

entourage. In certain cases, the student was viewed as a threat to this person's position. For example, the director of the préfet's cabinet or the secretary general who had not himself gone through E.N.A., often felt that the stagiaire might usurp some of his powers or might win too much favor with the préfet, thereby weakening his own influence. In this case, the préfet's collaborator would often issue directives to the student in an attempt to keep him occupied and under control. In other cases, the relationship between the stagiaire and the préfet's collaborator was one of close friendship and cooperation. This was most likely to occur with a director of the cabinet who had recently graduated from E.N.A. Here again, the stagiaire tended to be given directives. But, while in the former relationship, the style was hierarchical and the motive was to reduce the maneuverability of the stagiaire, in the latter case, the préfet's collaborator sought to advise the student in order to reduce his problems of determining how to behave in order to win the favor of the préfet and get a good grade for the stage.

Written instructions by the school administration provide additional coverage of behavior during the stage. While these instructions delineate, with relative precision, the types of activities in which the stagiaire should participate, they provide a much less detailed form of instrumental and comportmental coverage. In fact the instructions explicitly emphasize that the student learns how to fulfill his tasks and how to behave largely by using his intuition, simply living through the experience, and following the examples set by the préfet and his collaborators.[5]

Without stipulating a detailed code of conduct for the stagiaire, the written instructions do provide some general behavioral guidelines: Most importantly, the stagiaire should establish close working relationships with the préfet and his associates; he should seek out tasks, but avoid confining his activity to a limited domain; he should assume responsibility and make decisions on his own initiative without having to be told exactly what to do by his superordinates.[6] Thus, the instructions effectively inform the students that a successful stage is one in which the stagiaire acts in ways which win the confidence of the préfet, his associates, and the school administration, but that these superordinates will not directly tell the students what specific pattern of action will achieve this goal. In fact, the stage seems calculated to select out those students who can learn how to act in a way to satisfy their superordinates without the aid of direct coverage.

The interview results reinforce the impression of the stage gathered from reading the instructions. Respondents repeatedly noted the importance of observing the behavior of the préfet and his collaborators as a means for choosing a suitable mode of conduct for themselves. Furthermore, the students often tried to discover how their superordinates thought on a variety of issues and then used this knowledge to decide when they should not express their personal views and/or what opinions they should express. Concomitantly, there was a notable lack of mention in interviews of superordinates directly telling the stagiaires how they should perform a given task or how they should behave. Rather there was frequent mention of a student going to the director of the cabinet or the secretary general to solicit advice on these questions. Finally, the interviewees suggested that there was indeed a "proper" way (in the minds of their superordinates) of conducting a stage, and the student had to try successfully to determine what this was, if he wanted to receive a good grade.

The major parts of this argument are clearly reflected in the following quotations from three interviews:

I had what I think was a successful stage. In fact, I am sure of it from a personal point of view and as a result of the grade I received. I succeeded essentially because I tried to respond perfectly to everything that the préfet expected of me. In other words, while privately holding opinions on departmental problems and on the style of relations the préfet had with his subordinates, I never expressed an opinion opposed to his own. . . . Even during informal and social relations with the préfet, I felt that I was not just speaking with anyone. In the background, there was always the fact that I was his hierarchical inferior. Even if our conversations were relatively free, there was this desire to please him which was relatively apparent in what I did and said.

The letters sent to parliamentarians had to be written in an absolutely impeccable prose form, and the préfet himself set the example. When I wrote a letter, I would first read a certain number of letters written by the préfet, and then try to put myself in his place to know exactly what he would have written.

The préfet believed he was an example from which the young stagiaire could draw inspiration for the rest of his career. He thought that by watching him take decisions, the stagiaire would be inspired and would model his future behavior on him.

In sum, the stage is also characterized by assumed coverage. Few directives are issued to the stagiaires. Those directives that do exist seek essentially to define the students' tasks and many of these are transmitted to the student in a written, generalized form. But there are prescribed patterns of instrumental, comportmental, and ideological behavior. Finally, this prescribed pattern of behavior is perceived as externally imposed—i.e., the stagiaire acts in a way which he believes will satisfy his superordinates, even though he may personally dislike "having" to act in this manner.

But behavior toward authority during the stage (as compared to the dominant mode of interaction in the upper grades of secondary school) is not and could not be based on remembered socialization because the students come to the stage with few guides to tell them how they should behave. For the older secondary school pupils, as well as for the E.N.A. students in the classroom, there were past experiences in social units which provided rather precise guidelines for how to behave, but in the préfecture, the stagiaire cannot behave according to a series of directives which he received in another context. This absence of past experience in the social unit is partially counteracted by the written instructions, but these are both imprecise and insufficiently detailed. Thus, the prime determinant for the stagiaire's conduct becomes his own perception of how his superordinates think he should behave (his attempt to divine their desires) supplemented by observation and imitation of what and how things are done. Within this process, he is frequently aided by friendly counsel from the director of the préfet's cabinet or the secretary general. It might be noted that the school administration is not simply aware of this general phenomenon but feels that this is precisely what makes the stage a formative and worthwhile experience for the student. After all, a high-level civil servant will normally be asked by his superordinates to perform a given task without being told how to do it or what to say. Yet the civil servant must produce suggestions which his superiors are likely to find acceptable, and he must present his argument in a manner calculated to please them.

Hence, the distinguishing feature between the modes of authority interaction characteristic of the upper grades of the secondary schools and the stage is the *source* of behavioral direction—i.e., reference to previous incidents of direct coverage as compared to imitation, observation, friendly counsel from those already habituated to the procedures, and general written instructions. In both cases, subordinates live within a world of assumed rules which they perceive as being externally imposed upon them.[7]

Dual Guides to Action

Under routine conditions, E.N.A. students regard their own behavior as being determined by the prescriptions of their superordinates rather than by internalized norms. Not only are these prescriptions unexpressed, but, in addition, any failure to comply is noted at a time when it is too late to modify one's behavior—i.e., the sanctions (low grades) are distributed only at the end of each exercise, either the stage or a class. Thus, without exaggeration, it might be said that the E.N.A.s are acting as their own "jailors," and they are fully aware of this. Such a situation naturally gives rise to strong and consistent feelings of constraint. On a priori grounds, there should be an outlet for such feelings.

Rebellion—e.g., the chahut—might serve such a function. However at the National School of Administration—at least until the May crisis of 1968—incidents of insubordination were, to all intents and purposes, nonexistent. To the extent that the general model of authority relations learned (and/or acquired and/or adopted) in secondary schools serves to delimit and define one's adult behavior and dispositions toward authority in all other social units, the hypotheses developed in Part I should have enabled us to forecast this outcome; and they do. Specifically, the assumed-coverage pattern should endure as long as both the goal sought by membership in the unit is valued *and* the unit and its superordinates are perceived as acting in a way that seems effectively to achieve this goal for the subordinates. These two conditions have virtually always existed among E.N.A.s. The goal sought through membership in the school is a position as a high-level civil servant—a career which carries with it a great potential for prestige, power, and financial security. This is a highly valued goal: Membership in the unit demands important sacrifices of time (the student must devote literally every waking hour to properly fulfilling his tasks during the stage and the course of study) and financial earning power (for twenty-nine months he receives a much lower income than he would have if he took a regular job), but many more people wish to study at the school than are actually allowed to do so. The students have always—until 1968—perceived of E.N.A. as effectively achieving this valued goal for them. Going through the school was not only the best way but also a guaranteed way to obtain a position as a high-level civil servant. Moreover, each student expects and values an equal and fair chance to obtain the best of the positions open to E.N.A. graduates.

The chahut, therefore, cannot serve as a viable outlet for the prevailing feelings of constraint. However, this function is served by the routinely available, rhetorical denunciations of the "system" which are part of a dualistic, normative structure characteristic of many E.N.A.s. Specifically, prior to May 1968, many of the students condemned the school, but this had had no influence on their in-unit behavior. These criticisms appear to have been especially coherent and consistent for the members of the 1967 promotion. This is probably attributable to the fact that virtually all of them had read and been influenced by an essay entitled *L'Enarchie ou les mandarins de la société bourgeoise,*[8] a brilliantly written polemic against the school authored by two of its alumni. The authors lashed out against what they considered to be the class nature of E.N.A., which creates a series of handicaps for individuals who come from modest family backgrounds, condemned a number of practices which seemed essentially artificial and dysfunctional, and proposed a series of reforms which were viewed as capable of generating a new, healthier, and more "democratic" system.[9] The criticisms presented in this book were espoused (and supplemented) by a large proportion of the students who, however, continued behaviorally to conform to the tenets of the E.N.A. system.

Because it is so striking, an observation made during my second visit to E.N.A. (in February-March 1969) provides an excellent concrete example of a dualistic normative structure in action. The case centers on the behavior and rhetoric of a maître conducting a seminar on the E.N.A. system, specifically the school's academic program. As is customary, a couple of students had prepared reports for the session. These exposés adhered to the E.N.A.-Sciences Po model. After the reports, there was classroom "discussion," and, to conclude, the maître gave an alternative presentation. The form of his speech was predictable, but its content was quite unexpected (by me, at least): He gave a sweeping and thorough condemnation of the system of classroom reports, "discussion," and professorial counter-presentations. In other words, he denounced what he and his pupils were doing. At the end of the session, the maître asked me if I had found his class profitable. I responded, quite truthfully, that I had been fascinated, and wondered how it was possible for him to give such a presentation while running his class according to the tenets which he so vigorously condemned. His response was: "This is the way classes *have* to be run at E.N.A., but that doesn't mean that I have to like it." But, in point of fact, none of the maître's superordinates requested or demanded that he follow the E.N.A.-Sciences Po model. Rather, he, as all the other instructors, had simply been hired to teach a particular subject matter. However, as an alumnus of the school, he "remembered" how things "had" to be done. Since he did not normatively approve of this system, he behaved as people who have dual guides to action behave under routine conditions—i.e., they strongly condemn a system in which they participate while adhering to that system's rules, even though, in fact, they are not "forced" to do so.

The rhetorical, critical norms, which are part of a dualistic normative structure, may be actualized behaviorally in noncrisis times through support of another social unit which has as one of its goals the transformation of the core unit. There is evidence to suggest that this does occur for E.N.A. students. Specifically, despite the assumption that French high-level civil servants and E.N.A.s tend to be political moderates or conservatives, over fifty percent of the students were most favorably disposed toward the political parties of the left (on the basis of the responses given to the political preference item included in the questionnaire distributed in February-March 1969). Of particular significance is the very high level of support given to the P.S.U. (Parti Socialiste Unifié)—thirty-seven percent (N = 32) for the 1967 promotion and twenty-seven percent (N = 16) for the 1968 promotion. This was clearly the most revolutionary party of any significance at that time and the one most likely, if it obtained power, to carry through a fundamental reform of the high-level civil service and E.N.A. Thus, support for this party can be viewed as an actualization of the rhetorical critiques of the E.N.A. system. The significance of this support is accentuated when it is realized that, among the general population, the level of sympathy for the P.S.U. fell below five percent.

The rhetorical, critical norms also seem to have been somewhat actualized in 1971-1972. In September 1971, sixty-eight of the one hundred members of the "Charles de Gaulle" promotion addressed a letter to the Prime Minister calling for a serious reform of the school; without which, they would not accept positions in the *grands corps* (assuming their classement permitted such a choice). In June 1972, twelve openings were made available in the Conseil d'etat, the Inspection des Finances, and the Cour des Comptes. Six of the signatories were among the top twelve graduates: Four of them took positions in the prefectoral corps. And it was only with the twenty-first student that all the positions in the grands corps were filled. So nine of the sixty-eight critical students took the action they had foreseen, and thereby, operationalized their rhetorical condemnations of the E.N.A. system.[10]

Finally, the rhetorical, critical norms were also actualized in the reform proposals enunciated by the students during the crisis which began in May and ended in July 1968. The events of this period are unique in E.N.A.'s history. This uniqueness, however, is not inexplicable. Rather, it stems from a change in the students' perceptions of how effectively the school was achieving the valued goals they sought from membership.

Crisis Authority Relations

THE DEVELOPMENT OF THE CRISIS

In March and April of 1968, a significant proportion of the promotion held a series of general ideas which were critical of the system in which they were functioning. Some were more discontented than others, but virtually all were willing to accept the system as it was, if for no other reason than that they saw little possibility of changing it. In order to jump the significant hurdle between this vague, ideological critique and an organized reform movement in rebellion against one's superordinates, some rather important catalyzing events were needed. These occurred during the month of May and led the students to perceive the school as not acting effectively to achieve for them the goal sought through membership (a condition which has been hypothesized as leading to the alternating pattern of authority relations). Then there was a favorable response by superiors to a student demand for a suspension of courses to permit them to elaborate a reform of E.N.A. This attempt to satisfy the students' desires—to appease them—marks the beginning of the real crisis.

The first event which moved the future high-level civil servants toward rebellion was the university crisis. Specifically, during the week of May 10, the promotion sent a letter to *Le Monde* criticizing the "police brutality" in repressing student demonstrations. A short letter, filled with carefully worded phrases so as not to offend too strongly, published in a highly "respectable" newspaper, during a period of revolutionary turmoil which threatens to topple an apparently well-established regime, would seem of little significance, but this was not the case with the E.N.A. letter. First, such a thing had never happened before—not during the tense moments of May 1958, not during the Algerian War. E.N.A. students had traditionally adopted the "nonpolitical" stance expected of civil servants. Second, the students themselves viewed this as a rather serious step. While the large majority was ideologically in agreement with the text, out of seventy-three who voted on sending in the letter, only forty-eight cast favorable votes, and this figure was achieved only because most students believed they would not be sanctioned for this action now or later in their careers. Third, the act was only possible because the ground had been prepared by a small group (approximately six) of left-wing activists who were extremely sympathetic to the cause of the university students in revolt and who were generally respected and well-liked by their classmates.

Once the text of the letter was voted, the E.N.A. students returned to their classes. The majority seemed to feel that the present events might interest them as citizens of the state but, in their capacity as future civil servants, did not personally concern them. Assumed coverage persisted and the goal-attainment effectiveness of the school was not called into question.

The second significant event occurred on the afternoon of May 20. While the E.N.A.s were in their seminars debating, academically, a particular aspect of the French economy or in the library studying a series of official documents, a commando group of Occident (an extreme right-wing, neofascist French student group) utilized E.N.A. as a passageway to the back entrance of Sciences Po and attacked the students occupying that school.[11] This event had a strong influence on the E.N.A. students. First, they saw themselves in a rather ludicrous position: While they were following their normal course of studies as if nothing had happened, their school was being used as a road by an armed band. Second, no one at E.N.A. had much sympathy with either the tactics or the ideas of the members of Occident. Third, the people being attacked were students at Sciences Po, and most E.N.A.s were alumni of this school and had a strong sense of empathy with the victims.

If during March and April, many of the E.N.A. students believed their school should be reformed, now, in May, with the student rebellion in the universities and the workers' strikes which had paralyzed France, they must have felt that reform was a genuine possibility. The Occident raid demonstrated that E.N.A. was, in fact, already deeply involved in the societywide crisis, even if the students were still going to their regular classes and acting as if everything were normal. Yet these events were not sufficient to bring about the crisis. Rather, they created an environment hospitable to rebellion.

The third event, which served as a detonator, was the distribution of the grades for the stage. The director of stages announced on May 20 (the same day as the Occident raid) that the grades were ready, and during the next few days, students learned how their year's work and that of their classmates had been evaluated. It was quickly seen that the grades received by the former civil servants were significantly lower than the ones given to those who had taken the students' entrance exams. For the former civil servants this was quite a shock, since most had expected to be more successful in this phase of their studies, because of their work experience. In searching for an explanation of the low grades, many leaned toward a condemnation of the E.N.A. system which seemed to favor those who came from the upper levels of the social class hierarchy—an uncommon trait among the former civil servants. The handing out of the grades also had a "revolutionizing" effect on two other categories of students. First, many received grades which were in strong contradiction with their personal perception of how their préfet had judged their performance during the past year. Having returned to Paris with the idea that they had done an excellent job, they suddenly found themselves given mediocre grades; for them, this was direct and personal "proof" that E.N.A. was not functioning effectively for all the subordinates in the sense that the grades they received were unjust. Second, in discussing the grades, most of the students seemed to perceive a high correlation between one's social origin and the grade received for the stage. This convinced other members of the promotion, who had received what they considered to be fair grades, that E.N.A. was not functioning effectively, since it seemed to be prejudiced against students coming from modest backgrounds.

Now, the promotion moved rapidly toward open revolt. On May 25, a general assembly of the students voted that there should be a relatively long suspension of courses, during which time the students themselves could develop a reform of E.N.A. On May 27, student representatives met with M. Michelet, the Minister of the Public Service at that time, and obtained the following agreement: (1) There would be a one-month suspension of all courses, during which time the students would work out a proposed reform of the school. (2) A reform commission, on which student representatives would have an important voice, was to be created to examine the proposed project. (3) This commission would begin working on June 20, by which time, of course, the students' proposals were to be presented in the form of a written document. Thus, the government had decided to accept the students' demands, thereby demonstrating "weakness" and triggering off the school crisis.

THE GENERAL STYLE OF AUTHORITY RELATIONS DURING THE CRISIS

The reform effort began on the afternoon of May 29, after the results of the interview with Michelet were communicated to the entire student body. Under the direction of the delegation and the student activists, the promotion was divided into six commissions, each of which was assigned a general problem upon which they were to work to develop a reformed and improved system for training high-level civil servants.[12] Each commission was to elect a *rapporteur* who would go to a daily session *(assemblée des rapporteurs)* in which the work of each group would be discussed. Then, after each commission had outlined a series of options, there was to be a general assembly to decide, by majority vote, which options were to be further developed and which were to be removed from consideration. Next, each of the six commissions was to prepare a final report. These reports were to be incorporated into a single document containing the students' proposals for reform. Finally, this document was to be approved by the whole promotion in a general assembly, published, and used to guide the reform commission which was to be created by June 20. In fact, as a result of increasing levels of conflict with their superordinates which obliged the students to devote all their energies to seeking resolutions of these problems, a synthesized report was never prepared nor, obviously, approved by the majority of the promotion.

Throughout this period of reform activity, which lasted until the month of July, authority relations took on the basic characteristics of a chahut. Interactions between students and their leaders were highly directive, with the latter quite consistently and effectively orchestrating the behavior of the former. Normal superordinates were unable to control the activities of the students. When they did try to issue directives, there was a systematic refusal to comply. Finally, the crisis brought with it the festiveness which has been associated with chahuts. During routine periods, fellow students were rather separated from each other, having at most friendship-type relations with only a couple of other members of the promotion. In addition, there was a deeply entrenched spirit of competitiveness and oneupmanship. Finally, when addressing each other, the E.N.A.s at times used the formal vous.

All this changed dramatically at the end of May. The whole promotion seemed to become welded together into a single, "communal" body. Students got to know each other as human beings for the first time; there was a strong and pervaisve sense of cooperation and a profound rejection of competitiveness; the use of the informal form of address (tu) became universal.[13]

To illustrate the crisis style of authority relationships, the interactions between the students and their leaders will first be examined, and then the relations between the promotion and the school's administration will be analyzed.

Leader-Led Relations: Throughout the crisis, the students were led by about eight individuals: the president of the delegation, the chief rapporteur who was to be in charge of synthesizing the reports prepared by the working groups, and the rapporteurs of the six commissions. These leaders had a great deal of actual authority over their classmates and also some nominal authority. In form, all (with the exception of the chief rapporteur) were "elected" to their positions. In fact, the democratic process had not functioned very smoothly. The rapporteurs were elected by the members of their commission, but within each commission, there was an activist minority who had participated in the societywide crisis during the first weeks of May and had decided prior to the meetings of the commissions who would be elected. These nominees either defeated a weak opponent or were unchallenged. The president of the delegation had been chosen months before the crisis with the view that he would have only a small role to play in the promotion's life. But, even in his case, election had been secured by the work of an active minority. As far as the chief rapporteur is concerned, he was overtly coopted for the post by the president of the delegation.

The relationship between the rapporteurs and the students in their commission was rather authority-laden. Acting more like sergeants than discussion group leaders, the rapporteurs not only directed discussion within the group but also decided what their commissions were going to do, when they were going to do it, who was to do such and such, and when the group was going to meet. The compliance rate with these directives was extremely high. When there was disagreement with the reform proposals being evolved, these conflicts were "resolved" by splitting the group into smaller sections composed of like-minded individuals. Each of these subcommissions also was characterized by having a directive leader and submissive followers.

The chief rapporteur and, especially, the president of the delegation had a great deal of influence over both the rapporteurs and the other members of the promotion. As a consequence of their frequent discussions with the rapporteurs, they were able to play a large role in formulating the reform proposals presented by each commission. Of even greater significance, in general assemblies (meetings of the whole promotion), when the president and the chief rapporteur agreed on a particular tactic—which was typically the case—they were able to win the support of virtually every other member of the class, although frequently only after lengthy public debate. Such a level of success is particularly noteworthy, because during the crisis contradictory tactics were chosen at different times. Those observers of French society who emphasize the highly "individualistic" nature of the French might well be shocked by the malleability of these E.N.A. students who are in the process of being trained to lead the nation. However, their behavior was consonant with what we would have expected on the basis of the secondary school findings and the normal pattern of behavior toward authority at the National School of Administration—from their routine experiences, the young E.N.A.s had learned not to overtly disagree with the points of view expressed by their "superiors" and to act in ways calculated to please them.

An interesting and accurate indicator of the style of leader-led relations during the crisis was the seating positions occupied in meetings. Most of the rooms within which commissions met had tables arranged in the form of a rectangle with one side missing (see Figure 3.1). In all cases, the rapporteur sat in the middle of the table perpendicular to the others (i.e., X on Figure 3.1). The practice was that members of the group, as they entered the room,

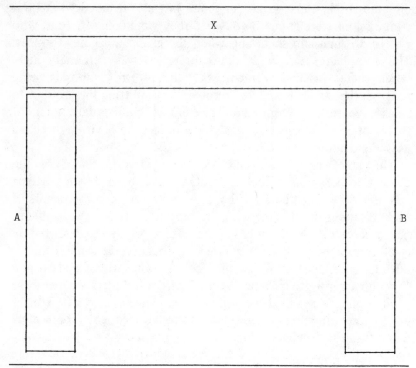

FIGURE 3.1: Seating Positions at the Commission Meetings

sat down in chairs along the outside of the two parallel tables (i.e., A and B on Figure 3.1). Only if these places were occupied would newcomers go to the head table, sitting in those chairs farthest from the rapporteur. This practice derives from the normal classroom environment at E.N.A., where the maître always occupies the head of the table. The durability of this custom, despite the fundamental change of circumstances—i.e., from a normal to a crisis period and from a teacher to a fellow student—is one of the signs of the permanence of subordinate behavior toward accepted superiors.[14]

The seating practices which prevailed at the assemblée des rapporteurs accurately reflect the hierarchical relationships between leaders and led as well as between different levels of leadership. These sessions were open to all members of the promotion. Their purpose was to provide a forum where the president and chief rapporteur could transmit information to the

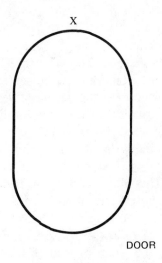

FIGURE 3.2: Seating Positions for the Meetings of Rapporteurs

rapporteurs and where the leaders could learn what each of the groups was doing. These meetings took place in a room with a large oval table. Given this geometrical shape, there were two theoretically suitable positions for the leader. However, given the location of the door, the actual vantage point was the round part of the table facing this entranceway (see X on Figure 3.2). The president always sat here and the chief rapporteur sat next to him. (Interestingly enough, one of the first "acts" of the chief rapporteur, after being coopted for this position, was to leave the place he had occupied along the flat side of the oval table and move to the head of the table next to the president. This change could be viewed as a consummation of his promotion in rank.)

The distinction between leaders and followers was also clearly revealed in seating practices. Only the rapporteurs and individuals they believed should participate in a particular session were allowed to sit at the table; any others who went to the session went to chairs placed against the walls of the room. The inviolability of this arrangement was brought out a couple days after the reform movement began. One of the observers came in and sat down at the table. The president told him he could not sit there; the student retorted that he needed a place to write; the president noted that there was a small table in the corner of the room; the observer went to this table and moved it to the end of the oval table near the door. Now the student was sitting directly opposite the president who sharply reacted, saying: "You are a comrade, like everyone else, and no more!" (The observer's act violated another unwritten rule of the seating arrangements—i.e., never sit directly opposite the leader unless there is no other available space. A violation of this rule implies a challenge to the leadership.) In the end, the student sat in one of the places provided for his "kind." Significantly, the president attacked the observer for attempting to stand out, for trying to be more equal than anyone else. That the observer was trying to break down the equality between himself and others of his "kind" is unquestionable. But this was not only an attempt to break down an equality within the stratum of followers, it also sought to break down the inequality between the strata of leaders and led. It seems that the president of the delegation was a fervent believer in equality within but not between strata.

Student-Superordinate Relations: For approximately two weeks after the beginning of the reform movement, there was no attempt by any superordinates to interfere in the student's work. Then, on June 13, three student leaders met with the General Director of the Administration and Public Service (effectively, the hierarchical superior of all civil servants). He told them that, contrary to the provisions of the agreement with Michelet, a reform commission could not possibly be convened before July 15, because the new Government would not be formed before the first week of July. In addition, he indicated that one of the central, probably the most important, reform proposal—i.e., that there would no longer be a classement—could not possibly be considered.[15]

The "superordinate offensive" continued with an announcement on June 15, placed on the bulletin board by the director of the school, that there would be examinations on July 10. This signified quite clearly that an end to the system of classement would not be accepted, and it threatened to halt the reform movement, because if the students were going to take exams in a month, they would have to stop their present work and start studying.

The students responded very strongly against these directives.

At a general assembly held on June 18, they voted, virtually unanimously, to (1) demand a change in the style of the course to be given in July; (2) immediately put into effect a form of *cogestion* (i.e., student participation in the decision-making process); (3) refuse to take exams in July, and (4) refuse to take any examination until the reform commission had been convened and had made decisions on the various student proposals.

On the day after this general assembly, the president of the delegation met with the director of the school, who was outraged by these votes. In particular, the director was disturbed by the conditional motion (no exams before the reform commission decides), and he announced that there would be no further discussions with the students; from now on, all decisions would be made unilaterally by the Administrative Council of E.N.A. (effectively, the school's board of trustees).

During the next week, there was no further action by either subordinates or superordinates. The director of the school was attempting to behave in an authority-laden manner, but the students did not seem to perceive him as being forceful and showed no signs of complying.

On June 26, three days after the Gaullist victory on the first ballot of the legislative elections, the director of studies called a general assembly to reopen the dialogue. The core section of his speech was devoted to pointing out certain "disadvantages" of the motions which the students passed at their June 18 general assembly—"disadvantages" which jeopardized the possibility of reform as well as the careers of the students.[16] He went on to note that the Administrative Council was meeting the next day, and, as a consequence of the conditional motion, might well act very severely toward the students, and then many problems would ensue. The only feasible way out of this dilemma would be a rescheduling of exams for the end of July and a reduced program to be covered on these tests. This, he stated, was, of course, only his personal point of view, and he did not know if it would be acceptable to the Administrative Council.

The way in which the director of studies presented his ideas is at least as interesting as what he actually said. He spoke as if he were an outsider to the decision-making process at E.N.A., a friend who came to tell you what he had heard and how he personally saw the situation. He constantly reiterated that this and that was what he personally thought; that he, as an individual, did not mind if the students took the exams or not, but he wanted to point out what might happen if they followed a particular course of action. This nondirective style, which almost made one forget that the man who was speaking held a key position in the E.N.A. hierarchy, was extremely effective. After the director of studies left, there was a long debate culminating in a vote to withdraw the conditional motion.

Thus, the rebellious promotion had compromised. However, two factors should be emphasized. First, the general, societywide atmosphere was very different now than it had been when the reform movement began. France was no longer paralyzed by a general strike, nor were most university buildings still being occupied by students. The forces of order, the government, seemed to have squashed the "mini-revolution," and the voices of reform and change had been muted. Thus, societal conditions were no longer supportive of the promotion's activities. The realization of this change and the consequent awareness of the government's newfound strength and momentum, made it incumbent upon the students to modify their position. Second, despite the withdrawal of the conditional motion, the students had not agreed to take examinations. In fact, they continued to support the motion refusing to take exams in July.

On June 27, the day after the conditional motion was withdrawn, the Administrative Council decided that there would be exams at the end of July. On the same day, the discussions between the director of the school and the promotion's leaders recommenced. These two acts were compromises on the part of the superordinates, aimed at appeasing the students. First, the directive that exams were to take place on July 10 was effectively rescinded. Second, despite his earlier decision to stop discussions (and bargaining) with the students, the director of the school was again meeting with the leaders. Such a stance of "reasonableness" by superordinates does not stop a chahut, for it does not lead subordinates to regard their superordinates as forceful—i.e., as authorities to be obeyed.

On July 1,[17] the dialogue between the student leaders and the director of the school was broken off, with the director saying that discussions could only continue after the students agreed to take the July examinations. The students severely rebelled against this announcement. On July 2, there was a general assembly. At this meeting, the student delegation resigned and a nonpolitical union was created to take its place. In reality, the former members of the delegation along with the crisis leaders became the officers of the union, with the president of the delegation becoming the president of the union. The reason for this change was twofold: (1) The delegation was an institution created by the school administration and regulated by the school's rules, but the union was the students' creation to make demands on the administration; and (2) civil servants in France have a right to form unions, and these have a legal right to strike. Then the students voted that if there were examinations in July, they would go on strike the day of the exams. The director of the school was informed of these votes on July 3. He immediately responded by posting a decree on the bulletin board announcing that the exams would be given on July 23.

THE RESOLUTION OF THE CRISIS

As of July 4, 1968, it did not seem likely that the crisis at E.N.A. would be rapidly resolved. The students seemed committed to the idea of not taking any examinations in July, and the school administration seemed equally committed to the idea that they were going to give examinations. Yet, only a week later, the crisis was resolved, not through compromise, but rather through an authority-laden intervention of a very high-level superordinate. The terrain was well prepared for this intervention: First, by convincing the students' president, in private meetings, of the wisdom of a return to normalcy, and, second, through a general assembly called by the director of studies, in which he acted as if the crisis was already over and got many students, for at least a period of time, to accept this pretense.

The first of these preparatory moves became apparent on July 9 during an information session called by the president to tell the promotion what he had learned from his contacts and discussions during the past few days. His basic points were: (1) classes must begin again; (2) if the students took their exams in July, the Government would be responsive to the reform proposals, but if the exams were not taken in July, then they would have to be taken in August (otherwise there would be too great a loss of face for the Government) and then there would be no guarantee of responsiveness; (3) the scope of the examinations might possibly be reduced; and (4) the general director of the administration and the public service would be coming to E.N.A. to address the promotion.

This analysis of the situation was publicly rejected by a good number of the students. They argued that the so-called guarantees were not in writing and were simply an attempt by the administration to obtain a return to normalcy. Furthermore, they claimed that, with a slight increment of pressure on the superordinates by a united promotion, the students' goals could be achieved.

The second act designed to prepare the scene for ending the crisis was a general assembly on July 10 called by the director of studies. During this session, he ignored the continuing crisis and simply described the program of studies to be followed beginning in September. This presentation was followed by a series of questions from the students which conformed to the speech's style—i.e., they could well have been posed if the crisis had never existed. Finally, one of the members of the promotion got up and said, "Well, then there will be no application of the reform." The director of studies responded that he had always said that reforms do not come quickly, and that, in any case, it had always been dubious that they could have much effect on the students actually at E.N.A. Before the session closed, a few more reform-related topics were discussed. In his responses, the director of studies indicated that: (1) he has ready to talk with the union leaders and would not overlook them; and (2) he questioned the legality of having a strike to avoid the exams—i.e., while, according to their statute, the students are partially civil servants and, therefore, have the right to strike, they are also students, and such activities as taking examinations are part of this role where the right to strike is not recognized.

This session with the director of studies was over at about 3:00 p.m. Most of the students stayed in the same room to listen to a representative of French businessmen who had been invited to E.N.A. to discuss the effects of the national crisis. At 4:00 p.m., this meeting was interrupted by an announcement that in a half-hour the general director of the administration and public service would be coming to the school to speak to the students.

At 4:30 p.m., this high-level superordinate arrived and walked to the front of the room. Taking a series of notes from his pocket, he began by noting how pleased he was to meet this promotion, about which there had been so much talk. Then, he made five basic points. First, two months of reflection had been very profitable for the promotion. He had personally read all their reports. On the question of access to the high-level civil service, their ideas were extremely interesting, but there were important lacunae in other parts. Second, while the promotion had made many contacts with people outside E.N.A., it had behaved a bit like parliament—i.e., "a house without windows." The students did not seem to have been totally cognizant of what had been going on throughout the society: The dissolution of the National Assembly and the ensuing legislative elections required a total reconsideration of the situation, which, however, the students did not make. Third, the "executive power" had promised both a reform commission on which the students would participate and increased student participation in the activities of the school. These promises would be kept. Fourth, there was no valid reason not to take the examinations on July 23. (According to the students, this statement clearly implied that if the exams were not taken, there would be sanctions.) The students should not forget that the state was paying for their studies. Finally, he was persuaded that the students understood him, wished them good luck, and walked out.

This performance, for that is what it was, took less than a half-hour. The entire speech had been delivered in a harsh and glacial tone. There was no overt attempt to threaten the students. (This, in fact, would have been out of place, because the speaker acted as if he already had the situation under control.) Having completed his remarks, he simply folded up his notes and walked out of the room—i.e., there was obviously nothing to be discussed. All that was said could be summed up in a single word: "Comply." The question now was: How would the students react to this "authority-laden" behavior?

After the high-level civil servant left, there was a long discussion among the students. The president, as well as some of the other leaders of the reform movement, seemed ready to submit, but others were not. After about an hour and a half of arguing, the meeting broke up. But instead of going home, many of the students stayed talking in small groups about what had happened and how the students should react. As the general discussion had indicated, there were sharp divergences in opinion. However, even those who were in a fighting mood doubted their chances of accomplishing anything now. In other words, defeatism was the students' reaction to the authority-laden speech.

A general assembly was called for 5:00 p.m. on the following day, July 11. About thirty minutes after the scheduled beginning time, the president and some of the other leaders finally arrived. After clearing up a few bits of business unrelated to the crisis, the president began reading a speech he had written. The first part was a long sardonic analysis of the students' behavior during yesterday's sessions with the director of studies and the general director of the administration and public service—all of which was cleverly done to imitate the style of General de Gaulle. Then, in a very serious tone, the president proposed his plan of action. He made three major points: (1) the students should take their exams on July 23; (2) since this could be interpreted as a capitulation on their part, they should have a strike on July 22; (3) he was engaging his personal power on this proposal—i.e., if it were rejected, he would resign.

Although the president requested that there be no debate on his program, just a simple vote of approval or disapproval, he was not to have his way. During this discussion some students viciously attacked the president's plan. The high point of the session occurred when the chief rapporteur got up to make a short speech. He began by saying that what was going on was totally inadmissible. The president had decided all of this without consulting the other leaders, and this was not democratic. As a result, the chief rapporteur said he was resigning from the union's administrative council. Then he went on to note that after the promotion withdrew the demand for an end to classement (which had been viewed as a maximalist position), the only thing left was the July examinations. But now it was impossible to vote for a strike on July 23 because such a vote would result in the resignation of the president and without his leadership the strike would be impossible (the president being the only person with contacts among the superordinates). Finally, the chief rapporteur turned directly toward the president and said: "You will have your majority; but now you are the president of the party of fear! "

Throughout this diatribe, the president had remained totally calm. Now he requested the right to respond. He said that while he had not consulted the entire administrative council of the union, he had spoken to many members of this group and listed some of the names. (However, before he could go any further, some of those with whom he had supposedly spoken noted that he had not done so.) Then the president said his mandate required him to make certain decisions. The most democratic thing was for him to take his responsibilities alone with the aid of certain contacts; now, democratically, the promotion could either accept or reject his program.[18]

This attack and counter-response was followed by more discussion before the students finally settled down to voting. The vote took place by secret ballot, and for the first time during the crisis the result of a vote was not virtually unanimous. Forty-two voted to take the exams, thirty-four to strike, and eleven cast blank ballots. There is good reason to think that the eleven blank ballots were cast by students who agreed with the chief rapporteur's argument. Thus, while in fact a majority, albeit a demoralized and very weak one, was against taking the exams, the vote meant that the students would take their examinations on July 23.

Now, the crisis was over; the superordinates had won. On July 12, the president met with the school administration and afterward sent a letter to each member of the promotion noting that they would only be examined on one-third of their full program. This was a much greater reduction in the scope of the examinations than the students had hoped for. The atmosphere at E.N.A. totally changed overnight. Previously, it had been a beehive of activity from morning to evening; now the corridors and the rooms were silent. The only students in the school were in the library studying for the exams. The majority of the promotion was not to be found; many had gone to their family's summer homes where they could study without interruption for the next two weeks.

No synthesized reform project was ever made. Rather, the separate reports drawn up by the commissions and subcommissions were combined, resulting in a document with many contradictory arguments. In the fall of 1968, a reform commission was created on which the students had a very limited representation. After more than six months of deliberation, this commission made a report which basically refused to accept any of the substantive changes in the E.N.A. system that had been proposed by the students.[19] The only significant and durable effect of the reform movement was to create a set of shared experiences to be remembered by the members of the 1967 promotion.

Conclusion

The style of E.N.A. authority relations described in this chapter seems in basic conformity with the secondary school findings. The normal mode of authority relations which exists during the stage and in the seminars is one of assumed coverage. In both social units, there is a prescribed pattern of subordinate behavior which is perceived by the students as being externally imposed, even though superordinates do not issue numerous detailed and precise directives. The stagiaire learns how to behave primarily by following the written instructions given to him by the school's administration, complying with the limited number of task-centered directives issued by the préfet and his collaborators, seeking out advice from his nominal superiors, and, most importantly, observing and then attempting to imitate the behavior of his superordinates. Most E.N.A. students learn the prescribed pattern of seminar behavior at Sciences Po; those who did not attend this school try to imitate their classmates.

The crisis occurred as a result of a combination of rare circumstances which led the students to question E.N.A.'s effectiveness. Their critiques of the system (part of a dualistic normative structure) provided a genuine desire for change and led them to see the May crisis from a particular vantage point. But, while the societywide crisis was the necessary factor for the development of the E.N.A. crisis, it was not a sufficient condition.

For the crisis actually to occur, the students must have perceived the school as functioning ineffectively for them personally—the distribution of the grades for the stage led to this perception.

The secondary school findings further suggest that, under these conditions (i.e., with the subordinates perceiving their unit as not performing its valued goal well), the style of authority relations will follow the alternating pattern. This is exactly what took place at E.N.A. First, the superordinates did not effectively control the activities of the subordinates. The students, in an organized fashion, systematically refused to comply with their directives —e.g., the end of classement cannot be part of your reform proposal; or you will take exams on July 10. Second, the insubordination was being guided in a rather authority-laden manner by a group of chahut leaders (i.e., the president, the chief rapporteur, and the commissions' rapporteurs). Third, there was a festive atmosphere, characterized by a strong sense of community and a lack of competitiveness. The chahut at the National School of Administration only ended when the director of the administration and public service came to the school and directly told the students, in an authority-laden manner, that they must comply. At that point, there was an immediate return to order and assumed coverage.

While the E.N.A. findings seem in general agreement with the analysis of authority based on the study of secondary schools, some additional information, which may or may not be specific to the National School of Administration, is also provided. First, the breakdown of assumed coverage was followed by a chahut that continued until there was a brief incident of authority-laden behavior; this was immediately followed by a return to assumed coverage. In other words, there was no prolonged period of alternation between the chahut and the authority-laden modes of interaction. Furthermore, once the authority-laden mode was invoked, it was immediately withdrawn in favor of a return to assumed coverage.

Second, throughout the crisis, there was a constant attempt to resolve (or to put it more precisely, to avoid) conflict among the students.[20] This goal was achieved in two different ways. During the general assemblies, there were constant calls for unanimity and, to facilitate consensus, all questions to be voted upon were posed in sufficiently general terms to provide an ideological bandwagon aboard which virtually everyone could climb. The major effect of using this technique was to increase the role played by the leaders, who, as a result, had almost unhindered power to determine what the specific policies of the promotion would be. Within the commissions, conflict was avoided by a process of subdivision—i.e., when competing points of view existed in the group, rather than searching for a compromise acceptable to all, the group broke up into smaller sections each composed of like-minded individuals.[21] The result of this process of subdivision (groupusculation) was a series of homogeneous groups, each of which could prepare a coherent report on the specific problem with which it was dealing. However, a simple amalgam of these disparate proposals would inevitably be a report filled with contradictions. To avoid this outcome, a group charged with preparing a unified and coherent reform document was created. Although this group never actually fulfilled its task, if the process had been completed, it would have resulted in placing enormous power in the hands of the synthesizers, whose suggested final report would simply have been accepted or rejected by the entire promotion in a general assembly (and the possibility of rejection would have been virtually nonexistent). Thus, the very high value attributed to conflict-avoidance led to placing enormous power in the hands of a small minority of the students.

NOTES

1. Naturally, I do not wish to suggest that no E.N.A. student at *any* time expresses a personal view or openly disagrees with one of his maîtres de conférence. Rather, I am saying that *modal* seminar behavior adheres to this pattern. As one interviewee put it, to support his notion that he and his comrades in a given seminar showed some intellectual independence: "We were somewhat independent. This independence usually took the form of asking questions—i.e., if a position was taken that differed from that of the maître de conférence, it was not expressed brutally, but rather in the form of a question asking if he did not think that such an opinion could be defended. His opinion would be asked on someone else's opinion."

More significant deviations are quite atypical. To the extent that they do exist, it is only among the students who come from the very highest social echelons, and, as a result, have learned how to guard cordiality without totally sacrificing the ability to disagree.

This situation may have changed in the past couple of years, since students are no longer graded on their classroom participation.

2. At least some aspects of this behavioral pattern exist at other French institutions of higher education. And, the emphasis on form more than on content can be traced back to the *lycée dissertation* (essay).

3. *Ecole National d'Administration, Epreuves et statistiques des concours de 1967* (Paris: Imprimerie nationale, 1968), pp. 106-111.

4. Since almost all of the *stagiaires* have at least some experience in a préfecture, and since the large majority only have this type of stage, I will refer exclusively to the authority relations of a student sent to work with a préfet.

5. To quote from the instructions: "The stage is the only pedagogical instrument capable of transmitting to future civil servants, *by example, imitation, and lived experience,* the practical rules of behavior and ways of thinking and acting which cannot be taught by the classical methods of transmitting knowledge" (Ecole Nationale d'Administration, "Instruction sur le stage auprès d'un Préfet," mimeo [1968], p. 1; italics added).

6. Ibid., pp. 2-18.

7. In this discussion of the stage, no mention has been made of the written work required of each student—i.e., the *compte-rendus* (two short summaries of the stagiaire's activities which he sends to the school's administration) and the *mémoire* (a research paper examining an issue of importance to the local region). Most importantly, because it contradicts the other aspects of the stage, the student is given a detailed and precise series of written rules defining tasks, instrumentalities, and comportment for researching and writing-up his mémoire (see Direction des stages, Ecole Nationale d'Administration, "Thèmes de mémoires de stage 1968," mimeo, D.S. 194 [1968]·; and Le Directeur des stages de l'Ecole Nationale d'Administration aux élèves en stage de 1ère année, "Instruction sur le mémoire de stage," mimeo, No. 195 [1968].

My interpretation of this apparent anomaly is as follows: The issuing of detailed directives in written form, combined with an absence of directives issued personally by a superordinate to a subordinate is a way to teach subordinates assumed coverage while practicing it. This strategy is utilized when (a) the subordinate has little past experience in social units which can guide him in what he is presently doing, and (b) the superordinate(s) wish to make sure that everyone does the same general task in a particular way. The latter factor does not exist for the stage, because the superordinates will largely judge the students according to their ability to select, on the basis of observation and intuition, the proper way of doing things. However, the mémoire is primarily an exercise to determine the stagiaire's ability to propose a realistic solution to a problem existing in the region where he is working (ibid., p. 3). Now, if the school wishes to judge specifically the capacity of the student to propose solutions, an attempt must be made to eliminate all other factors which might influence the jury's appreciation of the mémoire (e.g., the length); this, in fact, seems to be the purpose served by the detailed written directives regarding the mémoire.

8. Jacques Mandrin [pseud.], *L'Enarchie* (Paris: Editions de la Table Ronde, 1967). The authors are actually a couple of radical civil servants in the *Inspection des finances.*

9. It might be noted that the idea that E.N.A. should be reformed is widespread and far antedates the publication of *L'Enarchie.* Furthermore, high-level civil servants (especially alumni of the school) have been among the most vocal exponents of this view. (See, for example, Alain Gourdon, "Les grands commis et le mythe de l'intérêt général, *Cahiers de la république,* No. 1 [1956] and "L'E.N.A.: situation et perspectives," a special issue of *Promotions,* a journal published by the E.N.A. alumni association, No. 70 [1964].)

10. For further details, see Ezra Suleiman, *Politics, Power and Bureaucracy in France,* pp. 89-94. I should point out that the critical students did not disobey the rules

of the system, which only dictate that students choose positions according to their classement. In the past, there have been top-ranking students who did not select the grand corps.

11. This tactic was used because the back door of E.N.A. and the back door of Sciences Po is only separated by a 100-yard-long garden, which in normal times is crossed many times each day by young E.N.A.s on their way to use the excellent library resources available at Sciences Po.

12. The six general problem areas were: the university training to be received prior to entering E.N.A.; access to the top positions in the civil service; the school's program of studies; E.N.A.'s internal organization; "democratization" of the upper levels of the civil service; and careers to which E.N.A. should lead.

13. It should be remembered that it is this human contact devoid of competition which tends to characterize festive occasions for adults, just as games and pranks define such occasions for children.

14. In the American seminar system, seating arrangements are not as rigidly defined as in the E.N.A. case. One often finds different professors, who give seminars in the same room, sitting in different places. One reason for this is the table arrangement: In the United States, it is usually continuous—i.e., either a complete rectangle or a full circle. At E.N.A. the table arrangement is typically discontinuous and, as a result, contains an obvious "key" or central position.

In the seminar rooms at the Institut d'Etudes Politiques of Paris, the professor's position is sometimes even more clearly indicated. In some of the classrooms, there is a table arrangement similar to the one existing at E.N.A. but, in addition, there is a small desk midway between the ends of the parallel tables which becomes the instructor's vantage point. Both the practices at E.N.A. and at Sciences Po are, however, no more than modifications of the high school practices in which the teacher's desk is on a raised platform.

15. Three factors seem to explain why, at an earlier stage, there had been no attempt to interfere with the students' reform activity. First, many high-level civil servants had believed that the young E.N.A.s would content themselves with suggesting mild reforms of the system which the administration would find acceptable and perhaps even desirable. However, ending classement would have a profound effect on the civil service; in particular, it would reduce the great prestige of the grand corps, whose members were naturally very hostile to such an idea. Second, with order reestablished throughout France, the superordinates of E.N.A. believed they could now reassert control over the school. Finally, there were strong indications that, in the upcoming legislative elections, there would be a large Gaullist majority which would not tolerate a significant change of the status quo at E.N.A.

16. More specifically, he cited three "disadvantages." First, the chances for a successful reform seemed to be in jeopardy, because he did not think a minister in a new and strengthened government would give in to the conditions being stipulated—e.g., we shall not take examinations until the reform commission has met and made its decision. One possible effect might be a decision not to have any reform commission. Second, in all likelihood, when there were exams, some students would probably take them, while others would not. This would cause a distortion of the classement, and, as a result, he clearly implied that no positions in the grands corps might be offered. Finally, each student should realize that he was taking certain chances—i.e., a refusal to take the examinations might lead to sanctions (although the word "sanctions" was never used).

17. This was the same day courses began again but in a very different form than was traditionally the case. This time the students were not to be graded on their classroom participation.

18. This "debate" between the two leaders of the promotion is strongly reminiscent of recent French politics: The president's decision-making style and his notion of "democracy" were very similar to General de Gaulle's, while the chief rapporteur criticized this method and conception as the leaders of the Gaullist opposition criticized de Gaulle.

19. *Rapport de la commision d'étude des problèmes de L'Ecole Nationale d'Administration* (Paris: La Documentation Française, 1969).

20. It seems that this goal was more than simply a response to feared sanctions (i.e., no individual can be severely punished since the entire group is acting in the same manner), because unanimity within the promotion was just as eagerly sought during the first two weeks of reform activity when the administration seemed to support the students as during the last weeks of the crisis when there was overt conflict between superordinates and subordinates.

21. During the first week of the reform work, this process of subdivision affected every one of the commissions. In the case of one of the groups, a half-dozen subcommissions were created, each having no more than three members and one having only a single member.

PART III

BEHAVIOR TOWARD AUTHORITY IN FRANCE

It hardly seems possible that there can ever have existed any other people so full of contrasts and so extreme in all their doings, so much guided by their emotions and so little by fixed principles, always behaving better, or worse, than one expected of them. At one time they rank above, at another below, the norm of humanity; their basic characteristics are so constant that we can recognize the France we know in portraits made of it two or three thousand years ago, and yet so changeful are its moods, so variable its tastes that the nation itself is often quite as much startled as any foreigner at the things it did only a few years before. Ordinarily the French are the most routine-bound of men, but once they are forced out of the rut and leave their homes, they travel to the ends of the earth and engage in the most reckless ventures. Undisciplined by temperament, the Frenchman is always readier to put up with the arbitrary rule, however harsh, of an autocrat than with a free, well-ordered government by his fellow citizens, however worthy of respect they be. At one moment he is up in arms against authority and the next we find him serving the powers-that-be with a zeal such as the most servile races never display. So long as no one thinks of resisting, you can lead him on a thread, but once a revolutionary movement is afoot, nothing can restrain him from taking part in it.

Alexis de Tocqueville, *The Old Regime and the French Revolution*, pp. 210-211.

Chapter 4

DESCRIBING AND EXPLAINING AUTHORITY IN FRANCE: A THEORETICAL SUMMARY

The Dependent Variables

ROUTINE AUTHORITY

Assumed Coverage: If the concept of authority rapidly crosses one's mind, there is a tendency to conceive of an explicit superordinate-subordinate relationship in which the hierarchical superiors issue rules or directives to be obeyed by the subordinates. Moreover, if a very high level of obedience is obtained, this (it might be assumed) is at least to some extent a function of effective sanctioning power in the hands of the superordinates. Finally, if a group of subordinates in a given social unit follow a uniform and rather rigid pattern of behavior, this is likely to be attributed either to very effective socialization into that unit or to "authoritarianism"—i.e., a very high level of attempted behavioral control supported by effective sanctioning power.

The French experience with assumed coverage (hypothesized to be the normal, routine mode of authority interaction) challenges these assumptions. The defining characteristics of assumed coverage are: (1) subordinate behavior *is* determined basically by general rules (written instructions), remembered socialization, observation and imitation of superordinate and peer behavior, and/or "advice" solicited from superordinates; (2) subordinates *perceive* their behavioral patterns as being forced upon them by superordinates; and (3) superordinates *in fact* rarely issue directives to subordinates and do not (or cannot) enforce compliance through the use of sanctions.

Two points deserve special emphasis. First, the concept of assumed coverage denotes a particular way in which behavior, whatever type it may be, is determined. Thus, varying degrees of subordinate freedom of control may be involved—both apparently democratic and apparently authoritarian relationships are compatible with this mode of authority interaction.[1] Yet, given the high degree of control over subordinate behavior in E.N.A. and in the secondary schools, it may be hypothesized that assumed coverage in France *tends* to define a relatively rigid and tightly constricted pattern of behavior.

Second, and of special import, the question arises as to whether superordinates have a way of enforcing compliance with assumed coverage. In other words, what happens when, during a period of assumed coverage, a subordinate does not follow the expected behavioral patterns? Although the evidence relevant to this point is limited, it all points in the same direction: superordinates do not or cannot stimulate compliance through sanctions. At E.N.A., during the stage and in the seminars, noncompliance was severely sanctioned (by poor grades), but at a time when this sanction could not effect the extent of compliance with the expected behavioral pattern. This is a logically comprehensible situation, because noncompliance was rarely an indication of rebellion but rather a suggestion that the student involved was not capable of doing as good a job of observing and imitating the desired behavioral patterns as an ideal high-level civil servant should. Hence, sanctioning noncompliance with poor grades was, from a systemic perspective, totally rational (given the system of classement in which grades determine the specific civil service position one will obtain at graduation and, consequently, one's career potential).

While the secondary school study provides no data on teachers' sanctioning practices during assumed coverage, some relevant information (not previously presented) can be culled from interviews with teachers and administrators in regard to sanctioning noncompliant teachers. Teachers rather consistently seemed to feel that their own in-class behavior was tightly controlled by school administrators and ministerial directives. This perception, combined with the fact that direct coverage of teacher behavior is virtually nonexistent, suggests that normally teachers function under assumed coverage. Now teachers, in effect, always comply with the expected behavioral patterns learned from written rules and from previous experiences in the classroom both as pupils and as student-teachers assigned to assist experienced instructors). Furthermore, and of crucial importance to the present argument, there are no effective sanctions for noncompliance. Once a secondary school teacher is assigned to a particular school, the "omnipotent" ministry and rectorate have virtually no control over him: If he does not follow the established curricula or even if he decides not to teach at all (e.g., allowing students to use class time to do their homework while he reads the newspaper), he cannot be fired nor can he be transferred against his will to another school. The principal has no more effective control over teachers than the ministry. The only sanction that can be administered is a very weak one which affects the rapidity with which a teacher receives salary increments. Teachers are graded by their principals and by inspectors from the académie. A teacher will automatically receive a salary hike every four years, no matter how ineffective or unconscientious he may be. If a teacher is given a very high evaluation by the principal and by the inspector, he may be given a raise in less than four years, but to all intents and purposes not more frequently than every three years. Since each increase in salary is small, the sanctioning power derived from the grading system is insignificant. Hence, from the perspective of a rational cost-benefit analysis, conscientiousness and compliance have little, if any, material payoff. Yet—and this is the crucial point—virtually every teacher is totally compliant and attempts, to the utmost, to satisfy the perceived wishes of superordinates, while at the same time complaining about the lack of freedom he has in the school.

A second set of supportive examples drawn from the secondary school context comes from interviews with school administrators. The following summary of an interview with a principal of a lycée depicts, in a clear and anecdotal fashion, the general perspective of administrators:

> Principal: I have very little ability to determine how the school runs. I am like the head of a factory making objects according to given specifications. [He suggests that the different types of pupils he is to train are like raw materials to be converted into blue, green or red "bic" pens.] I have no choices to make. I supervise the "manufacturing process" to ensure its conformity with the instructions I have been given by the ministry.

> Investigator: But doesn't the principal of a lycée, such as yourself, have the power to influence, if not determine, certain aspects of the way in which the school functions?

> Principal: Not really. We just carry out the ministerial and rectorial directives which are so complete and precise that there is virtually nothing left for a principal to decide. This is unfortunate because there are many things I would like to do differently, but I cannot.

> Investigator: What would happen if you tried to do something different from the way it was specified in the ministerial directives.

> Principal: Oh, I would be sanctioned!

> Investigator: How? Would they reduce your salary?

> Principal: No, they cannot do that.

> Investigator: Well, would they demote you or transfer you to another, less desirable school?

> Principal: Well, no. They cannot do that either.

> Investigator: Then, how can they sanction you for not following the written directives?

> Principal (pause): Well, I guess they really could not do anything to me.

In sum, the evidence from the E.N.A. and secondary school contexts suggests that when assumed coverage prevails, there are no effective sanctions for noncompliance with the prescribed behavioral patterns. In fact, this does not have important systemic consequences, because virtually all subordinates seek to totally comply with the prescribed patterns. (Some E.N.A.s may not comply but, in almost all cases, it is because they do not know how, not because they want to disobey.)

This finding is at variance with a frequently espoused view of French attitudes toward authority: Frenchmen will only accept authority when *forced* to do so.[2] Rather, the case studies of E.N.A. and the secondary schools suggest that—to slightly modify this proposition—Frenchmen will only accept authority when they *perceive themselves* as forced to do so. The difference between these two propositions may appear negligible, but it is the difference between obtaining compliance only through the exercise of force, or, in fact, "voluntarily."

Dual Guides to Action: People living under assumed coverage perceive their own behavior as being determined by the prescriptions of others rather than by internalized norms. Were they habitually being given orders, there would be the possibility of noncompliance with specific directives. But, in the case of assumed coverage, not only is behavior tightly controlled by what is perceived to be an outside source, but there is no possibility of rebellion or disobedience against the source of the directives. As a result, French citizens, living under assumed coverage, may be expected to have strong and constant feelings of constraint. On a priori grounds, there should be an outlet for such feelings. This function seems to be partially served by the chahut, in which subordinates may "retaliate" against their perceived (and in the case of authority-laden interactions, their actual) "oppressors." However, the chahut occurs rather infrequently. Therefore, of greater importance, because they are routinely available, are the rhetorical denunciations of the "system" which are part of the dual guides to action.

Specifically, the French have a set of norms supportive of the assumed coverage behavioral patterns; it is those norms which, for example, lead them to attempt to divine the expectations of their superordinates. In addition, many subordinates have a second set of norms, segregated from the first, which is highly critical of the way in which the system functions. This second set of guides to action gives rise to rhetorical denunciations of the unit's practices and (possibly) membership in or support of other social units which have as one of their goals the transformation of the core unit.

THE ALTERNATING PATTERN: CRISIS AUTHORITY

Among both E.N.A. students and the older pupils in the secondary schools, assumed coverage is the modal, but not the exclusive, form of authority interaction. Under specified conditions (which in the case of E.N.A. seem to have been virtually unique in the spring of 1968) subordinate-superordinate relations become authority-laden or turn into a chahut. Before examining the conditions which are responsible for a movement away from assumed coverage, the two types of nonroutine authority interactions as well as perceived forcefulness—the axis upon which the alternation between the authority-laden and the chahut modes rotates—must be defined.

The Authority-Laden Mode: The essence of the authority-laden mode is not "authoritarianism" minus an explicit attempt to control what opinions are expressed. Rather, the core characteristic is simply that actual superordinates issue directives to subordinates who comply. This meaning is arrived at by juxtaposing this "exceptional" condition against the normal type of authority interaction.[3] Among the defining traits of assumed coverage, the one that most clearly distinguishes it from authority-ladenness is the absence of direct coverage. Routine authority relations in France exclude direct subordinate-superordinate interaction. The authority-laden mode is explicitly defined in terms of the existence of such interaction. In the secondary schools, direct coverage was extensive and long-lasting; at E.N.A., it only occurred very briefly and was highly specific. Yet, in both cases, we are dealing with the authority-laden mode, for there was attempted and effective direct coverage.

Perceived Forcefulness, the Basis for Legitimacy: Extrapolating from the secondary school study, superordinates who avoid appeasement and vacillation while exhibiting self-confidence and self-control will be perceived as being forceful. The E.N.A. case study provides only a single, rather fleeting glimpse of authority-laden behavior by an individual perceived as being forceful—i.e., the thirty-minute speech by the general director of the administration and public service. While he avoided appeasement and vacillation and appeared self-confident and composed, these were not the specific characteristics which his intervention immediately evoked. Rather, (1) his speech was delivered in a firm, glacial tone of voice; (2) he presented himself as a spokesman for a power (the Government) which was great, true to its original promises, and in total control of the society, but not desirous of sanctioning the students for their previous behavior, although quite capable of doing so; and (3) he acted as if the "crisis" at E.N.A. were already resolved—i.e., as if the situation were under his control. Of these characteristics, logically the most crucial was the last, for the first two elements can be viewed as specific ways in which a superordinate may transmit the impression that, in fact, he already dominates.

Thus, on the basis of the E.N.A. study, to be considered forceful, a superordinate must convey the impression that he has the situation under control—i.e., must act as if he were already in charge, even though he is, in fact, trying to obtain such control—and buttress this impression with something observable —e.g., the Government for which the high-level civil servant is speaking had, to all intents and purposes, ended the societywide May crisis. This basis for attributing legitimacy to a superordinate in no way contradicts the bases isolated in the secondary schools; in fact, there is overlap—it is a rather economical, although incomplete way of synthesizing the complex of bases located in the high school study. However, given the context in which legitimacy was evoked in E.N.A., it may be that this new basis of forcefulness is especially relevant to ending a chahut and re-establishing order.

While the general conceptual and empirical referents of "forcefulness" should now be clear, readers must be especially warned not to equate it with charisma.[4] Such an association would be incorrect. The empirical referent of forcefulness is a type of behavior and not a type of leader. While it is likely that French leaders who have been referred to as "charismatic" are forceful under the appropriate circumstances, it is not necessary to be charismatic in order to obtain legitimacy. Furthermore, a given individual—e.g., someone who is "charismatic"—may at times be viewed as forceful, and at other times as being a superordinate under conditions of assumed coverage.

The Chahut: When assumed coverage gives way to nonroutine authority interactions, unless superordinates behave in a forceful fashion, there is a chahut. The chahut is a special type of rebellion; it is not just any act of insubordination, a departure from convention, or a "rumble." Its core defining characteristics are:

(1) Insubordination is organized—it is a group phenomenon.

(2) There are leaders who guide and control the activities of the rebels.

(3) There is an atmosphere of gaiety, joy and special human companionship, as if this communal undertaking were a festival.

This conception conflicts with existing views of the chahut group as characterized by an absence of internal leadership. According to Jesse Pitts, the originator of this view, a defining quality of the "delinquent peer-group community" (i.e., the chahut group) is the "jealous egalitarianism which the members show toward each other."[5] Although many students of French society have adopted Pitts' interpretation,[6] no one, until quite recently, has conducted field work which could test his view. However, a study, only now being completed, of political socialization in France, Great Britain, and the United States does examine Pitts' hypothesis and provides evidence which strongly challenges his impressions, while supporting the interpretation of the chahut presented in this work. Specifically, Sidney Tarrow, Fred I. Greenstein, and Mary F. Williams reach the following (preliminary) conclusion:

> French children are strikingly passive in response to the assertion of leadership from within their ranks. They do not express the censure of the assertive leader that we expected from the peer-group's characterization in the literature as a "delinquent community."[7]

The Independent Variables

Two interrelated independent variables and an observed pattern of behavior can explain whether the routine, assumed-coverage pattern or the alternating pattern will occur: (1) the value attributed to the goal to be achieved by membership in the social unit, (2) the subordinates' perception of how effectively the unit and its superordinates are functioning to achieve this goal, and (3) the superordinates' directive-issuing practices. Specifically, it is hypothesized that when (1) a high value is attributed to the goal, (2) subordinates perceive their superordinates and the unit as acting effectively to achieve this goal, and (3) superordinates issue virtually no face-to-face directives to subordinates, assumed coverage will prevail; otherwise, there will be an alternation between the authority-laden and chahut modes.

DEFINING THE INDEPENDENT VARIABLES

The term "goal" is central to both explanatory variables. What precisely is meant by "the goal to be achieved by membership in the unit?" How is the researcher to determine the specific goals sought by joining a given organization? I asserted that completing one's education was the goal in secondary schools, and the goal of E.N.A.s was to achieve a position in the upper echelons of the civil service. But by what criteria were these—rather than, for example, the seeking of human contact or intellectual growth—isolated as the goals sought by membership in these respective social units?

In theory, to empirically define goals is an extremely complex process, involving some attempt to determine the subordinates' motivation in joining a given organization. A crucial problem with this strategy, however, is that people belong to many social units which they did not consciously join. Furthermore, a major aim of this study was to describe and explain behavior toward authority in just such an organization—i.e., the nation-state. A second, more general, problem relates to the operational difficulty of determining people's motivations. A stab may be taken at discovering motivation through sophisticated questionnaire techniques calculated to overcome resistance to giving such information, but, unfortunately, there would still remain the difficulty of locating unconscious motivation. A final problem with making the goal sought from membership in a given social unit the operational equivalent of motivation for joining or remaining in a group, is that each member may have had a different motivation, and to explain his future behavior there would be a constant need to return to his idiosyncratic goal. While such a strategy might be desirable when social science has become more scientific, at this stage of development, there are no ways of realistically operationalizing this method.

What then is meant by "goal to be achieved by membership in the unit?" The starting point for determining the goal is the social unit, rather than its individual members. Each organization in a society has, literally by definition, a rather clear-cut, identifiable purpose for which subordinates are most likely to join it, were membership voluntary. For example, universities provide an education which is required for practicing certain professions; law schools train lawyers; work organizations provide an opportunity to earn money and have a given standard of living; and political parties seek to advocate and defend political philosophies and policies, as well as to elect public officials who will support and implement the party's views. Thus, were Crozier's Industrial Monopoly studied, or for that matter any work organization, the employee's goal, in these terms, is simply a certain amount of buying power in the society. And, turning to the nation-state, the goal of government is, minimally, to protect its citizens from violence and, at least in most modern nations, to avoid general economic crises.

While such an operational definition of "goal to be achieved by membership in the unit" is quite clear, at least one important objection might be raised. To take a concrete example, a bank employee may be offered jobs in many firms, receiving in each the same salary, but he will choose one position over another because the atmosphere is more pleasant or the people seem more friendly. This, of course, is true, and I do not even question the fact that people join groups for reasons other than, or in addition to, "the goal to be achieved by membership in the unit." In fact, should the theory presented in this book appear to have value, it might be worthwhile to develop it further by expanding the empirical notion of what constitutes a goal. Yet, given the current state of the theory, the simple, although possibly disturbing, definition of goal which has been presented will be used. At least, it has the great advantage of being applied without confusion to phenomena in the real world. And, it might be noted, such an advantage is not to be minimized. For even the most sophisticated and intellectually convincing notion is valueless if it cannot be operationalized and if its empirical referents are not clear-cut.

The key concept of the second independent variable is "perceived." For assumed coverage to persist, subordinates must perceive their unit as acting effectively to achieve for them the valued goal sought through membership. The difference between perceived and actual conditions is conceptually clear. Furthermore, there is no need to point out that, empirically, there may be a great difference between the perceived and the actual—if for no other reason than for any event there is only one actuality, but people rarely, if ever, approach unanimity in their perceptions of that event. And people act in the world according to "how they see it" not "how it really is." Yet, many scholars are uncomfortable with theories using perceived conditions as an explanatory variable. They somehow feel that this allows the researcher to present ad hoc conclusions which fit his desires. Obviously, such a possibility exists, but it also exists when dealing with "actual" conditions and practices. For, in fact, the actual is often the perceptions of scholars, while the perceived is the perceptions of the participants, either directly or through the intermediary of an observer. Thus, to a large extent, the difference between actual and perceived conditions is a difference between who is doing the perceiving.

The two independent variables do not alone fully explain all breakdowns of assumed coverage. The secondary school research implied—i.e., among teachers of the older students, those who gave too many orders were subject to the chahut—and logic supports the notion that superordinates, on their own initiative, may bring about a crisis. Specifically, assumed coverage persists only as long as superordinates do not attempt to directly cover subordinates' activities. However, if they do issue numerous face-to-face directives, they immediately change the form of interaction to the authority-laden mode, which could be transformed into a chahut if they lacked forcefulness. Since this relationship is true by definition, superordinate directive-issuing tendencies cannot properly be called an independent variable. Rather, an explanation of why superordinates may cease conforming with the basic tenets of assumed coverage is needed. Since my research was not directed at superordinates, it does not provide an answer to this question. However, Crozier's case study of the postal money order clerks, in which crises were engendered by superordinates is suggestive. Specifically, superordinates turned to direct (face-to-face) coverage at times of "traffic peaks" when the routine setup did not allow the unit to handle the additional work load.[8] This suggests that *superordinates' perceptions* of how effectively the unit's functional tasks are being accomplished may be the independent variable which explains their decision to initiate direct coverage. Such a hypothesis, of course, is simply based on speculation. What is not based on speculation is the notion that assumed coverage may give way to the alternating pattern simply by superordinates issuing face-to-face directives to subordinates.

Although in the cases studied, the differences between issuing many or virtually no face-to-face directives was clear—largely because the intervening points on this dimension were unpopulated empirically—theoretically, this distinction is gross. Likewise, there are numerous points on the "value attributed to the goal" scale between high and low and on the "perceived effectiveness" dimension between effective and ineffective. Ideally, these dimensions should be fully defined to permit precise classification of given empirical situations. If this were the case, then, for example, it might be concluded that (1) variations in perceived effectiveness have different behavioral outcomes, (2) variations in perceived effectiveness can be clustered and associated with a limited set of categories of behavioral consequences, or (3) there is a clear dividing line between perceived effectiveness and perceived ineffectiveness, and perceptions which fall into one category have the same behavioral outcomes, which, however, are distinct from the behavior linked with the other category of perceptions. Unfortunately, theorizing has not reached this stage of precision. Rather the independent variables have been treated as if they were dichotomous (since gross distinctions of this sort could be reliably made). This strategy is not ideal, but it is a first step toward a more sophisticated theory.

THE INTER-RELATIONSHIP BETWEEN
INDEPENDENT AND DEPENDENT VARIABLES

The three, dichotomously conceptualized independent variables may cluster in eight distinct ways. (For the purposes of expositional clarity, superordinate directive-issuing practices will from now on be included under the rubric of independent variables. Consult Figure 4.1 for a listing of these possible clusters.) Only one combination supports the routine pattern of authority interactions, and any other combination has as a common consequence, the alternating pattern.

It may be hypothesized that the four clusters including a low valuation of the goal sought by membership in the unit (and, hence, supportive of the alternating pattern), are only likely to occur within organizations in which membership is not voluntary. This seems to be the case for two reasons. First, it is highly improbable that people would choose to join a social unit, if its goal was not valued. Second, it seems likely that, if a person who had valued a unit's goal when he became a member stops valuing that goal, he will, if permitted, resign. Thus, these four clusters are only likely to occur within organizations in which membership is not a function of voluntary choice—specifically within primary and secondary schools, the army (since France has universal military training), jails, and asylums. However, even within this

---

Independent Variables

    1. Value attributed to the goal to be achieved by membership in the social unit
        1a — High valuation
        1b — Low valuation

    2. Subordinates' perception of how effectively the unit and its superordinates are functioning to achieve the unit's goal
        2a — Acting effectively
        2b — Acting ineffectively

    3. Superordinates' directive-issuing practices
        3a — Virtually no face-to-face directives
        3b — Many face-to-face directives

Possible Clusters

    1) 1a and 2a and 3a   Supports Routine Pattern

    2) 1a and 2a and 3b
    3) 1a and 2b and 3a
    4) 1a and 2b and 3b   Supports

    5) 1b and 2a and 3a   Alternating
    6) 1b and 2a and 3b   only probable within social
    7) 1b and 2b and 3a   units in which membership is   Pattern
    8) 1b and 2b and 3b   not voluntary

FIGURE 4.1: Clustering of the Independent Variables

type of social unit, there is a strong tendency for subordinates to acquire a high valuation of the unit's goal—to avoid severe cognitive stress. For example, among inmates and prisoners, it is improbable that most would value the unit's goal—i.e., isolating them from the normal world and freedom—and, hence, the normal form of authority interaction would be the alternating pattern. Yet, even in these social units, with goals seeming to run against the very essence of human desires, some subordinates acquire a high valuation of the goal (having become so habituated to their routine as to fear returning to the outside world) and, consequently, adhere to the assumed-coverage mode.

Although the conditions associated with a breakdown of the routine, assumed-coverage mode have been discussed in the context of the case studies, the process by which the alternating pattern is supplanted by assumed-coverage has not yet been examined. The secondary school study provides no helpful evidence, since a given group of students established assumed-coverage relations with certain teachers and participated in the alternating pattern with other teachers, but never seemed to change forms with a given teacher. The E.N.A. study, however, does provide some information. Specifically, there was an immediate return to assumed coverage following the authority-laden intervention of the director of the administration and the public service. Thus, the return to routine does not seem to require a change in the objective conditions which led to the crisis. Yet, the return to assumed coverage, by definition, does bring with it a change in subordinates' perceptions of how effectively superordinates and their unit are functioning. The E.N.A. case suggests that such a change occurs as soon as a chahut is replaced by authority-ladenness. Once a chahut is stopped by forcefulness, the superordinates can "choose," so to speak, either to maintain the authority-laden relationship which has been established or to stop issuing directives and return automatically to assumed coverage.

There seems to be a clearly logical reason why crises, created by subordinates' perceptions of superordinate and/or unit ineffectiveness, which include a chahut, should be terminated more or less quickly, according to the superordinates' desires, following demonstrated forcefulness. The independent variables strongly imply and the secondary school study explicitly asserts that the

French tend to act in a specific goal-oriented method on the basis of cost-benefit analysis.[9] Thus, one joins a social unit to achieve a valued goal. Subordinates adhere to assumed-coverage as long as the unit functions effectively to achieve this goal. When the unit is perceived as functioning ineffectively, there is a breakdown of assumed coverage, and, depending on the forcefulness of super-ordinates, the chahut or authority-laden modes prevail. If assumed coverage is succeeded by a chahut, subordinates may have fun, but absolutely nothing is done to improve unit effectiveness. Further-more, no matter how ineffective the unit may have been before, during the chahut its ineffectiveness is total. Thus, when super-ordinates do finally demonstrate forcefulness and "force" a return to order, there is a marked perceived improvement in unit effectiveness, even if, objectively, effectiveness is no greater than it was when the crisis began. Thus, when the chahut gives way to authority-ladenness, subordinates automatically perceive the unit as functioning more effectively to achieve the valued goal sought by membership. At this point, retaining for a more or less prolonged period the authority-laden mode of interaction before returning to assumed coverage is a decision which lies entirely in the hands of the superordinates. On intuitive and impressionistic grounds, it might be hypothesized that the return to routinized behavior will be rapid unless superordinates seek to change the content—i.e., the rules—of assumed coverage.

But what is the probable sequence of events if assumed coverage is terminated by subordinates' perceptions of ineffectiveness and followed by authority-ladenness? Although the case studies provide no direct evidence, it may be deduced that authority-ladenness will give way to the chahut and the above-described sequence of events, *unless* superordinates during the authority-laden phase act in ways to objectively improve unit effectiveness, and which result in a corresponding change in subordinates' perceptions of effectiveness. This outcome seems most likely because there is no reason to assume that the utilization of the authority-laden mode, in and of itself, will cause a change in perceived effectiveness. There is, however, one situation in which the movement from assumed coverage to authority-ladenness will be normally followed by a return to routinized behavior—i.e., when the cause of the breakdown of assumed coverage, rather than being perceived ineffectiveness, is superordinates' exerting direct coverage over subordinates' activities. In this case, if superordinates demonstrate forcefulness, there will be a return to assumed coverage as soon as they wish.

Throughout the preceding discussion, it has been implicitly assumed that the chahut always fails. Logically, this need not be the case, even though chahuts in the secondary schools and E.N.A. never succeeded in toppling the existing leadership stratum. If the actual superordinates perceive of the chahuteurs as about to win, in an attempt to avoid the full consequences of capitulation, they might decide to hand nominal power over to someone who is admired by and acceptable to the chahuteurs, yet someone whom they could tolerate. If the chahuteurs win, we would expect a change of official leadership in the social unit, with the chahut leaders either becoming superordinates or playing a key role in selecting the new "management." The new superordinates, who gained power through the chahut, would seek to establish authority-ladenness and create a new set of rules of the game. Whether and when this relationship would either be converted into assumed coverage or lead to a new chahut, should follow the conditions previously stipulated.

Theoretical Overview

In the following chapter, an attempt will be made to determine if the model of French behavior toward authority, derived from the two case studies, can provide a meaningful description and explanation of French citizens' basic behavior and dispositions toward national political authority. If this task is successfully accomplished, an argument presented in the Introduction (that an empirical understanding of social authority within a given society can be employed to increase comprehension of corresponding aspects of the government-citizen relationship) passes beyond the stage of plausibility and moves toward the realm of empirical tenability. Hence, a clear and concise formulation of the model's basic propositions and hypotheses is required as a backdrop to the forthcoming analysis of French political authority. Figure 4.2 schematically presents the key hypotheses; Figure 4.3 graphically summarizes the main arguments of this chapter by portraying the most probable sequences of, and connecting links between, the modes of authority behavior.

In more formal terms, the major hypotheses and propositions are as follows:

Proposition 1: Modal authority relationships within French social units are of the assumed-coverage, chahut, or authority-laden modes.

Proposition 1.1: Assumed coverage is the usual, the routine, the normal form of authority interaction in social units where membership is voluntary.

Proposition 1.2: The alternation between the chahut and authority-ladenness (i.e., the alternating pattern) is the crisis form of authority interaction in social units where membership is voluntary.

INDEPENDENT VARIABLES

I-1: Value attributed to the goal to be achieved by membership in the social unit
    I-1a: High Valuation
    I-1b: Low Valuation

I-2: Subordinates' perception of how effectively the unit and its superordinates are functioning to achieve the unit's goal
    I-2a: Acting Effectively
    I-2b: Acting Ineffectively

I-3: Superordinates' directive-issuing practices
    I-3a: Virtually no face-to-face directives
    I-3b: Many face-to-face directives

DEPENDENT VARIABLES

D-1: Assumed Coverage

D-2: Alternating Pattern

- -

Hypothesis 1: If *1a and* 2a *and* 3a than D-1.

Hypotheses 2 - 5: If 1b (and either 2a or 2b and either 3a or 3b) then:
    i. people are unlikely to voluntarily join the social unit, and if already members likely to leave; or
    ii. if "forced" to retain membership, D-2.

Hypothesis 2-8.1: If perceived forcefulness then authority-laden mode.

Hypothesis 2-8.2: If not perceived' as forceful then chahut mode.

Hypothesis 6: If 1a and 2a and 3b ⎫
Hypothesis 7: If 1a and 2b and 3b ⎬ then D-2.
Hypothesis 8: If 1a and 2b and 3a ⎭

FIGURE 4.2: The Basic Hypotheses

High Values, Perceived Effectiveness, and No Directives

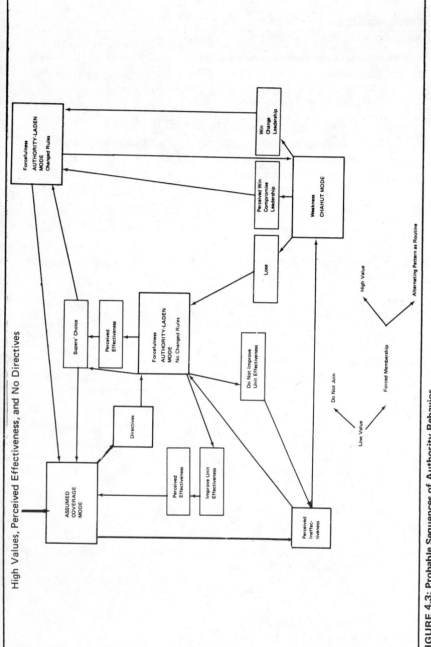

FIGURE 4.3: Probable Sequences of Authority Behavior

KEY TO FIGURE 4.3

"High Value"/("Low Value"): Subordinates attribute a high (low) value to the goal to be achieved by membership in the social unit.

"Perceived Effectiveness"/("Perceived Ineffectiveness"): Subordinates perceive the unit and its superordinates as functioning effectively (ineffectively) to achieve the unit's goal, which they highly value.

"No Directives"/("Directives"): Superordinates issue virtually no face-to-face directives (many face-to-face directives) to subordinates.

"Forcefulness"/("Weakness"): Subordinates perceive of their superordinates as being forceful (not forceful).

"Improve Unit Effectiveness"/("Do Not Improve Unit Effectiveness"): Superordinates act (do not act) in ways to objectively improve unit effectiveness.

"Perceive Win Compromise Leadership": Superordinates perceive of the chahuteurs as about to win and decide to hand nominal power over to a compromise leadership, acceptable both to the actual superordinates and to the chahuteurs.

"Win Change Leadership": The chahuteurs win and select a new set of superordinates.

"Changed Rules"/("No Changed Rules"): Superordinates seek (do not seek) to change the content—i.e., the rules—of assumed coverage.

"Supers' Choice": The selection of alternatives is made entirely by the superordinates.

"Do Not Join": If subordinates have the choice, they will not join the social unit.

"Forced Membership": Subordinates are compelled to join the social unit, membership is not voluntary.

> Proposition 1.3: In social units where membership is not a function of a voluntary choice, the alternating pattern may be the exclusive form of interaction with authority.

> Proposition 1.4: During the alternating pattern, the amount of forcefulness attributed to superordinates by subordinates determines whether the authority-laden or chahut mode will be established.

Proposition 2: Many Frenchmen have a dualistic normative structure. One set of norms is consonant with expected authority behavior; a second set, segregated from the first, is critical of the established way of doing things.

> Proposition 2.1: The critical norms give rise to rhetorical denunciations of the actual functioning of the social unit and may be behaviorally actualized through membership in or support of another social unit which has as one of its goals the transformation of the core unit.

Proposition 3: Subordinates perceive those superordinates who avoid appeasement and vacillation while exhibiting self-confidence and self-control as forceful.

Proposition 3.1: To end a chahut, superordinates—to be perceived
as forceful—must convey the impression that they have the
situation already under control (even though this, in fact, is what
they are trying to accomplish) and must buttress this impression
with something observable.

Hypothesis 1: If and only if subordinates attribute a high value
to the goal to be achieved by membership in a given social unit,
and they perceive this social unit and its superordinates as
functioning effectively to achieve this goal for them, *and*
superordinates issue virtually no face-to-face directives to subordinates, then authority relations will follow the assumed-
coverage pattern.

Hypotheses 2 through 5: If subordinates do not value the goal
to be achieved by membership in a given social unit, and
(hypothesis 2: they perceive the social unit and its superordinates
as functioning effectively to achieve this goal for them, and
superordinates issue virtually no face-to-face directives) or
(hypothesis 3: they perceive the social unit and its superordinates
as functioning ineffectively, and superordinates issue virtually no
face-to-face directives) or (hypothesis 4: they perceive effective
functioning, and there are many face-to-face directives) or
(hypothesis 5: they perceive ineffective functioning, and there are
many face-to-face directives), then they are unlikely to voluntarily
join the social unit, and, if already members, they are likely to
leave the social unit; but if they do not withdraw—for instance,
because membership is not voluntary—then authority relations will
follow the alternating pattern.

Hypotheses 6 through 8: If subordinates attribute a high value
to the goal to be achieved by membership in a given social unit,
and (hypothesis 6: they perceive the unit and its superordinates as
functioning ineffectively to achieve this goal for them, and
superordinates issue many face-to-face directives) or (hypothesis
7: they perceive ineffective functioning, and there are virtually no
face-to-face directives) or (hypothesis 8: they perceive effective
functioning, and there are many face-to-face directives), then
authority relations will follow the alternating pattern.

Hypothesis 2-8.1: If and only if (under any of the seven
conditions specified respectively in hypotheses 2 through 8)

subordinates perceive their superordinates as being forceful, then authority relations will follow the authority-laden mode.

Hypothesis 2-8.2: If and only if (under any of the seven conditions specified respectively in hypotheses 2 through 8) subordinates do not perceive their superordinates as being forceful, then authority relations will follow the chahut mode.

NOTES

1. The word "apparently" is used because the concepts of democracy and authoritarianism include, for example, besides a notion of level of control over subordinate behavior, different styles and degrees of participation and responsiveness. However, by definition, assumed coverage excludes both attempts by subordinates to influence the directive-issuing process and responsiveness by superordinates to such attempted influence, because, in fact, directives are not issued. In the sense that there is no participation or responsiveness under assumed coverage, it looks, given our everyday conceptual apparatus, rather authoritarian; but, as has been emphasized in the case studies, this perception is misleading.

2. One of the earlier exponents of this view was Robert Dell, who conceived of the French as having both a "democratic spirit" and "respect for authority." Fused with this respect is its natural adjunct "Frondisme"—i.e., the tendency to evade compliance with any law when this can be done with impunity (*My Second Country (France)* [New York: John Lane, 1920], pp. 31-34). Among more contemporary analysts, those who have seen "individualism" as a defining aspect of the "French character" have also tended to view Frenchmen as only accepting authority when forced to do so. (See, for instance, Jacques Fauvet, *The Cockpit of France*, trans. Nancy Pearson [London: Harvill Press, 1960], pp. 17-29.)

3. Such a procedure stems from the following logical tenet: The "abnormal" or exceptional can only be understood in terms of the "normal" or usual. Thus, for example, the concepts of "genius" and "moron" only have meaning when we know what is normal intelligence.

4. For an interesting discussion of charisma and charismatic leadership, see Ann Ruth Wilner, *Charismatic Political Leadership: A Theory* (Princeton: Center of International Studies, 1968).

5. This quote is from his most recent statement: Jesse R. Pitts, "La communauté délinquante," *Esprit* (January 1970), pp. 69-70. See also, Pitts, "Continuity and Change in Bourgeois France," *In Search of France.*

6. See, for example: Michel Crozier, *The Bureaucratic Phenomenon,* p. 241; and Stanley Hoffmann, "Protest in Modern France," in *The Revolution in World Politics,* ed. Morton A. Kaplan (New York: John Wiley, 1962), pp. 78-79.

7. S. Tarrow, F. I. Greenstein, and M. F. Williams, "Associational Incapacity in French Children: Some Evidence from a Study of Political Socialization in France and England," mimeo, 1970, p. 32. I am grateful to the authors for permitting me to refer to and cite from their preliminary findings.

8. M. Crozier, *The Bureaucratic Phenomenon,* p. 20.

9. In Weber's terms, they tend toward "instrumental rationality (Zweckrational)." See Max Weber, *Economy and Society: An Outline of Interpretive Sociology,* eds. Guenther Roth and Claus Wittich (New York: Bedminster Press, 1968), Vol. I, pp. 24 ff.

Chapter 5

AN ANALYSIS OF FRENCH
POLITICAL AUTHORITY PATTERNS

A complete analysis of political authority in any society would examine the nature of citizen behavior and attitudes toward the various units of political authority as well as the overall character of the regime. Such an analysis might also study governmental authority patterns—i.e., the nature of authority relations between and within segments of the government. To the extent that the school-based model defines a pattern of authority interaction that is *universal* in French society, it can be applied to the problem of how people behave toward authority within all political and governmental units. However, such a task would easily require a special volume, and, therefore, the scope of analysis must be severely restricted. Specifically, attention will be directed toward describing and explaining citizens' general behavior and dispositions toward the national government. This choice is arbitrary, but, given limitations on space and time, it seems to be the wisest selection, because this phenomenon has attracted the attention of most students of French politics.

From the outset, the reader should be aware of certain limitations in the forthcoming analysis. First, there is insufficient independent data on French dispositions toward political authority to determine with certainty if the same independent variables are operative in the political sphere as those which were observed in the secondary schools and E.N.A. As a result, to the extent that the analytical model fits French political realtiy, the hypotheses avoid refutation, even though they are not definitively "validated." This, of course, is of little concern to those who follow Karl Popper; adherents to other schools of the philosophy of science may regard this as a major limitation.

Second, the model was developed in the context of relatively simple social units in which it was not difficult to locate and isolate superordinate-subordinate interaction. But, for the French citizen, there is a very large number of different types of political superordinates—these run the gamut from the police officer and local governmental authorities to the national government and the President of the Republic. The model, as it now stands, fails to provide criteria which might suggest differences in citizen behavior toward these various levels of political superordination. Furthermore, the absence of sufficient information, as well as limitations of time and space, prevent analysis of the similarities and differences between citizens' behavior and dispositions toward each of the types of governmental superordinates—only the general nature of dealing with diffuse national political authority will be discussed.[1]

Third and most significantly, the model is limited by its own nature. In other words, it cannot describe or explain a whole variety of phenomena associated with French political behavior —e.g., the specific content of political authority relations, ideological conflict, the multiplicity of political parties—because it is not designed to describe and explain such phenomena. The model focuses attention on behavior toward authority. A typical set of behavioral sequences was located rather than a typical content of behavior or typical ideological ways of behaving in politics. This is of crucial significance and is a major reason for the difference between existing descriptions of French political behavior and the one presented in this work. Since this point is so important, before applying the model to the overall nature of political authority in

France, the model's interpretation will be compared to existing "theories."[2]

Comparing the School-Based Model's Interpretation with Other Interpretations of French Political Authority

INTERPRETATIONS OF FRENCH POLITICAL AUTHORITY

Most, although not all, observers have adopted a bimodal interpretation of French political authority.[3] Some of these "two-France theories" focus on the nature of the government, while others examine citizens' dispositions and behavior toward political authority. The bimodal conceptions of the French government will be considered first. The two elements are always (1) a liberal, "democratic," or weak form of government and (2) a strong, "authoritarian," or personalized regime. These two types of political systems are rarely seen as *simply* existing synchronically.[4]

Paul Seippel and J.E.C. Bodley were two of the earliest exponents of the view that the French political system oscillates, over time, between two different styles of government. According to Seippel, the alternation is between "self-government" and a "consolidating power" *(pouvoir reparateur);* while Bodley views the rotation as being between a purely "centralized" system and a mixed one with "parliamentary" and "centralized" elements.[5] Much more commonly, these "two Frances" have been labeled "democracy" and "authoritarianism." Helen Hill seems to have been the first person to apply these terms to the nature of the French political authority structure.[6] Her interpretation was popularized by Walter Rice Sharp, who wrote of France's "clashing political traditions" and explicitly cited Hill's conception as the basis of his view.[7]

Among the more recent conceptions of diachronic bimodality are those of Raymond Aron and Jean Laponce. Although their analyses are not identical, both see an alternation between regimes in which the political parties are dominant and those in which there is a "power above parties."[8] A more sophisticated and detailed version of this interpretation has been put forward by Stanley Hoffmann. He describes an oscillation between routine, parliamentary political authority—characterized by having a "non-directive leader, or the perfect broker"—and crisis regimes of "heroic leadership," which occur "when change cannot be delayed any longer."[9]

Another contemporary interpretation of diachronic bimodality has been presented by Nicholas Wahl and Henry Ehrmann. Wahl argues that France has both an "administrative tradition" of politics, which is closely associated with executive dominance, and a "representative tradition" characterized by the supremacy of parliament. Each of these traditions is actualized in different "sets of political institutions" which "have ruled France *consecutively*" since the eighteenth century.[10] Similarly, Henry Ehrmann conceives of the French government as having two "different forms of [political] authority"—the "representative and plebiscitarian traditions." The former is virtually identical to Wahl's tradition bearing the same name. On the other hand, the plebiscitarian tradition is characterized by "practices of direct democracy"—i.e., the absence of intermediaries between the ruler and the ruled.[11] Both Wahl and Ehrmann agree that the alternation in power of these two traditions has been the defining characteristic of French politics since the Revolution. Furthermore, their interpretations are not purely diachronic: They conceive of an alternation between regimes in which one or the other tradition *dominates,* but without eliminating its alternative.

These conceptions of the nature of the French political authority structure have more in common than simply a view of two different governmental styles which alternate in power. All the contemporary interpretations focus on the relative potency of the legislative and executive branches. It is this criterion which lies at the basis of their vision of bimodality. Those conceptions, which were presented in the early part of the twentieth century, tend for the most part to use the content of the relationship between the government and the governed as the determining factor for classifying some regimes as "democratic" and others as "authoritarian."

Two distinct types of two-France theories focus on citizens' dispositions and behavior toward political authority. One conception sees Frenchmen split between conflicting groups which orient themselves toward politics in different ways; the other conception regards each Frenchman as having two sets of dispositions toward political authority.

The interpretation which views French society as being segmented into two different groups is probably the oldest and most widely adopted of the two-France theories.[12] One of the earliest exponents of this view was Ernest Renan. He said:

> One reads in the old hebraic legends that Rebecca, feeling within her the two children she was carrying, consulted the Lord. "Two nations are within you," was the reply He gave her. Inside of our country, as within Rebecca, two peoples are struggling with each other, each trying to suffocate the other.[13]

The most popular version of this interpretation is to view the French as belonging either to the "Red France" of the left of the "Black France" of the right.

The red-black duality was first suggested by Stendhal in *Le Rouge et le Noir*. This conception was openly adopted by many writers of the pre-World War II generation—e.g., Paul Seippel and Roger Soltau[14]—and even certain contemporary scholars, such as Gordon Wright,[15] have at least paid lip service to this conception. More importantly, this interpretation has been refined. For example, André Siegfried stressed the existence of two political "tendencies" which attracted the French and labeled them the "left" and the "right." He went on to argue that even though these were the only "real" tendencies in the society, power tended to fall into the hands of the "center"—i.e., a coalition of the more moderate elements of the "left" and the "right."[16]

Much of Siegfried's contribution was simply a permutation of labels from "red" to "left" and from "black" to "right," thus permitting the duality to be used as the basis for a continuum. It was only with François Gouguel's *La politique des parties sous la Troisième République* that the view of France having an ideologically based segmentation was to obtain important elaboration and additions. Goguel replaced the societally generated terms of "left" and "right" with the analytical concepts of tendencies toward "movement" and "established order." He argued that the division into two durable and stable ideological blocs is peculiarly French. While other scholars may have agreed with him, he was the first to clearly outline the geographical and social class continuity of support for each of the two tendencies.[17] Finally, he modified and made more precise the idea which Siegfried implies, that the ideological duality of the society is not replicated at the political level.[18]

Goguel's views were quite influential, with such widely read studies as Jacques Fauvet's *The Cockpit of France (La France déchirée)* openly adopting the basic elements of his interpretation.[19] Concomitantly, Siegfried's concept of the "left" versus the "right" persisted either in its original or in amended form. François Bourricaud, for example, sees French politics in terms of a left-right conflict. But, he argues, there is normally a lack of union within each bloc. It is only in times of crisis that the various factions of the left and those of the right have realized the similarities between them. At these times, there is a conservative-left conflict, while otherwise a struggle takes place among the various factions.[20]

Another offshoot from the Stendhalian conception was also "fathered" by André Siegfried. He argued that there was a "cleavage" in "French Public opinion" between "two schools of thought, the one favoring autocratic government and the other the rule of the people."[21] Similarly, David Thomson seems to see a tension in French society between individuals who are more favorably inclined toward "liberty" than toward "equality," toward "democracy" than toward "government," and people who take the reverse position.[22] According to Nicholas Wahl, France is characterized by the "coexistence of two primitive patterns of politics, the state-minded administrative pattern and the individual-oriented representative pattern." These are both "competitive and hostile, because they are supported by hostile groups in society."[23] In a similar vein, Eric Nordlinger interprets French politics as a conflict between two political subcultures. On the one hand, there is the "France of hierarchical order," which is peopled by individuals having "directive" dispositions toward political authority. On the other hand, there is the "France of idealistic egalitarianism," whose members have "acquiescent" dispositions toward authority.[24]

Those two-France theories which conceive of each Frenchman as having two sets of dispositions toward political authority, tend to see insubordination and submissiveness as the two elements. Robert Dell, one of the earlier exponents of this view, argued that the French have adopted a utilitarian conception of obedience, as a function of a "natural dislike of the authority to which submission is too readily given when it cannot be evaded." Given this "attitude toward authority," after enduring "abuses for years without any effective protest," the French will suddenly "break out and smash up everything" when the "situation becomes absolutely unbearable."[25]

Stanley Hoffmann has argued that the Frenchman's "attitude" toward political authority is characterized by a "mixture of defiance and dependence,"[26] generated by a simultaneous "need for and fear of authority."[27] And Roy Macridis suggests that there is a dualism in the French political culture between "the search for authority" and "the deep distrust of it."[28] Finally, Henry Ehrmann argues that the French tend "to both distrust government and expect much from it."[29]

Other two-France theories which conceive of the individual as having dual orientations toward authority are posed less explicitly in submissive-insubordinate terms. Roger Soltau argued that the French citizen tends to have two "attitude[s] of mind" toward authority. On the one hand, most have "at some time been fascinated by the vision of "a beneficent despot . . . a despot to obey their bidding." This "dormant enthusiasm" for "Bonapartism"—i.e., "the idea that the best form of government is the absolute rule of a democratically selected aristocrat"—is brought to life "in times of crisis." On the other hand, there is the normally dominant force of "Republican reluctance to entrust to any man for a long time powers which he might use for the overthrow of the Republic."[30] Raymond Aron views the French as possessing both a "taste for personal independence" and a tendency to have "constant recourse to the state."[31] Jesse Pitts refers to the "tension" within each individual between "aesthetic-individualistic" and "doctrinaire hierarchical" aspects.[32] And, according to Charles Morazé, "the great majority of Frenchmen have two political souls: one as citizen," who identifies himself with the state, "the other as subject, who considers that the State is the others." The former role is congenial to making sacrifices, while the latter "demands subventions and protection, and revolts if these are not obtained."[33]

To sum up, most interpretations of the nature of French political authority fall into the category of two-France theories. There are, however, three distinct types of two-France theories: (1) the diachronic bimodal conception, which conceives of France as alternatively being subjected to two different types of government: a weak, "democratic," liberal regime, and a strong, "authoritarian," personalized one; (2) the segmented-society view, which sees Frenchmen divided into two conflicting ideological groups: there are the red, left, progressive, individualistic, democratic Frenchmen and the black, right, conservative, state-minded, authoritarian Frenchmen; and (3) the schizoid-individual view, which argues that each Frenchman has two distinct sets of dispositions toward political authority: he both fears, dislikes, distrusts, and seeks to avoid submission to authority and concurrently needs, seeks, and depends upon political authority. Many scholars have simultaneously adopted more than one of these interpretations, arguing, for instance, that the French political system is characterized by diachronic bimodality because the society is segmented and/or because Frenchmen have dualistic dispositions toward political authority. In fact, one could argue that these three types of interpretations are closely interrelated because the elements in each of the conceptions are consonant with the elements in the others.

THE MODEL'S INTERPRETATION OF FRENCH POLITICAL AUTHORITY

The "theories" which have been discussed locate one (or a combination) of the following phenomena as the central element(s) of French political behavior: the relative strength of the executive and legislative branches of government, the content of relations between citizens and government, the fragmentation and conflict between groups adopting contrasting ideologies, and the competing tendencies within the French toward submissiveness and insubordination. According to the school-based model, the defining characteristic of French politics and political behavior would be a particular recurrent (if not regular) cycle which has a formal pattern to it.

Besides differing from other theories in focusing on typical sequences of behavior in French politics rather than a typical content of behavior or typical ideological ways of behaving in politics, the model is different in not being derived from political behavior as such, but from early learning processes. One of its hoped-for theoretical advantages is that it would not only make sense out of French politics but also describe and explain French "political behavior" in quite different contexts—the contexts of the early experiences in the family onward.

Finally, the theory presented in this book differs from others, not all others, but many others, in suggesting that the French, in general, have a genuine need for behavioral coverage—either assumed or the type of direct coverage that comes from authority-ladenness or the chahut. They seem to seek and require direction, and that casts serious doubts on the widespread notion that while there is such a France that longs for authority and direction, there is also a considerable France that longs for the absence of authority, or anarchy, and exhibits it whenever possible. The model makes this "anarchic" behavior all of a piece with the directive-seeking behavior.

Up to this point, no evidence has been presented to support the contention that the model can provide a meaningful description and explanation of the overall pattern of French citizens' behavior and dispositions toward national political authority. The model's political utility will first be assessed by determining if it can explain the overall sequence of events in French politics from the beginning of the Fourth Republic to the death of President Pompidou. Then I will go on to ask if it provides a plausible account and explanation of the very short and dense sequence of events referred to as the May crisis of 1968. Since it is generally much easier to fit an explanation to a very prolonged pattern of events than to a very short one, and since it is most difficult of all to find a single model that will explain something like France over the last generation as well as French behavior over the period of a couple of months in a given year, the procedure which has been adopted should be considered a particularly demanding assessment of the model's political utility.[34]

Applying the School-Based Model

RECENT FRENCH POLITICS

According to the school-based model, the usual form of government in France would follow the assumed-coverage mode: Political superordinates would issue relatively few overt directives, although there might be numerous codified instructions, and citizens would be highly compliant with a detailed series of understood rules about how they should behave toward their government. Assumed-coverage rule would endure as long as the modal citizen perceived the government as acting effectively to achieve the valued goal sought from membership in the polity (i.e., a societal environment in which the pursuit of an individual's familial and vocational goals was facilitated rather than obstructed).[35] In other words, assumed-coverage government would persist until: (1) economic conditions deteriorated to a point where they seriously threatened or in fact sharply cut into the individual's earning power; (2) domestic peace was rudely disrupted by internal agitation; or (3) foreign military involvement impinged upon and became destructive of the country's domestic life.[36]

Of course, these are not the only goals valued by political subordinates. Certain subgroups of the population may, for example, consider the welfare aspects of the state as having greatest importance, and their behavior toward the government would be a function of how well they perceived this goal as being achieved for them. Other segments (e.g., the Communists, the Poujadists, and the early Gaullist R.P.F.) might systematically perceive the regime as functioning ineffectively to achieve the political goals they value. This would occur either because they value different goals (which are not being satisfied by the actual regime) or because their conception of what constitutes effective achievement of a desired goal is more demanding than the perception of the general population. Such groups would not establish assumed-coverage relations with the government; rather, their interactions would always follow the alternating pattern. Thus, I am simply suggesting that, according to the model, the modal political subordinate (the large majority, although not necessarily the overwhelming majority of citizens) would consider the regime to be functioning well when the economic environment was healthy and neither internal agitation (by, for instance, such chahut groups as referred to above) nor foreign military involvement seriously disturbed domestic tranquility.

When either a healthy economic environment or domestic tranquility broke down, assumed-coverage government would move toward an authority-laden regime in which the political system impinged directly on the citizens. (In addition, assumed coverage might rapidly be replaced by authority-ladenness on the initiative of political superordinates—they would simply start directly covering citizens' political activities.) Political authority would not only be directive, but also, in contradistinction to the assumed-coverage form, it would not leave the Frenchman alone: He would be both called to action and acted upon. During the transition period from assumed coverage to authority-ladenness, there would probably be chahuting (i.e., organized insubordination toward superordinates who were not perceived to be forceful, strong individuals). Chahuts might also be interspersed with authority-ladenness. The movement back toward assumed-coverage government would be predicated upon a change in the citizens' perceptions of how effectively the political system was functioning.[37] A convincing demonstration by the political authorities of their forcefulness might well be sufficient to change the subordinates' perceptions. It should be noted that, during the authority-laden phase, a new set of rules of the game may have been implemented; if so, they would continue to be followed once there was a return to assumed coverage.

The Fourth Republic was basically an assumed-coverage regime.[38] Citizens were more or less divorced from political authority. During this period, France gradually but steadily recovered from the economic morass in which it had been left as a result of World War II. Although French workers were not, in an absolute sense, well off, their lot in life had continued to improve under the assumed-coverage regime. Domestic tranquility was seriously challenged in late 1947 by a series of important Communist-led strikes, but the government was able to halt the destructive process before it spread to other segments of the population. With regard to foreign military involvement, France fought for nine years (from 1945 to 1954) against Ho Chi Minh's rebel forces in Indochina, but this conflict had not seriously intruded on the ordinary Frenchman's life, because France's professional army—rather than draftees—was doing the fighting, and this army did not interfere in the government's domain of policy-making.

During most of the Fourth Republic, the modal political subordinate may not have been proud of his regime, and he may even have intellectually condemned its chronic cabinet instability, but, at least, he was left alone by the government which was providing him with an environment in which he could lead a satisfactory familial and vocational life. In 1957, this situation started gradually to change. France was suffering from severe inflation. The ensuing economic difficulties were sharply resented because the growth of the French economy after World War II and the commencement in 1954 of a period of real prosperity had not prepared the French for this type of setback. In 1957 and during the early months of 1958, there were numerous protests and strikes for higher salaries. Industrial workers, government employees, farmers, and even police participated in these demonstrations.

Alongside this domestic unrest, and of much greater significance, was the disastrous Algerian War, which by the beginning of 1958 was having a profound effect on internal French life. Sons were being called to fight in this war, and many were being killed or wounded. Furthermore, the French settlers in Algeria and the military commanders were unwilling to accept anything less than victory over the rebels, but they believed the government was leading France toward a compromise. These two groups posed to the assumed-coverage regime a challenge which it could not meet.

The army leaders and French settlers in Algeria (perceiving the government as not effectively functioning to protect their valued goal of *Algérie française*) began to test their political superordinates to determine if they were authorities to be obeyed—i.e., forceful and strong—and found the government to be very weak. The result was a full-blown chahut in May 1958, with the army assuming full powers in Algeria, taking control in Corsica, and threatening to invade mainland France. The army and settlers demanded that the government turn power over to General

Charles de Gaulle. In other words, they wanted a forceful political leader who, they believed, would change the political system's policies to achieve the goal they valued.

During May 1958, there were Frenchmen who actively demonstrated for and against the military rebels. These forces often clashed in the streets, but it seems that the major portion of the population was inactive, simply hoping for any government which could restore order.[39]

As is well known, these events led to the investiture of General de Gaulle as the last premier of the Fourth Republic on June 1, 1958. He was given complete power to revise the Constitution and to make governmental policy during the next six months. On September 28, 1958, eighty percent of the voters approved the Gaullist Constitution and, thereby, inaugurated the Fifth Republic.

Until the end of 1962, the normal style of relationship between government and governed was authority-laden. General de Gaulle made a large number of television and radio addresses to the French people calling for their support and cooperation. In addition, between September 1958 and October 1962, there were four referenda in which the voters were asked to approve de Gaulle's policies and proposals. Throughout this period, there was, in general, a very high degree of compliance with governmental directives. However, certain subgroups in the society were quite dissatisfied with the Algerian developments: They perceived the political system as not effectively functioning to satisfy the most basic goals they sought from it. Their reaction was to test the government's authority through chahuting. The most significant of these protest groups were the military leaders and French settlers in Algeria, who had been instrumental in bringing de Gaulle to power. By late 1959, these groups clearly saw that the general was not the staunch defender of *Algérie française* that they had believed him to be. From that point until the end of 1962, the settlers and army leaders, as well as their sympathizers, used every means at their disposal to prevent the government from giving up Algeria. At first there were simply demonstrations in Algeria; then there were settlers' revolts and an army revolt; and finally, there was the creation in May 1961 of the O.A.S. (*Organisation de l'armée secréte,* the Secret Army Organization), which was to use sabotage and attempted assassination as a last-ditch means to keep Algeria French. The political authorities responded with forcefulness to the various acts of subversion and, thereby, retained their legitimacy in the eyes of the overwhelming majority of the population.

The demise of the assumed-coverage Fourth Republic regime was directly linked to the inability of this government's leaders to assert their mastery over the Algerian problem. Now that the war and organized terrorism were over (in late 1962), there was no longer a need from the perspective of the political superordinates for a continuation of the authority-laden regime. As a result, the Fifth Republic entered a new phase characterized by assumed coverage. The rules of the political game were quite different from those which had existed before June 1958. These new rules had been instituted during the four years of authority-laden government. But the way in which authority was exercised was quite similar. This assumed-coverage phase lasted until the end of 1967. During this period, the French adhered to the new rules, but were no longer called upon to respond to direct appeals for support of particular policies. Furthermore, from 1963 through 1967, there were no referenda.

In 1967-1968, assumed-coverage rule broke down both because of subordinates' perceptions and because of governmental direct coverage. On the one hand, university students and industrial workers perceived their vocational units as malfunctioning and saw this as a by-product of the government's social and economic policies. On the other hand, there was sudden and "unjustified" governmental directiveness toward students. I am referring here to the imposition of the Fouchet reforms on the universities. This led to the May crisis (i.e., a chahut) which was resolved when the incumbent political superordinates reasserted their forcefulness and, thereby, won back legitimacy. The leader (General de Gaulle) had, however, been severely and permanently weakened by these incidents. First, the fact that the chahut had occurred under his rule strongly suggested that it could happen again. Second, one of the potential functions to be served by authority-ladenness is to bring about change in the unit, but since it was under the assumed-coverage rule of General de Gaulle that the perceived ineffectiveness had developed, it was likely that Frenchmen would not consider him well-suited to the task of bringing about those changes which were desired.

From the end of the May crisis until the April 27, 1969, referendum, the French regime was not particularly authority-laden, save vis-à-vis the students. Following June 1968 and with the monetary crisis of November 1968, the French perceived the regime as potentially dysfunctional. During the same period, General de Gaulle felt there was a need for authority-laden government to bring about certain necessary transformations (particularly a restructuring of regional government). Thus, he called for a referendum on April 27, 1969. The majority of the citizens responded by rejecting the proposals, thereby engaging in a formalized chahut which sought to get rid of what seemed to them a weakened leader and to avoid future dysfunctions. Their action achieved this goal, for de Gaulle resigned.

The newly elected President of the Republic, Georges Pompidou, began his tenure in office by trying to reestablish assumed-coverage government according to the basic rules of the Fifth Republic. Of course, as might be expected, there was some chahut testing, to determine the forcefulness of the Pompidou government, by those groups which did not perceive the regime as functioning effectively to achieve for them the valued goals they sought from the government. But this was rather short-lived.

Citizen-goverment relations during the years of "Pompidolisme" adhered to the assumed-coverage mode. This is not surprising, since France avoided both foreign military involvement and serious internal agitation, while economic conditions of growth and development prevailed.[40] Perhaps nothing better exemplified the "nonheroic" leadership of the second president of the Fifth Republic than the astonishing rapidity with which discussion and analysis of his personality and policies ceased after his death in April 1974. The only referendum (an instrument of governing which does not "fit" with assumed coverage) called during Pompidou's rule was responded to with "enthusiastic" apathy—the level of non-voting was significantly higher than it had ever been in a twentieth-century national election.

The most important deviation from assumed coverage occurred in March-April 1973. A sudden exertion of direct coverage by the government over students led to a breakdown of routine and testing of the political superordinates to determine their force-fulness. Specifically, beginning on February 27, lycée and then university students (and still later, pupils in technical schools) launched a series of strikes and demonstrations in opposition to the "Debré Law," which was to suppress military deferments for students. During March, the protest movement grew both in magnitude and in scope. However, order was restored by the end of April, following a "hard-line" position taken by the government during the first ten days of April and then the Easter vacation which removed momentum from the protesters.

This brief historical tracing has demonstrated that the school-based model can account for the overall sequence of events in French politics for the past generation. At the outset, let me note that most of the two-France theories could equally well describe the historical sequence of events in French politics. For example, Wahl's conception of the Fourth Republic as a regime in which the representative tradition was dominant while the administrative tradition is dominant in the Fifth Republic is quite tenable. One could also argue that the Fourth Republic responded to the desires of one segment of the population, while the Fifth Republic is more palatable to the other section. Or these two regimes might be seen as alternatively responding to the two orientations each Frenchman has toward political authority.

The question arises whether any of these two-France theories can explain the breakdown of the Fourth Republic *in 1958.* Those who view France as segmented into conflicting groups or who see each Frenchman as a fragmented, schizoid individual would be able to account for the change by saying that before 1958 one group or one tendency was dominant, but afterward the other group or tendency reigned. This sort of explanation, however, seems ad hoc—that is to say, there are no precise, defined, and operationalizable variables which explain when one or the other element will dominate.

The model's classification of political regimes is likely to cause some concern, since one rarely finds the Fourth Republic and the post-1962 Fifth Republic placed in the same analytical category. Rather, the two cases are usually cited as examples of the distinct types of French political authority. The difference between existing interpretations and the one which has just been presented is simply a function of the dimension upon which the regimes have been classified. The model focuses on the mode or *form* of authority interaction rather than its *content*. In this sense, it conflicts with some strongly entrenched traditions, specifically in the study of French politics and, more generally, in political science.

One of the major contributions de Tocqueville made in his study of the French Revolution was to direct attention away from the change caused by the Revolution in social class composition of the governmental elite and toward the centralized, monarchical nature of political power which characterized both the ancien régime and its successors.

> That ancient institution, the French monarchy, after being swept away by the tidal wave of the Revolution, was restored in 1800. It was not, as is often supposed, the principles of 1789 that triumphed at that time (and are still incorporated in the French administrative system); on the contrary, it was the principles of the old order that were revived and have been endorsed by all successive governments.[41]

De Tocqueville's emphasis on the "centralization of power" common to both pre- and post-Revolutionary France was at least partly responsible for the almost universal tendency to classify French political regimes according to the content of the authority relations established between government and governed. A second, and probably more crucial, reason for this focus on content has been the almost total acceptance in modern political science of some form of a democracy-dictatorship continuum which classifies governments according to the *amount* of authority they possess.

Thus, the model's focus on the form of authority interaction runs counter to some rather well-established tendencies. The difference in focus results in developing different dimensions upon which regimes are to be classified. Hence, it is not the case that one categorization is correct and the other is in error. Rather, to return to the case of French political authority relations, the conflicting ways in which regimes are classified by the school-based model and the two-France theories are both correct. Therefore, the key question is not one of "correctness," but rather which dimension permits the development of explanatory theory?

THE MAY CRISIS

The Preconditions: The model suggests that assumed coverage will break down whenever (1) subordinates do not perceive the unit and/or its superordinates acting effectively to achieve for them the valued goal sought from membership, or (2) superordinates start exerting direct coverage over subordinates. Both conditions seem to have existed in the pre-May days among university students (i.e., those who played the major role in instigating the crisis), and the first condition was clearly present among workers (without whose participation the events would not have assumed the massive dimensions of a challenge to the very existence of contemporary French society).

The beginning of the 1967-1968 academic year was marked by the imposition of the Fouchet reforms[42] and a great deal of student protest, much of it directed against these reforms. The Fouchet plan sought to modernize the content of a university education. Specifically, it attempted to create a system to cope with the recent "knowledge explosion" and to better prepare students for research. From now on, an undergraduate program was to be divided into two stages, neither of which strongly resembled the curricula in force before 1967-1968.[43] The new system would probably not have been as controversial it it had only been applied to incoming students. However, it was decided that students who had already completed part of their education (and had, therefore, learned the university's mode of assumed-coverage) would now have to follow the Fouchet reforms. As a result, these reforms were a case of direct coverage exerted over the task-centered activities of continuing students. For many students, part of the work they had completed would now be irrelevant, and they would have to take additional courses —thereby prolonging the time they must spend in the university— to prepare for the new examinations. This sudden, imposed change in the rules of the game was deeply resented and led many students to participate in the wave of protests, beginning in November 1967 and culminating in May 1968, against the government and the university.

More crucial for understanding the bases of the May crisis were the perceptions of workers and students about how effectively their vocational units were achieving for them the goals sought by membership. Both attributed a very high value to the goals they sought through membership in the university and in their industrial organizations, respectively. Young men and women who wanted to obtain positions considered prestigious in French society knew that this goal could only be attained through a university education. Their entire career potential was to be determined by their educational experience.[44] Blue-collar workers may have been dissatisfied with the status of their occupations, but most were resigned. What they really valued was their salaries, which, since the end of World War II, had permitted them to live increasingly well.

While both university students and workers valued the goals they sought through membership in their vocational units, neither group perceived its organizations (in the pre-May days) as functioning effectively to achieve these valued goals for them. In two distinct but overlapping ways, the university did not seem to be functioning effectively. First, among students who spent the normal number of years at the university, only about fifty percent would, in fact, get a diploma.[45] Of course, without a diploma, the time spent at the university, from the perspective of obtaining a special position in society, was wasted. Second, many university graduates, especially those receiving degrees in the Faculty of Letters, were unable to obtain positions commensurate with their training. Unfortunately, there are no available statistics on the job placement of university students, so we do not know how severe the actual underemployment situation was. Yet, on the perceptual level, it was clearly of crucial significance. During the student protests beginning in November 1967 and going up through the early months of 1968, the problem of *débouchés* was central in their critiques. In addition, polls of university student opinion conducted after the May crisis clearly isolate job placement as the major post hoc explanation for participation in the crisis. A poll conducted in September 1968 by the French Institute of Public Opinion (I.F.O.P.) discovered that, when asked to rank three phenomena in the order of their importance in generating the events of May-June 1968, fifty-six percent of the respondents placed the job placement issue first, thirty-five percent ranked the poor organization of studies at the top, and only seven percent put the refusal of the society of consummation in the first place.[46] Even more striking are the results of a poll conducted by the *Institut Français de Polémologie.* Specifically, among the students who actually participated in the crisis, seventy-two percent said they had been fearful about their future employment possibilities.[47]

In the pre-May days, workers began to perceive the government as acting ineffectively to achieve their valued goal of a salary. One factor leading to this perception was the "ordinances" affecting the French comprehensive system of social security which were published in late August 1967. Specifically, the new laws made the following important changes:

(1) workers would have to increase their financial contribution to the system from six percent to six and one-half percent of their salary;

(2) the benefits they were to receive were to be reduced—e.g., seventy percent rather than eighty percent of one's doctor and dentist bills were to be reimbursed, and support, under the family allowance provisions,[48] was to be reduced for young couples without children;

(3) the previously unified social security system was to be divided into three sections: medical insurance, family allocations, and old age; and

(4) the members of the proposed administration councils for the three sections were to be selected by workers' unions and business associations.

The unions quickly and vigorously began protesting against all these aspects of the new system. However, from the model's perspective, the key element, which contributed to the workers' developing perceptions of governmental ineffectiveness, was the increase in rates combined with the reduction in benefits. This was equivalent to a de facto reduction in workers' salaries—i.e., the valued goal sought from membership in the vocational unit.

More significant than the change in the social security system was the issue of job security. First, the general unemployment rate had increased by almost fifty percent during the twelve months preceding January 1968. Second, and more importantly, a sizable proportion of workers personally feared they might become unemployed. This point is strikingly supported by a survey conducted by I.F.O.P. during the first few days of February 1968.

When asked: "Do you think you may lose your present job during 1968?" seventeen percent of the workers responded affirmatively.[49]

This situation clearly demonstrated the growing ineffectiveness of the employers (and of the government, since it plays a key role in determining economic conditions) to satisfy the goal which workers valued. The young workers were especially hard hit by these developments. Seeking living quarters for the first time, they had to pay much higher rents than the older workers paid for comparable lodgings. Moreover, they were usually the first to be fired, not only because of their lack of seniority, but also because of the poor training they had received in government apprenticeship and vocational training programs which were dated and ill-adapted to the needs of modern industry.[50] And while the unemployment rate for the general population was still less than two and one-half percent, among younger workers it was almost nine percent.[51]

Thus, both university students (especially those in the Faculties of Letters) and workers (especially the younger ones) tended to perceive their vocational units as functioning ineffectively to achieve the valued goals they had sought through membership in these organizations, and they attributed this ineffectiveness to governmental policy. In addition, the government, by applying the Fouchet reforms, exerted direct task coverage over the students' activities. As a result, there was, hypothetically, a movement away from assumed coverage toward the alternating pattern.

In the pre-May days (beginning toward the end of October 1967), demonstrations, marches, and strikes occurred very frequently. If we are to believe the words of the protesters, their discontent was based on the above-mentioned dysfunctional aspects of the workers' and students' vocational units. Many of these protests were directed against the government, which was perceived as creating a social and economic environment making it impossible for the vocational units to satisfy effectively the goals sought by their members.[52] All of these "rebellions" can be viewed as ways of testing superordinates to determine if they are "forceful" individuals who, thus, should be obeyed. In each case, the superordinates tended to respond calmly but firmly (and without massive force) to the protesters.[53] The result was a maintenance of order and an avoidance of the chahut.

The fact that the rebels in the pre-May days tended to perceive the government as being forceful is suggested in anecdotal form by the famous incident in January 1968 between Daniel Cohn-Bendit —one of the leaders, if not the major leader, of the student revolt in May 1968—and François Missoffe, Minister of Youth and Sports. The Minister had come to Nanterre to dedicate a swimming pool. On campus, Cohn-Bendit was insolent toward him and showed a lack of respect in public—i.e., he acted like a chahut leader. However, after the Minister left, Cohn-Bendit did not speak about Missoffe in public again, but rather sent the Minister a letter of apology!

The pre-May protests and demonstrations rarely involved direct confrontation between subordinates and superordinates in their place of work. Most of the testing was done outside the vocational organizations. Individual students and workers who were critical of their unit's effectiveness did not go to speak and argue directly with their superordinates, but rather joined or helped found organizations to represent their interests. These organizations presented demands to the leaders of the vocational units and successfully called upon the subordinates to support these demands through street demonstrations and strikes. One of the most salient characteristics of these pre-May protests was the important role played by new or informal groups. Although the workers had a series of powerful trade unions (especially the very progressive C.F.D.T. and the Communist-dominated C.G.T.) and the university students had U.N.E.F. (the National Union of French Students) to defend their interests, these traditional groups often failed to perceive the degree of discontent among their adherents. As a result, radical students (e.g., Daniel Cohn-Bendit's Movement of March 22) and young workers often played an initiatory role in protest movements and wildcat strikes. This, however, is not to suggest that the entrenched interest groups were inactive. In fact, they led the protests most of the time. What is interesting is that sometimes they were not aware of the poignancy of their clientele's critiques and thereby lost some of their control to newly formed or informal groups.

The concept of dual guides to action may help explain this style of protest, which avoids direct, face-to-face contact with superordinates in the unit and which includes the creation of new "pressure groups." An individual with a dualistic normative structure (a characteristic of Frenchmen who are critical of the way in which their social unit functions) will rarely express his opinions to his superordinates within the organization. Rather, he is prone to join or support groups which actively seek to transform it. If he does not perceive any existing groups as performing this role, we may logically assume he will help found organizations to represent his interests.

The Outbreak and Development of the Crisis:[54] Despite the high level of worker and student protest during the first few months of 1968, it is not difficult to locate the actual beginning of the crisis. On the afternoon of Friday, May 3, approximately 400 students gathered in the Sorbonne to protest the closing of Nanterre's Faculty of Letters and the appearance before the Council of the University of six Nanterre students.[55] To protect themselves against a possible attack by extreme right-wing groups, they had a security guard armed with clubs. The rector of Paris' académie, Jean Roche, asked these students, especially the armed marshalls, to leave the Sorbonne, because he believed their presence increased the possibility of conflict. At the same time, police took up positions outside the university to prevent any other students entering. The leftist students in the Sorbonne refused to leave, but promised to avoid any incidents. Then, on the rector's orders, police entered the university and surrounded the protesters. The organizers of the meeting agreed to cooperate with the police and the evacuation took place peacefully. The leftist students entered police vans to be taken to headquarters to have their identities checked.

While the Sorbonne was being evacuated, other students had gathered around the building. Seeing their classmates being taken by the police, they falsely believed their comrades were being arrested and began hurling insults at the police. Soon tensions had mounted to a very high level, and the police decided to clear the area by using tear gas. Throughout the evening there were violent manifestations in the Latin Quarter. Many people were wounded, 596 protesters were stopped and questioned by the police, and 27 students were arrested (of these, 4 were sentenced to prison terms of two months and the rest were freed on May 5). Furthermore, the rector decided that courses at the Sorbonne would be provisionally suspended beginning on May 4.

The most crucial of these events was the evacuation of the Sorbonne by the police. The use of such direct and massive force by the superordinates suggested (within the French conception of authority) that they lacked forcefulness. For, as in the case of the secondary school teachers, if the superordinates are "strong," they do not employ force to obtain compliance with their directives; and, in fact, it is the weak teachers who use force and give the largest number of sanctions. This perception of the police-led evacuation of the Sorbonne as a sign of the authorities' lack of forcefulness was widely held. For instance, *Le Monde's* editorial article on the events was entitled "Un manque de sang-froid" ("An Absence of Composure or Coolness") and clearly suggested that the use of police force by the rector demonstrated that the authorities were no longer in control of the situation.[5][6]

During the following week, the university situation continued to worsen. Under the leadership of U.N.E.F. and S.N.E. Sup. (an organization of radical university teachers with a relatively small membership), there were large demonstrations (with 20,000 to 25,000 students participating) on May 6 and 7. These marches were in protest against the two-month imprisonment of four students arrested on May 3. Both of these dmonstrations culminated in violent conflict with the police. The protest leaders said they wanted to negotiate with the government but that three conditions must first be accepted: (1) removal of the police from the Latin Quarter, (2) amnesty for the imprisoned demonstrators, and (3) reopening of the closed Faculty of Letters. (These conditions amounted to a demand for a return to the pre-May 3 situation.)

The response of the university authorities to these demands was ambivalent. At a meeting of the Council of Ministers on May 8, Minister of Education Alain Peyrefitte, took a hard-line position, saying all of the difficulties had been caused by a handful of "agitators" and "elements foreign to the university." But later during the same day, at a session of the National Assembly, Peyrefitte said, "Courses will begin again as soon as professors and students can maintain order against agitators, should there be any; in other words, I hope tomorrow afternoon." Reversing his position again on the following day, the Minister of Education vetoed a decision taken by the rector and the deans to reopen the Sorbonne.

This vacillation between appeasement and severity has already been isolated as a defining characteristic of chahuted superordinates. University students responded to this vacillation with a large demonstration on May 10 which degenerated into a massive conflict with the police and the first night of the barricades. In the process of momentarily restoring order, 367 people were wounded (32 seriously), 460 protesters were taken into custody, 188 cars were burned or damaged, and entire streets were unpaved.

On the following day (Saturday, May 11), Georges Pompidou, the Prime Minister, who had just returned from an official visit to Iran and Afghanistan, gave a very conciliatory speech. Implicitly disavowing the actions of the government during his absence, he promised to reopen the Sorbonne and to free the arrested students. This speech marked the beginning of a period of increasing concessions by the government which were met by intensifying levels of strife. Hitherto the crisis had largely been restricted to Parisian students in the Faculty of Letters, but this new appeasement tactic was to be accompanied by a massive extension of the crisis, eventually leading to the total paralysis of France.

Immediately following Pompidou's speech, a group of students occupied the Censier center of Paris' Faculty of Letters.[57] Then, on May 13, these students momentarily left Censier to join in the occupation of the Sorbonne. These events, as well as the freeing of the students who had been arrested on May 3 and sent to prison on May 5, were a direct consequence of the Prime Minister's conciliatory policy.

The real significance of May 13, however, stems from the mass demonstrations and the general strike which occurred in France on that day. These protests were organized by the labor unions and the F.E.N. (*Fédération de l'Education Nationale,* a grouping of the main teachers' associations) with the cooperation of the leftist political parties. The call for a 24-hour general strike and mass demonstrations occurred just before Pompidou's speech and was in direct response to the "police repression" of the student protesters on the night of May 10. However, the undreamed success of this movement (which rallied between 200,000 to 1,000,000 demonstrators in the streets of Paris and a few hundred thousand more in large provincial cities) is largely attributable to the Prime Minister's speech, which seemed to suggest that the government was weak and no longer capable of warding off or controlling demands made by the citizens.

Although workers played the major role in the May 13 demonstrations, they were not yet full participants in the crisis. However, on May 14, a move was made in this direction when workers, on their own initiative, occupied the Sud-Aviation plant in Nantes. On the same day, General de Gaulle left France, as scheduled, for a four-day official visit to Rumania, and Georges Pompidou made another appeasement speech in the National Assembly announcing the government's readiness to make the "necessary gestures" for a return to calm.

Within the next few days, France became totally paralyzed. More than 10,000,000 workers were on strike; universities throughout the country were occupied; schools were either closed because of teachers' strikes or occupied by pupils; public transportation was no longer functioning; the airports were closed; gasoline was very scarce, if it could be found at all; banks and post offices were closed; department store employees were on strike; garbage was piling up on city streets; and the radio and television was silent except for periodic newscasts.

On May 24, two days after the parliamentary opposition had failed to overthrow the government on a motion of censure, General de Gaulle spoke to the French people by radio and television. His short speech was very conciliatory in both substance and tone. Only brief and passing reference was made to the need to restore order. The major emphasis in this speech was on the positive aspects of the crisis: It had shown the need for transformations of the French economy and university. The General proposed a referendum (to take place on June 16) whereby the people could decide if they had confidence in him to lead the nation in this process of renovation.

Following the General's speech, there was, if anything, a worsening of the crisis. On the same evening, there were large student-worker demonstrations in Paris and in the provinces which degenerated into riots. While earlier incidents of violence in Paris had been confined to the Latin Quarter, on May 24, there was a geographical extension of the conflicts. Among other incidents, the Stock Market (La Bourse) was set on fire and windows in the Ministry of Justice were broken.

On May 25, representatives of trade unions, business organizations, and the government met to discuss and seek a resolution to the economic crisis. These meetings, which lasted twenty-five hours, were chaired by the Prime Minister. Negotiations led to a series of conclusions (called the *Accords de Grenelle*)[58] which gave the workers a series of very important material benefits. In fact, these concessions were substantially greater than anything won by the workers since 1936. But when the union leaders went to the factories to announce the results of the negotiations, the workers refused to accept the accords.

On May 28, Alain Peyrefitte resigned as Minister of Education. This was another concession to the protesting students. On the same day, François Mitterand (candidate of the united left in the 1965 presidential elections) announced that he would be a candidate for the succession to General de Gaulle following the (hypothesized) defeat of the June 16 referendum; and that "if it was necessary," he was ready to form a provisional government. Mitterand noted that others (specifically Pierre Mendès-France) could also "legitimately" head up such a provisional regime. Then, on May 29, Mendès-France announced his readiness, if requested by a united left, to assume this responsibility. Meanwhile, a few hundred thousand workers marched in Paris calling for a "popular government" and chanting "adieu de Gaulle."

In sum, despite the important concessions made to students and workers, the crisis had continued to grow since the Prime Minister's conciliatory speech of May 11. From a protest which was largely confined to students in the Faculty of Letters in the Parisian region, the ranks of the rebels had swollen to engulf large, and critical, segments of French society. By May 29, France was in a state of total paralysis; universities, schools, and factories were occupied; few of the nation's essential services were functioning; demonstrations and protests were rampant; and preparations were being made to form a provisional government.

So far the general train of crisis events has been examined. From this sequential perspective, it seems clear that the events of May were a chahut. However, during this period, were the rebels organized as well as guided and controlled by leaders? Furthermore, was there a holiday-like atmosphere of gaiety? If this were a chahut, these characteristics should have been present. In fact, they were.

The activities of the rebels were orchestrated by a limited group of leaders. However, as was the case of the reform movement at E.N.A., there was a strong tendency to break down into small, somewhat homogeneous groups. This characteristic of the rebellion has frequently been discussed under the rubric of *groupusculation*.[59] Specifically, there was a large number of groups, literally hundreds,[60] which either were created during the crisis or had existed before, that served to organize the revolt. Within each of these groups there seem to have been a well-defined set of leaders who guided the activities of their peers. Most of these groups, especially those created during the crisis, had a very small, cohesive membership. Above this level of organization, there was a set of general chahut leaders—Daniel Ben-Saïd, Daniel Cohn-Bendit, Alain Geismar, and Jacques Sauvageot were the most important—who coordinated the activities of all rebels. Of course, they did not have total control over the chahateurs, and there were important conflicts between different *groupuscules*. It is this characteristic which has led some observers to view the events as being "spontaneous" or "anarchic." Yet, and this is the crucial point, these conflicts were between chahut groups, and, to all intents and purposes, all rebel activities were being guided and directed by leaders.

The holiday atmosphere of the May crisis is only too clear. Frequently, for the first time in their lives, strangers stopped on street corners to discuss the events with each other. During the month of May, the French had more human contact with each other than they ever seemed to have had before. In addition, everyone felt an atmosphere of excitement and often of joy. It is these characteristics which led E. J. Hobsbawm to write an article on the crisis entitled "Birthday Party."[61] Similarly, Raymond Aron analyzed the May events from the following perspective:

> The French suffer from an overly rigid system and from an overly authoritarian hierarchy. Why do they remember with ecstasy periods when they knock everything down? In these crisis periods, when the system falls apart, they have an illusion of brotherhood—they feel this brotherhood—of equality—and they live it—then they reconstruct again

the hierarchical straitjacket in which they had been enclosed. The French, since 1789, always retrospectively magnify their revolutions, immense holidays during which they live out everything they have been deprived of in normal times, and they feel as if they are fulfilling their aspirations, even though it is only in a day-dream.[62]

While I obviously disagree with Aron's exclusive concentration on the festival aspect of the crisis, since this is only one of the characteristics of a chahut, I do agree that this is one of the defining elements.

Thus, the May events, both from a sequential and from a content perspective, fit the conception of a chahut rather well. Now, it must be determined if the model's suggestions on how a chahut may be terminated are upheld by the crisis.

The Resolution of the Crisis: On May 30, General de Gaulle gave a brief and very forceful speech which was only broadcast over the radio (since the strikes made television facilities unavailable). Lucien Rioux and René Backmann describe the style of the speech perfectly:

> 4:30 P.M. Everywhere in France, life has stopped. In factories, offices, and on the street, people gather together around transistor radios. 4:31 P.M. General de Gaulle speaks. His voice is distinct and authoritarian. It does not try to convince. It gives orders.[63]

The content of the speech was similar. No mention was made of the need for reform or of the other positive aspects of the crisis which had dominated the General's remarks six days earlier. He began by noting that he was the "holder of the national and republican legitimacy" and had a "mandate from the people" which must be fulfilled. Substantively, de Gaulle announced that: (1) Pompidou would remain as his Prime Minister at the head of a renewed cabinet; (2) the National Assembly would be dissolved, and new legislative elections would occur within the time period specified by the constitution; and (3) the announced referendum would have to be postponed. More importantly, the General warned that if the present situation continued (thereby preventing the people from freely expressing their opinions at the polls, as they had recently been prevented from living, studying, teaching, and working), in order to maintain the Republic, he would have to use "other means than the immediate vote of the country." In any case, to counteract the "totalitarian" party[64] which had stood behind the recent crisis, de Gaulle told the people they must organize themselves for "civic action." Furthermore, to halt subversion, the préfets were to become *"Commissaires de la république"* (Commissioners of the Republic).[65]

This speech was preceded by preparations calculated to enable de Gaulle to back up his forceful remarks with action, should it be necessary. On May 29, the General left Paris, apparently to go to Colombey-les-deux-Eglises. But, rather than going directly there, he secretly went to Baden-Baden to consult with General Massu and other military chiefs of the French forces in Germany. However, the public soon learned where the General had been and with whom he had "secretly" met. In addition, on the evening of May 29, motorists (the ones still fortunate enough to have gasoline) who came into Paris noticed a great deal of troop movement on the outskirts of the city, and quickly passed on this news to anyone they saw. As a result, all Paris was soon aware of the new developments.

The forceful speech was followed by events which seemed to demonstrate that de Gaulle, in fact, already had the situation under control. Immediately after the General's address, there was a massive pro-de Gaulle demonstration in Paris. It was estimated that as many as one million people marched along the Champs-Elysées to show that "de Gaulle is not alone."[66] Then, on May 31, there was a series of large demonstrations in the provinces in support of the General. And, on June 1, gasoline was suddenly available throughout the country.

De Gaulle's speech combined with these indicators that the authorities were back in control immediately began the process of resolving the crisis. By May 31, there was already some movement toward a return to work, and the political parties and trade unions had announced their acceptance of and willingness to participate in the elections. By June 7, most of the important businesses and industries, both public and private, were functioning again. The major exceptions to this general rule were the continuing strikes in the automobile and metallurgy industries (which were largely resolved by June 18, and completely so by June 26) and the conflict with radio and television employees (which was not of vital importance because these media were providing their basic services and was finally resolved on July 12).

With France beginning to function again and with most of the workers back on their jobs, the strength and significance of the protest had been sharply reduced. (After all, a few hundred thousand young people demonstrating and occupying university and school buildings may be disturbing and dangerous, but it is relatively insignificant when compared with the entire working force of a nation on strike.) However, following the General's speech and its immediate aftereffects, even the students seemed to feel they were now simply participating in a holding action. There were a few more large-scale student demonstrations (including one which resulted in significant street violence on June 11), but now the government seemed to have much greater control over the protests. On June 14, the Odéon Theatre, which had been occupied since May 16, was taken over by the police. Similarly, the Sorbonne, held by the students since May 13, was evacuated on June 16. And by the end of June, all university buildings were back under governmental control.

At this juncture, it is interesting to note the preparations students had made for any attempt by the authorities to evacuate them and their actual reaction to these attempts. Let us take the example of the Sorbonne. The occupiers had made preparations to ward off an assault by the police. They had not only stockpiled Molotov cocktails, tear gas bombs, and cobblestones, but also had constructed a series of brick walls, approximately a foot thick, to cut off corridors from the invaders and to provide safety for those under seige. Small openings were left in the upper portion of the wall, so that projectiles could be hurled at invading police. Despite these preparations, when police actually arrived at the Sorbonne on the morning of June 16, the students agreed to leave the building on the sole condition that no one would be arrested. This pattern of rapid surrender was the rule for the evacuation of all university buildings. The only opposition ever given to the police was at the *Ecole des Beaux Arts* (School of Fine Arts), where after leaving the building, one of the former occupiers threw a Molotov cocktail.

By the end of June not only had there been an almost complete restoration of normalcy, but the results of the legislative elections which were held on June 23 and 30 gave the Gaullist party (U.D.R.) a majority of the seats in the National Assembly for the first time. The elections were an unexpectedly large triumph for the forces favorable to the policies of General de Gaulle: of the 485 seats in the legislature, the U.D.R. and its Republican Independent allies now occupied 358.

In sum, the resolution of the crisis began almost immediately after General de Gaulle's speech on May 30. The restoration of order did not occur all at once. Rather, as might have been expected, since the subordinates had to be sure that the authority was forceful, the return to order took place bit by bit. What is of crucial importance is that, with each test of wills between the authorities and a section of the workers or the students, the government always won. The Grenelle accords, which, prior to de Gaulle's May 30 speech had been unequivocally rejected by the workers, were now found quite acceptable. When the workers stopped their active protest, the university students were rapidly and peacefully evacuated from the buildings they had occupied, and the crisis was truly over.

On the basis of this survey of the May events, the school-based model seems to provide a good explanation for the outbreak, development, and resolution of the crisis. In the pre-May days, workers and university students held attitudes which moved them away from assumed coverage toward the alternating pattern. The lack of forcefulness on the part of the authorities seemingly instigated the chahut, which persisted until General de Gaulle gave a convincing demonstration of the government's strength. Then there was a rapid return to authority-ladenness and a resolution of the crisis. Finally, once order had been restored, there was a gradual movement toward assumed-coverage practices.

It is difficult to imagine how the various types of two-France theories might be applied to the May events. Those who view France as alternating over time between two governmental styles cannot even start to come to grips with the crisis. Observers who have characterized the French as split into two conflicting groups (e.g., the left and the right) can certainly label the demonstrators as belonging to one of these segments while the government and its supporters belonged to the other. But this in no way helps us to explain why the May crisis occurred when it did, why it evolved as it did, or why it was resolved following General de Gaulle's speech of May 30. Finally, the conception of France as peopled by fragmented individuals who both need and fear authority can certainly explain why something like the May crisis could occur, but it can explain neither why it occurred when it did nor the evolution of events.

NOTES

1. While we would expect to find differences among relationships with political superordinates, these differences should be of the type found between authority relations in lycées and in C.E.G.s—i.e., differences of degree, not of kind.

2. Quotation marks have been used here because real theories, in contrast to most "theories" of French politics, not only describe but also provide explanations (as compared to historical tracings) of the phenomenon to be analyzed.

3. Maurice Duverger, in contrast to virtually all his colleagues, has opted for a unimodal conception of the French political authority structure (see *La démocratie sans le peuple* [Paris: Seuil, 1967]). According to him, the lack of citizen participation in public affairs is the most crucial characteristic of the French style of government. Under the Fifth Republic, the people choose a "supreme chief" whom they cannot control between elections, while under preceding regimes, they chose "500 second-rank chiefs" over whom they had no control between elections (p. 11). Thus, the French government has always been a "democracy without the people."

According to Charles Morazé (*Les Français et la république* [Paris: Armand Colin, 1956]) and Dorothy Pickles (*The Fifth Republic* [New York: Praeger, 1960]), France since the Revolution has oscillated among three forms of government. Morazé's trimodal interpretation suggests that parliamentary "center" rule gives way to monarchist, rightist regimes which are succeeded by revolutionary, leftist governments before there is a return to parliamentary rule (pp. 101-102). Pickles argues that the process of change goes from constitutional monarchy to a republic, to some form of dictatorial government, and then back again. But she adds that, with the advent of the Fourth Republic, this traditional trimodality seems to have given way to a bimodality between republican and dictatorial forms of government (pp. 9-12).

4. Roger Soltau (*French Parties and Politics 1871-1921* [London: Oxford University Press, 1930]) is one of the rare scholars who has thought that France is simultaneously exposed to two different types of political authority structures. According to him, there is a contradiction between the "democracy of the central government and the autocracy of the local administration" (p. 20). Of course, it has been quite common among students of French politics to note the existence of an efficient administration alongside the ineffective and unstable political regime. But Soltau seems virtually alone in suggesting that the only type of bimodality in the structure of political authority worth stressing is one that exists synchronically.

5. Paul Seippel, *Les deux Frances* (Payot, 1905), p. xxii and J.E.C. Bodley, *France* (London: Macmillan, 1907), throughout.

6. Helen Hill, *The Spirit of Modern France*, World Affairs Pamphlets No. 5 (New York: Foreign Policy Association, 1934), p. 14.

7. Walter R. Sharp, *The Government of the French Republic* (New York: Van Nostrand, 1938), p. 10.

8. Raymond Aron, *France: Steadfast and Changing* (Cambridge, Mass.: Harvard University Press, 1960), pp. 121 and 135; and Jean Laponce, *The Government of the Fifth Republic* (Los Angeles: University of California Press, 1961).

9. Stanley Hoffmann, "Heroic Leadership: The Case of Modern France" (paper delivered at the 1966 annual meeting of the American Political Science Association), pp. 7-13.

10. Nicholas Wahl, "The French Political System," in *Patterns of Government,* eds. Samuel Beer and Adam Ulam (New York: Random House, 1962), pp. 278-280; italics added. See also his *The Fifth Republic: France's New Political System* (New York: Random House, 1959), pp. 15-30.

11. Henry Ehrmann, *Politics in France* (Boston: Little, Brown, 1968), pp. 7-9. See also his "Direct Democracy in France," *American Political Science Review* 57, No. 4 (December 1963), pp. 883-901.

12. In addition to the conception of France as politically characterized by bimodal segmentation, there have been quite a few interpretations stressing multimodality. Robert Dell argued that there were four "political tendencies" in France: socialism, bourgeois leftism, centrism, and rightism (*My Second Country [France],* p. 138). In addition, Dorothy Pickles and Gordon Wright have conceived of France as divided into more than two ideological segments. According to Ms. Pickles, France is cleaved into three segments which have conflicting views as to what Republicanism means. For one group, which is composed of socialists and some radicals, "the revolutionary tradition . . . is an integral part of the Republican tradition." A second group, dedicated to radical Republicanism, "emphasize[s] spiritual and intellectual equality," as the Socialists do, but in contrast to them, "allows economic equality often to take a back seat." A third group, the "right-wing republicans" are "less concerned with general principles and more with techniques of government, and, in particular, with the need for strong government" (*The Fifth Republic,* pp. 14-16). For Gordon Wright, the "partial truth [of the bimodal conception] obscures the more complex whole." He argues that the crucial French political problem has been the inability of the majoritarian democratic group to achieve agreement on fundamentals. This has come about as a result of an "almost irreconcilable contradiction" between "liberty" and "equality" within the "democratic tradition," a split already apparent in the writings of the philosophers of the eighteenth century. It persisted through the years, and, in our own epoch, political conflict in France has tended to be waged between the authoritarian right, the authoritarian left, "the libertarian right-center and the egalitarian left-center" ("France," in *European Political Systems,* ed. Taylor Cole [New York: Knopf, 1959], pp. 190-202).

13. Ernest Renan, "Questions contemporaines," in *Oeuvres complètes de Ernest Renan* (Paris' Calmann-Lévy, 1947), Vol. 1, p. 27.

14. See Paul Seippel, *Les deux Frances;* and Roger Soltau, *French Political Thought in the Nineteenth Century* (New Haven, Conn.: Yale University Press, 1931), pp. 486-494.

15. Gordon Wright, "The Red and the Black in Rural France," *Yale Review* (Autumn 1962), pp. 39-53.

16. André Siegfried, *France: A Study in Nationality* (New Haven, Conn.: Yale University Press, 1930), pp. 84-88.

17. Siegfried had suggested a vague geographical base for each of the tendencies (ibid.).

18. François Goguel, *La politique des parties sous la Troisième République* (Paris:

Seuil, 1957), pp. 19, 148, 548-552. It is interesting to note that Goguel was, in fact, Siegfried's student.

19. Jacques Fauvet, *La France déchirée* (Paris: Fayard, 1957), p. 90.

20. François Bourricaud, "France," trans. Caroline B. Rose, in *The Institutions of Advanced Societies,* ed. Arnold M. Rose (Minneapolis: University of Minnesota Press, 1958), pp. 445 ff.

21. André Siegfried, *France: A Study in Nationality,* p. 96. He further divides the "school of thought" favoring "the rule of the people" into three parts: a "parliamentary conception," "Bonapartism," and "government by committees" (pp. 96-100).

22. David Thomson, *Democracy in France Since 1870* (New York: Oxford University Press, 1964), pp. 36, 112.

23. Nicholas Wahl, "The French Political System," in *Patterns of Government,* p. 279.

24. Eric Nordlinger, *The Working-Class Torries: Authority, Deference and Stable Democracy* (Berkeley and Los Angeles: University of California Press, 1967), pp. 236-237. Nordlinger locates the basis for the congenital French political disease of instability in the failure to "mix" (either within individuals or in groups) "acquiescent" and "directive" dispositions toward authority. This conception is similar to one of Wahl's arguments. He wrote, "Mixed government has never existed in France because the aristocratic principle of command and the democratic principle of consent, instead of becoming blended within each institution and thus assuring balance and cooperation among them, individually became *fully* embodied in *different* and ultimately antagonistic institutions" (Wahl, "The French Political System," in *Patterns of Government,* pp. 278-279).

25. Robert Dell, *My Second Country (France),* pp. 31-34.

26. S. Hoffmann, *Heroic Leadership: The Case of Modern France* (paper delivered at the 1966 annual meeting of the American Political Science Association), p. 8.

27. Stanley Hoffmann, "Paradoxes of the French Political Community," in *In Search of France,* ed. Stanley Hoffmann et al. (Cambridge, Mass.: Harvard University Press, 1963), p. 9.

28. Roy Macridis, "France," in *Modern Political Systems: Europe,* eds. Roy Macridis and Robert Ward (Englewood Cliffs, N.J.: Prentice-Hall, 1968), p. 138.

29. H. Ehrmann, *Politics in France,* p. 10.

30. Roger Soltau, *French Parties and Politics,* p. 64. This conception is similar to the view of diachronic bimodality presented by Stanley Hoffmann in his article on "heroic leadership."

31. Raymond Aron, *France: Steadfast and Changing,* p. 76.

32. J. Pitts, "Change in Bourgeois France," in *In Search of France,* pp. 239-240.

33. C. Morazé, *Les Français et la République,* p. 20.

34. I am indebted to Harry Eckstein for suggesting this organizational scheme and its justification.

35. This definition follows from the idea that government is not usually of great cognitive centrality to the average citizen. Such an idea seems true on the basis of commonsense observation. In addition, this notion is not only implicit in elitist theories of democracy but also in the pluralist theories—i.e., the average citizen has political "resources" but rarely uses them. Further details on the relationship between the cognitive centrality of government for the ordinary citizen and the study of politics are presented in my "The Focus of Political Socialization Research: An Evaluation," *World Politics* 23 (April 1971), pp. 571-578.

36. These three conditions, of course, seem likely to lead to a breakdown of routine in many polities, and not simply in the French.

37. This would be so unless the cause of the breakdown was superordinates exerting direct coverage over subordinates; in this case, the return to routine would occur whenever the governmental leaders wished, assuming they had demonstrated forcefulness.

38. In fact, all French regimes seem to be basically of the assumed-coverage form. This is certainly the case for the Third Republic. Similarly, the Vichy government adhered to the assumed-coverage pattern from November 1942 to April 1944. And, as will be noted in the latter part of this section, the Fifth Republic since 1962 has been largely an assumed-coverage regime.

39. This is a logical deduction drawn from the results of a survey conducted by the French Institute of Public Opinion in January 1958. At that time, a sample of Frenchmen was asked, "If there were a military insurrection, what would you personally do?" Only seven percent said that they would either actively support or oppose the coup; eight percent said they would take a position of passive support or opposition; twenty-five percent did not respond to the question; and sixty percent said they would be inactive and neutral (of this sixty percent, four percent said they would take sides once they saw who was going to win) (*Sondages*, no. 3, 1958, p. 50).

40. A stimulating, but perhaps somewhat exaggerated, image of the French economy and its future, from the vantage point of the early 1970s, is presented in Edmund Stillman et al., *L'envol de la France dans les années 80* (Paris: Hachette, 1973).

41. Alexis de Tocqueville, *The Old Regime and the French Revolution,* trans. Stuart Gilbert (Garden City, N.Y.: Doubleday and Company, 1955), p. 60.

42. These reforms, although instituted by Alain Peyrefitte, carry the name of his predecessor, Minister of Education Christian Fouchet, who, in fact, thought up the new system.

43. The specific content of these reforms is irrelevant to the argument and, consequently, will not be discussed.

44. While there is not sufficient data on intragenerational occupational mobility rates in France or in other societies, it may be assumed, with a high degree of probability, that occupational mobility of individuals in the upper levels of French society is relatively low. This assumption is based on the structure of higher education in France, which is characterized by a series of distinct and difficult-to-cross paths leading to each and every type of profession. Furthermore, the individual must select one of these paths after high school, and the particular program of study followed in the secondary schools narrows the choice to a limited number of these paths.

45. Raymond Boudon, "Quelques causes de la révolte estudiantine," *La Table Ronde,* No. 251-252 (December 1968-January 1969), pp. 172-173.

46. "Les étudiants et la nouvelle université," *Réalités,* No. 274 (November 1968), p. 71.

47. Louise Weiss, "Télémaque 1969," *Guerres et paix* (no. 4, 1969-no. 1, 1970), p. 50.

48. The system of family allowances is basically one which gives money to French families according to how many children they have. However, couples without children have received some help.

49. *Sondages,* no. 2 (1968), p. 29. Unfortunately, I.F.O.P. had never posed this question before, and, therefore, I cannot compare workers' perceptions of their personal chances of becoming unemployed over time. Previously, I.F.O.P. had posed a less personal question about unemployment. Specifically, in 1955, workers were asked if there was reason for great fear of unemployment. At this time, eleven percent responded affirmatively (*Sondages,* no. 2 [1956], p. 27). If it is assumed that an individual is more

likely to perceive others becoming unemployed than himself, then the seventeen percent figure for 1968 seems extremely high.

50. Philippe Bénéton and Jean Touchard suggest that fifty percent of the unemployed were less than twenty-five years old. See their "Les interprétations de la crise de mai-juin 1968," *Revue française de science politique* 20, no. 3 (June 1970), p. 532.

51. This is an estimate made by the *Union Nationale des Associations Familiales.*

52. That, in fact, this is an accurate description of the frequency, nature of demands, and objects of the protests is strongly supported by the survey of significant events in France during 1967 and 1968 contained in *L'Année politique 1967* and *L'Année politique 1968.*

53. One important exception to this general rule was the strike at the S.A.V.I.E.M. truck factory outside Caen. After the workers were out on strike a couple of days, the trade unions and the university students' union organized a demonstration of sympathy for January 26, 1968. This demonstration gave way to violent conflict between the police and the protesters during which eighteen people were injured.

54. The May-June events in France have received very extensive written treatment. Besides observing the events, among book-length treatments I found to be of value are the following: Raymond Aron, *La révolution introuvable* (Paris: Fayard, 1968); Georges Chaffard, *Les orages de mai; Histoire exemplaire d'une élection* (Paris: Calmann-Lévy, 1968); Adrien Dansette, *Mai 1968* (Paris: Plon, 1971); Edgar Morin, Claude Lefort and Jean-Marc Coudray, *Mai 1968; la Bréche, Premières réflexions sur les événements* (Paris: Fayard, 1968); Alain Schnapp and Pierre Vidal-Naquet (ed.), *Journal de la commune étudiante: Textes et documents, novembre 67-juin 68* (Paris: Seuil, 1969); and Alain Touraine, *Le Mouvement de mai ou le communisme utopique* (Paris: Seuil, 1968). For an almost complete listing of the numerous analyses and interpretations of the crisis, see Laurence Wylie, Franklin D. Chu, and Mary Terrall, "France: The Events of May-June 1968, A Critical Bibliography" (mimeo, Council of European Studies, University of Pittsburgh, November 1971). A briefer, yet comprehensive, bibliography, can be found in the notes to Philippe Bénéton and Jean Touchard, "Les interprétations de la crise de mai-juin 1968."

55. The University of Nanterre had been one of the most active centers of unrest during the past academic year. Built in 1964 on the outskirts of Paris to meet the needs of the increasing size of the student body, Nanterre was composed of a Faculty of Letters and an annex of Paris' Law Faculty. The agitation at this school began in November 1967 with a ten-day strike by sociology students. After that, the protest became increasingly strong. On March 22, the students invaded one of the large meeting rooms, and the famous Movement of March 22, led by Daniel Cohn-Bendit, was formed. From then on, the protesters' critiques were no longer focused strictly on university problems but sought to attack the capitalist society.

56. B. Girod de L'Ain, "Un manque de sang-froid," *Le Monde,* May 5-6, 1968, pp. 1, 9.

57. In 1968, the Faculty of Letters in Paris had two centers: the Sorbonne and Censier. Censier (as Nanterre) was a recent addition to the university, created to help accommodate the increasing number of students.

58. This name was chosen because the meetings were held at the Ministry of Social Affairs on the *rue de Grenelle.*

59. For analyses and descriptions of the genesis and characteristics of various groupuscules, see, for instance, Daniel Ben-Saïd and Henri Weber, *Mai 1968: une répétition générale* (Paris: François Maspéro, 1968); Jean Bertolino, *Les Trublions* (Paris:

Editions Stock, 1969); and Richard Gombin, *Le projet révolutionnaire: Eléments d'une sociologie des événements de mai-juin 1968* (Paris: Mouton, 1969).

60. Alain Schnapp and Pierre Vidal-Naquet provide a rather extensive list of these organizations in the index to their *Journal de la commune étudiante,* pp. 853-857, 858-861.

61. *The New York Review of Books* 12 (May 22, 1969), pp. 5-12.

62. Raymond Aron, *La révolution introuvable,* pp. 31-32.

63. L. Rioux and R. Backmann, *L'explosion de mai: 11 mai 1968, Histoire complète des "événements"* (Paris: Robert Laffont, 1968), p. 464.

64. By this term, de Gaulle was referring to the French Communist Party, which, in fact, had been regarded by most leftists as playing a conservative, anti-revolutionary role during the crisis! The party's position has not been discussed, because this is extraneous to the purpose of this section.

65. This was the title given to de Gaulle's men who were sent from Algeria in 1944 to take control of liberated France for the provisional government and to keep the Communists out of power.

66. Under the direction of the Gaullist party and governmental leaders, the preparations for this demonstration had begun on Monday, May 27, and went into high gear on Wednesday, May 29, the day before the General's speech. (I am grateful to A. Nicholas Wahl for this information.)

Chapter 6

CONCLUSION

In the Introduction, I specified three major research goals: (1) to describe and explain how Frenchmen behave toward authority, (2) to determine if case studies of social authority behavior could be used to increase understanding of political authority, and (3) to further develop Michel Crozier's theory of French authority relations. Hitherto, I have dealt with the first two goals, but have only made casual or implicit reference to Crozier's notions.

The major portion of this chapter will compare and contrast Crozier's argument with the school-based model. Then, after discussing the breadth of the model's application, I will consider the pattern of voluntary association membership in France. Forecasts will be made about what this pattern should be. One of these forecasts can and will be tested—the results support the model's interpretation. Another forecast cannot be tested because appropriate data are not available. By identifying the requisite data and the findings which would support the model—any other outcome leading to refutation—the falsifiability of the theory is demonstrated.

Building on Crozier:
An Increased Understanding of France?

Crozier's theoretical analysis of bureaucratic authority—based on an empirical study of two government-owned and -controlled industrial organizations—occupies a very special position in the literature on France.[1] Two factors help to explain the fundamental and overarching importance of his research. First, he provides the first relatively systematic probe into the nature of French authority relations. Many, if not most, observers of French society and politics had sought to provide some understanding of behavior and dispositions toward authority. This tradition dates back to the writings of de Tocqueville, and among its contemporary exponents are found such contributors as Raymond Aron, Jesse Pitts, Stanley Hoffmann, Nicholas Wahl, and Laurence Wylie.[2] Nevertheless, no one before Crozier had attempted to provide a rigorous empirical analysis of French authority and to use this to explain behavior in a wide variety of social and political contexts. Furthermore, these other interpretations are effectively encompassed by and incorporated into Crozier's work.

Second, not only has the bureaucratic model superseded its predecessors, but it has become the accepted "paradigm" of the nature of French authority relations. Virtually all recent general studies of France which refer to authority take Crozier's argument to be a "factual" given.[3] The most important of these works are those of Stanley Hoffmann.[4] His goal has been to take the paradigm and use it to answer questions which were overlooked or given insufficient treatment in the original analysis. Finally, those systematic, empirical studies of the nature of French authority which have been stimulated by *The Bureaucratic Phenomenon* begin with the premise that the theory is not only accurate, but also that its major tenets are developed in sufficiently precise terms.[5]

According to Crozier, there are two independent variables which determine the nature of French organizational life. On the one hand, there is a very strong desire to avoid face-to-face authority relations which, by definition, involve situations of personal dependency. But, on the other hand, the prevailing view of authority in France is one which conceives of it as universalistic and absolute. The basic dilemma of Frenchmen is to find a means for simultaneously satisfying these apparently contradictory values. The solution is the bureaucratic system of organization,[6] characterized by:

(1) the existence of detailed and precise rules which govern the normal functioning of the unit;[7]

(2) a high degree of centralization of the decision-making process;[8]

(3) isolation between the various strata of the hierarchy combined with a high degree of egalitarianism within each stratum;[9] and

(4) an absence (or more precisely, a refusal) of participation.[10]

The "bureaucratic system" is not perfect. The impersonal rules fail to anticipate and control all areas of uncertainty. Around these areas of uncertainty, parallel power relations develop which result in certain individuals being dependent on others who have control over these uncertainties. But this sort of situation is very much an exception to the norm.[11]

There is one very important problem with the bureaucratic system—i.e., its inability to cope easily with change. The very characteristics of this system mean that change will be postponed as long as possible, not because Frenchmen dislike change but rather because they dislike disorder, and any transformation of the status quo carries with it the possibility of a breakdown of order. As a result, change only occurs when serious dysfunctions develop; it comes from the top down and is universalistic—i.e., it encompasses the whole organization, en bloc. Moreover, change is a deeply felt crisis, during which individual initiative prevails and dependency relations develop. Thus, there is a rhythm in bureaucratic systems between long periods of stable routine and very short periods of crisis and change.[12]

From this concise outline of Crozier's argument,[13] it is quite apparent that there are numerous similarities between his theory and the one presented in this book. But, especially at the explanatory level, and even to a certain extent at the descriptive level, there are important distinctions.

Crozier identifies two distinct, but interrelated styles of authority relations. The dominant pattern is the bureaucratic system of organization, normally functioning quite smoothly, but unable to bring about change. When serious dysfunctions develop, this routine breaks down and is briefly replaced by a crisis pattern. In general terms, the normal bureaucratic system is comparable to assumed coverage, and crisis authority is something like the alternating pattern.

Under the routine, "bureaucratic system" of authority,

> every member of the organization . . . is protected both from his superiors and from his subordinates. He is, on the one hand, totally deprived of initiative and completely controlled by rules imposed on him from the outside. On the other hand, he is completely free from personal interference by any other individual—as independent, in a sense, as if he were a non-salaried worker. Such a system of human relations devaluates superior-subordinate relations.[14]

This system, as is the case with assumed coverage, is characterized by an absence of direct coverage (personal dependency relations) combined with a rather high degree of control over subordinates' activities and an absence of participation.

There are differences between these two conceptions of French routine authority relations.[15] Most importantly, for Crozier, the exclusive controlling agent is a series of detailed, precise, impersonal rules; the idea of assumed coverage makes such rules part of a more extensive category which also includes remembered socialization, soliciting advice from superiors, and observation and imitation of peer and superordinate behavior. Besides having a broader conception of the source of behavioral direction, assumed coverage provides, on an individual-by-individual basis, a logic which explains why there is such a high degree of obedience with the impersonal rules of the "bureaucratic system" in France: subordinates perceive their behavior as being "forced" upon them by superordinates and believe acts of noncompliance will be sanctioned, even though, in fact, such is not the case.

There are more significant differences between the two theories in regard to crisis authority relations. Crozier argues that crises: (1) are the result of serious dysfunctions in the bureaucratic system, (2) bring change with them which is (3) decided upon and applied by the highest levels of superordination, and (4) are characterized by an assertion of personal authority and individual initiative.

The model developed on the basis of research conducted in secondary schools and E.N.A. strengthens Crozier's notion of crises in three ways. First, what constitutes a "serious dysfunction?" Without precise, empirical delimitation of this concept —and Crozier does not provide any—the reason the routine system breaks down can only be vaguely understood. The model may be used to develop an empirical definition of "serious dysfunction." Specifically, crises can be triggered by either: (1) the subordinates' perception that their unit and/or its superordinates are not acting effectively to achieve the valued goal sought through membership in the organization, or (2) superordinates issuing numerous face-to-face directives to subordinates.[16]

Second, what constitutes "change?" Crozier has dealt at great length with "change" in France. However, some very perceptive scholars have had difficulty in understanding and accepting his argument.[17] In part, this confusion stems from the variety of phenomena in regard to which Crozier discusses change. My findings are particularly suitable for dealing with one aspect of his conception: the idea that crises *always* are accompanied by "change" (in the sense of eliminating the "serious dysfunctions" which led to the crisis).[18] According to my model, if the breakdown of routine is a consequence of subordinates' perceptions, the return to assumed coverage will always be accompanied by a change in these perceptions, but not necessarily by any change in the objective conditions which gave rise to them. If the crisis is created by superordinates exerting direct coverage over subordinates, changes are likely to occur in the assumed rules which guide behavior during routine periods; such changes may also occur during crises (under authority-ladenness) generated by subordinates' perceptions. In sum, the model, in contradistinction to Crozier's theory, suggests changes (of "dysfunctional" conditions and in the content of behavior toward authority) *may* but do not necessarily accompany crises.[19] Existing empirical evidence tends to support this interpretation. For example, no "changes" took place as a consequence of the E.N.A. crises. Similarly, the entire university crisis which triggered the events of May 1968 did not eliminate the "dysfunctions" which caused this outbreak. In fact, writing about the May crisis, Crozier himself seems not to have seen any objective change.[20]

Third, the research in secondary schools and E.N.A. provides a means for further developing Crozier's notion that during crises there is an assertion of personal authority. While both authority-ladenness and the chahut—my two crisis forms of interaction—are characterized by face-to-face directives, this is by no means the only defining or important element of crisis authority. In addition, and of utmost significance, these two distinct, but connected, styles of subordinate-superordinate interaction are conceived of as alternatively being used according to the subordinates' perceptions of how forceful their superordinates are.[21] Furthermore, and this may contradict Crozier, during the chahut—a phenomenon which he really does not envision—there is an absence of equality among subordinates. Rather, there are peer leaders who guide their fellow subordinates in their acts of "negative . . . solidarity directed against superiors."[22]

The areas of disagreement between the two theories are enlarged by turning to their independent variables. This is in large part a function of the *types* of explanation provided. Crozier primarily wanted to explain the nature of organizational life in France; he isolated two factors for this purpose: (1) the desire to avoid face-to-face dependency relations and (2) the view of authority as necessarily being absolute and universalistic. My purpose, on the other hand, has not been to explain why authority relations in France seem almost exclusively of the assumed-coverage, authority-laden or chahut modes. Rather, I have attempted (1) to suggest why an infant born in France today personally acquires these modes of behavior toward authority rather than others, and (2) more crucially, to explain the conditions responsible for adopting one or the other of these patterns at any given time.

To compare the two models' forms of explanation, I shall begin by critically examining how well Crozier's variables can deal with the problem of locating conditions for a change in mode of interaction—the model's capability in this regard has already been fully discussed. Then I shall speculate on how the independent variables presented in this book would deal with Crozier's problem.

According to Crozier, the French attribute a high value to avoiding face-to-face authority relations, and they conceive of authority as necessarily being universalistic and absolute. To account for crises, he suggests:

(a) The bureaucratic style of organizational life excludes the possibility of change.

(b) As a result of the changing environment within which organizations function, if there is no internal change, serious dysfunctions will develop.

(c) These dysfunctions bring about, by necessity, a need for change which creates a crisis.

(d) Since the French fear disorder—a derivative from their *horreur* of personal dependency relations—the only kind of change which is tolerated is one that does not disturb the existing relations between strata in the organization's hierarchy.

The major problem with this analysis is its failure to specify conditions for determining when the desire to avoid face-to-face authority relations will be of paramount, or simply of secondary importance.[23] Crozier contends that small dysfunctions in the system are not rapidly resolved because of the fear that any alteration in the status quo might carry with it some face-to-face authority relations. Thus, dysfunctions accumulate until they are serious. This brings about a necessity for change. Change occurs in the form of a crisis and "dependency relations reappear." (But why? What value exists which supersedes the previously omnipotent *l'horreur du face-á-face*?) According to Crozier, it is the pattern of change and not the change itself which is really important, and this pattern of change is determined by the French dislike of disorder which stems from their fear of face-to-face authority relations.[24] But now it is the value attributed to avoiding dependency relations which is again supreme.

Other than providing a more precise and empirical meaning to the notion of serious dysfunctions, my research does not help to solve Crozier's problem. In fact, I have raised questions about whether the evidence really indicates that the French fear face-to-face dependency relations. Specifically, the school research suggested that the French may "fear"—i.e., seek to avoid—the chahut due to its dysfunctional aspects. However, since the chahut cannot exist without being accompanied by the authority-laden mode, both styles of interaction must be behaviorally rejected, *unless* either the unit and/or its superordinates are perceived as acting ineffectively, or superordinates start issuing many face-to-face directives to subordinates (under these conditions, of course, the rationale for rejecting the chahut disappears). Since the chahut from the perspective of superordinate-subordinate relations, is characterized by much disorder, it may be this rather than personal dependency relation which is shunned and "feared." Crozier also observes rather few disorderly and face-to-face relations, but he sees their relationship in exactly the opposite way: The French reject disorder because it may bring dependency relations with it.[25] The difference in interpretations may only be a function of the social units compared. For example, it could be argued that school children were accustomed to the authority-laden mode and, therefore, may not have attributed primary importance to avoiding it, while Crozier's adult workers had not been exposed on a regular basis to this type of authority interaction for many years and, consequently, may have developed a special intolerance for such relations. If this were the case, and there is no evidence to the contrary, the bases for the conflict between hypotheses can be noted along with the agreement in observational terms.

There are, however, two theoretical grounds on which evidence in favor of the school-based conception can be developed. First, if one simply assumes that there is a supreme value attributed to avoiding face-to-face authority relations, there is no logically consistent way to explain the existence of crises which inevitably involve personal dependency relations. But, if one assumes that what is valued by subordinates is the avoidance of the chahut *because* it militates against achieving the goal sought by membership in the unit, then it is logically consistent to view crises originated by subordinates as only occurring when the unit and/or its superordinates are perceived as not functioning effectively to achieve the goal sought through membership in the organization.

A second theoretical support for the notion that authority-laden interactions per se are not avoided may be derived from some tentative speculation about the basic values in French society which seem to support and perpetuate the particular set of authority interactions which prevails.[26] Crozier has argued that the "French bureaucratic system of organization" became established and has remained the modal form of authority interaction because it reconciles and simultaneously satisfies two contradictory French cultural values—i.e., fear of face-to-face dependency relations and the prevailing view of authority as necessarily being absolute and universalistic. There is no logical inconsistency here. However, there may be some discomfort with this explanation, since these supreme values are violated by the crisis forms (form, for Crozier) of authority interaction. Crozier does not confront this issue because crises are, in fact, explained by the changing environment within which organizations function and that causes the need for change within the organization. Organizational resistance to this pressure for change causes dysfunctions, thereby creating crises.

There is an alternative, more parsimonious argument, that can explain simply on the basis of cultural "values" both the routine and crisis forms of authority. Specifically, it might be suggested that the historical tendency toward political absolutism (the cause cited by Crozier for the development of the prevailing view of authority) brought with it a tendency to define everything with precision and clarity. As a result, the French never "learned" to deal with ambiguity or uncertainty in their organized lives. This argument, using the same elements cited by Crozier, seems somewhat more theoretically useful, because, while one of Crozier's basic "values"—avoidance of face-to-face dependency relations—is not *always* successfully realized, none of the three types of observed authority interaction—assumed coverage, authority-laden, and chahut—violates the value of ambiguity-avoidance. Quite to the contrary, within each form, subordinate behavior is rather well defined, whether the source of definition be remembered socialization combined with observation, imitation, written rules, and advice solicited from superiors, direct coverage, or peer directives. Thus, if there were a French cultural value (derived from a historical tendency toward absolutism) which resulted in ambiguity-avoidance, the pattern of authority relations, during both routine and crisis periods, would not violate this value.

Locating ambiguity-avoidance as the basic "cultural value" which perpetuates and supports the French system of authority relations is not an original idea. Contemporary scholars, other than Crozier, have given prominence to this "cultural value": to explain "complicity" during the Nazi occupation, Robert Paxton draws upon the Frenchman's "fear of social disorder as the highest evil";[27] and Stanley Hoffmann sees French dispositions toward change as being "based on the fear of insecurity."[28] But most relevant is an argument made seventy years ago by Paul Seippel. In his brilliant but neglected study, *Les deux Frances*,[29] he noted:

> [In France] social omnipotence is manifested in a hundred different forms. The individual no longer counts on himself for anything. He senses himself, in every respect, subordinated. He seeks his truth from a spiritual authority. . . . He has the cult of the all-powerful state; he counts on it to take care of his sons, first to give them a diploma, then a job. Every observer of modern France has noted the prestige of the civil service in this country. Well, this is nothing other than a lay form of monarchy. It also responds to the motivating force, which is going to continue to increase, of the most "policed" people [in the world] : *the fear of risk.*[30]

The "fear of risk" is precisely what is meant by avoiding uncertainty, disorder, insecurity, and ambiguity.

A Test of the Model

Before defining a basis for refuting the theoretical statement developed in this book, two points must be reemphasized. First, the model focuses on individuals occupying specific roles in given social units. Pierre Dupont, let us say, is a student at Paris' Faculty of Letters, a member of the French Communist Party, and a voter. From the model's perspective, separate, distinct clusters of his behavior toward authority would be examined if the unit of analysis were the university, the Communist Party, or France. In each of these three roles, his mode of interaction with authority would be explained by the value he attributes to the goal sought through membership in the particular unit, by his perception of how well the given organization and its superordinates are functioning to achieve this goal, by how forceful he perceives his superordinates to be, and by the superordinates' directive-issuing tendencies. The level of analysis is an individual's behavior and dispositions *within* a specific social unit: Dupont may well be following an assumed-coverage pattern in the university and an authority-laden mode in the party, while he chahuts his political superordinates.

Second, whenever I have suggested that a particular unit is functioning according to a particular pattern, this does not mean that all members of that unit are acting in this manner; rather, it simply means that this is the modal pattern. Similarly, the model does not argue that all Frenchmen in all social units act according to its tenets; again, it says this is modal.

The model implies that authority relations within all French social units (running the gamut from educational institutions and work groups to voluntary associations—e.g., trade unions—political parties from the Communists to the Gaullists, and governmental bodies—e.g., the parliament, a ministry, or a mayor's office) as well as the modal style of authority-based interactions between citizens and different types of governmental agents tend to conform to the basic pattern of oscillation between the alternating pattern and assumed coverage, with the latter normally—except when the unit's goal is not highly valued by the subordinates—being the routine (sometimes, the virtually exclusive) form. The actual applicability of the model can only be determined after there has been empirical research on the nature of these relationships. This research might well reveal important differences in the model's descriptive and explanatory power according to the unit being analyzed.

Depending upon the results obtained from such investigations, the idea that behavior toward authority tends to be consistent throughout a given society (i.e., universal) may be impugned. Refutation would not occur if the nonconforming social unit is composed of top superordinates—e.g., a ministerial cabinet or the national parliament—because the model proposes to explain and describe how the French behave as subordinates but does not offer anything other than clues about why they act as they do when they are top superordinates. Hence, there is no reason to demand conformity with the model's tenets within organizations primarily composed of superiors. In all other types of social units, the model should work, if the universality hypothesis is tenable. Given the notion of modality, it is obvious that this hypothesis may not be rejected by locating, for example, a specific school, a particular trade union, or a given political party, which fails to adhere to the model. However, if, within a type of social unit, authority does not modally conform to the tenets of the model, then the universality hypothesis is impugned. If such an outcome occurred, but rarely, this would leave the interesting question of why the model fits in most cases, but not in all.

Despite the frequent discussions of group life in France, there are few solid data on this phenomenon. As a result, scholarly interpretations are often in direct conflict with each other. First, many observers have suggested that there are relatively few formally organized groups in France, but others have noted a rather high level of organizational "comprehensiveness."[31] There also seems to be disagreement over the density of group life—i.e., the percentage of eligibles who actually are members.[32] Third, there is little parallelism between the conceptions of what kinds of groups exist.[33] These contradictory interpretations are an inevitable result of the lack of reliable data, especially in regard to the density and comprehensiveness of French group life.[34] In regard to a fourth dimension upon which we would want to classify group life—the extent to which organizational membership includes active participation—there are, to all intents and purposes, no usable data. Finally, the only point of agreement seems to be on the fragmented nature of group life—i.e., the same vocational interest usually is represented by competing groups, rather than by a single one.

The model is most suited to making forecasts about the extent of participation within groups and the density of group life. The notion of dual guides to action suggests that, to the extent Frenchmen join voluntary associations, occupationally related groups (e.g., trade unions) should have *comparatively* large memberships. This is so because adults spend the overwhelming part of their group life in work organizations. As a result, rhetorical condemnations of these organizations should be prevalent. Such critical feelings should lead many individuals to behaviorally actualize these norms through participation in and/or support of social units which seek to change the core unit.

The model's general hypotheses suggest that the modal Frenchman is not likely to join voluntary associations, especially if membership requires active participation. This forecast is derived from the following hypothesis: If people do not attribute a high value to the goal to be achieved through membership in a given social unit, they will not voluntarily join it. Since the goals individuals are most likely to highly value (e.g., their salaries and social interaction) tend to be achieved through vocational and informal or familial groups, they will not normally join voluntary associations. Furthermore, since the nature of French authority interactions gives rise to feelings of constraint when participating in an organized group, low levels of group membership may be expected unless (a) such membership was simply nominal and, hence, active participation were excluded—e.g., belonging to a cinema club so as to see certain classic motion pictures at reduced prices—or (b) there was an important pragmatic goal to be obtained, or possibly obtained, through such membership—e.g., more money. Although these two propositions could be expanded upon at great length,[35] my purpose is to test the model by determining if the predicted type of group life, in fact, exists. In other words, is active membership in formally organized groups relatively low (as the basic hypotheses suggest) except for voluntary associations which defend the interests of individuals in their occupational role (as the notion of dual guides to action forecasts).

There are no reliable data on the levels of participation in voluntary associations. If it were to be discovered that active participation in such groups were modal, then the model would be falsified.

The other aspect of the forecast can be investigated, because there are available data on the general tendencies toward joining groups (without regard to the behavioral meanings of such membership).

Duncan MacRae has pulled together some data on membership in voluntary associations gathered in France in 1951 and in the United States in 1955. While 41 percent of the Frenchmen as compared to 53 percent of the Americans belong to one or more voluntary associations, 30 percent of the French respondents belonged to occupational associations, but only 17 percent of the Americans.[36] Thus, if we compute the percentage of those joining any voluntary association, who belong to an occupationally related group, the French statistic is 73 percent while the American is 32 percent. This strongly supports the model's expectations. The strong tendency in France to join, among voluntary associations, occupationally related groups also seems to hold on a multinational basis. Extrapolating from Almond and Verba's data, we find that 43.8 percent of American respondents, 55 percent of Italian respondents, 61.3 percent of German respondents, 61.7 percent of British respondents and 72 percent of Mexican respondents who belonged to voluntary associations were members of occupationally related groups.[37] All of these percentages, except the Mexican one, are significantly lower than the French figure of 73 percent.

Additional support for the notion that Frenchmen are particularly likely to join occupationally related voluntary associations comes from evidence gathered by the French Institute of Public Opinion. In a survey of salaried workers conducted in 1955, 43 percent of the blue-collar workers, 36 percent of the white-collar workers, and 42 percent of the staff members belonged to a union.[38] In a more recent survey, conducted in July 1969 and limited to industrial workers, 31 percent of the respondents were union members. However, 61 percent of the sample supported union activity.[39] For a society which apparently does not have a very dense group life, the percentage of workers who join unions seems extraordinarily high. In addition, the 1969 survey suggests that a large majority of eligibles are supportive of union goals. These results are exactly what should be the case if dual guides to action are prevalent in French society.

Similar evidence is found among other economic groups. Sidney Tarrow points out that, according to surveys, at least 48 percent of French peasants belong to agricultural syndicates.[40] Among the eighty-two teachers I interviewed in secondary schools, 80 percent were union members. Finally, in his study of employees in seven Parisian insurance companies, Michel Crozier discovered (much to his surprise) that 38 percent belonged to the union and an additional 25 percent had once been members.[41]

The data which have been presented suggest not only that the level of membership in occupationally related voluntary associations is rather high—in a society in which membership in voluntary associations tends to be low—but also that, among non-members, such groups have a rather large level of support. This evidence supports the expectations derived from the model.

NOTES

1. Michel Crozier, *The Bureaucratic Phenomenon* (Chicago: University of Chicago Press, 1964). The original French title translates as: *The Bureaucratic Phenomenon: An Essay on the Bureaucratic Tendencies of Modern Organizational Systems and on Their Relationship in France to the Social and Cultural System.*

2. These authors' works are cited in Chapter 5. The other scholars referred to there have obviously also sought to understand French authority.

3. See, for example, Ehrmann, *Politics in France;* Hoffmann, "Paradoxes of the French Political Community" and "Heroic Leadership"; and Macridis, "France." These works are representative of many others which could have been cited. Macridis is a particularly interesting example because in the first ediction of the textbook (1963), he makes no reference to French social authority patterns, but in the second edition (1968), he both cites and accepts Crozier.

4. Hoffmann, ibid. Hoffmann has recently synthesized and revised his probing essays on authority in France. See *Decline or Renewal? France since the 1930's* (New York: Viking Press, 1974), Part II, pp. 63-184.

5. See, for example, Pierre Grémion and Jean-Pierre Worms, *Les institutions régionales et la société locale* (Paris: Copédith, 1968), pp. 3-4 and throughout.

6. Crozier, *The Bureaucratic Phenomenon*, p. 222. In this, as well as in all future references to Crozier, I will cite only one place in the book where he makes the particular argument.

7. Ibid., pp. 187-189.

8. Ibid., pp. 189-190.

9. Ibid., pp. 190-192.

10. Ibid., pp. 204-208.

11. Ibid., pp. 192-193.

12. Ibid., pp. 195-198, 224-227.

13. For a more detailed review of Crozier's work, see Eric A. Nordlinger, "Democratic Stability and Instability: The French Case," *World Politics* 18, No. 1 (October 1965), pp. 127-157.

14. Crozier, *The Bureaucratic Phenomenon*, p. 189.

15. The focus of my inquiry was on the way people live and deal with authority. Crozier approached his cases from a structural perspective and was equally concerned with both subordinate-superordinate relations and the style of interaction between various levels in the structure of superordination. Consequently, the data which I explicitly gathered are not relevant to discussing either the degree of centralization of the decision-making process or the extent of isolation between and egalitarianism within each stratum. However, none of the casual observations in either the secondary schools or E.N.A. suggests that either of these points requires modification.

16. Crises are not likely to arise from a low valuation of the unit's goal. This factor results in not joining the unit, leaving the unit, or establishing the alternating pattern as routine.

17. See François Bourricaud, "Michel Crozier et le syndrome de blocage," *Critique*, no. 282 (November 1970), pp. 960-978; and Ezra Suleiman, *Politics, Power and Bureaucracy in France*, pp. 383-389.

18. Some readers of a preliminary version of this section have wondered if I was not distorting Crozier's argument by saying that he believes crises always bring change with them. A quote from *The Bureaucratic Phenomenon* should settle the question: "Change will not come gradually on a piecemeal basis. It will wait until a serious question pertaining to an important dysfunction can be raised. Then it will be argued about and decided upon at the higher level and applied to the whole organization, even to the areas where dysfunctions are not seriously felt. Only in this way can the impersonality of the system be safeguarded. One may even contend that change will lead to further centralization, by providing a way to get rid of local privileges that have developed around the rules.

"Because of the necessarily long delays, because of the amplitude of the scope it must attain, and because of the resistance it must overcome, change in bureaucratic organizations is a deeply felt crisis. The essential rhythm prevalent in such organizations is, therefore, an alternation of long periods of stability and very short periods of crisis and change" (p. 196).

19. Unfortunately, I have no evidence on the basis of which an explanation can be constructed for why "change" will or will not take place during a given crisis.

20. Michel Crozier, "Révolution libérale ou révolte petite bourgeoise? Notes sur les structures de l'Université et la signification de la crise de mai," *Communications* 12 (1968), pp. 38-45.

21. At one point in his argument, Crozier suggests that during "periods of crisis" there is "submissiveness-rebellion" (p. 203). This proposition fits my conception of the alternating pattern, but Crozier never develops this idea nor gives it more than this passing reference.

22. Crozier, *The Bureaucratic Phenomenon*, p. 219. I have carefully chosen the phrase "may" contradict rather than "does" contradict, because Crozier's assertion about egalitarianism within each stratum is presented solely in the context of his description of normal, bureaucratic authority, but there is no suggestion that this phenomenon ceases to be a characteristic of in-stratum relations during crises.

23. There is also the problem of what it is that changes or does not change.

24. Crozier, *The Bureaucratic Phenomenon*, p. 226.

25. Ibid.

26. To fully accomplish this task would require a special book, for, in fact, I am touching upon an explanation of the development of the French pattern of authority. Such an explanation falls outside the domain of this work. Yet, since the question is an interesting one, I would like to make some tentative observations.

27. Robert O. Paxton, *Vichy France: Old Guard and New Order, 1940-1944* (New York: Alfred A. Knopf, 1972), p. 382.

28. Stanley Hoffmann, *Decline or Renewal?*, p. 70.

29. This work is virtually unknown today, yet it is a classic study of France which rightly belongs in the same category as Bodley's. The failure to read Seippel can probably be attributed to readers only superficially looking at his work and noting the general thesis, so common in his day, that France was irreconcilably split between the "red" and the "black." Below the surface of this general organizing scheme, however, he made a series of profound and insightful observations worthy of careful study.

30. Paul Seippel, *Les deux Frances* (Payot, 1905), p. 396.

31. This term was suggested to me by Philip Goldman of the Department of Political Studies, Queens University, Ontario, Canada. For views which stress the existence of relatively few formally organized groups, see Lucien Bernot and René Blancard, *Nouville, un village français* (Paris: Institut d'Ethnologie, 1953); Jesse Pitts, "The Family

and Peer Groups," in *A Modern Introduction to the Family,* eds. Norman Bell and Ezra Vogel (New York: Free Press, 1968); Arnold Rose, "Voluntary Associations in France," in *Theory and Method in the Social Sciences* (Minneapolis: University of Minnesota Press, 1954); and Laurence Wylie, *Village in the Vaucluse.* Two discussions which suggest that the level of formal group life is rather comprehensive are Jean Meynaud, *Nouvelles études sur les groupes de pression en France,* Cahiers de la Fondation Nationale des Sciences Politiques (Paris: Armand Colin, 1963), pp. 41-63; and René Rémond, "Participation électoral et participation organisée," in *La dépolitisation: mythe ou réalité?,* Cahiers de la Fondation Nationale des Sciences Politiques, ed. Georges Vedel (Paris: Armand Colin, 1962), pp. 84-97.

32. Henry Ehrmann *(Politics in France)* tells us that normally "actual membership in almost all associations amounts to only a fraction of potential membership" and goes on to cite statistics demonstrating that density seems to vary between fifteen percent and twenty-five percent (p. 173). Similarly, René Rémond ("Participation électorale et participation organisée") sees trade unions as being much more densely populated than political parties, even though actual members only represent about fifteen percent of those who are eligible (p. 93). In contradistinction to these authors, Eric Nordlinger ("Democratic Stability and Instability: The French Case," *World Politics* 18 [October 1965]) suggests that density is rather high. His argument is based on a survey reported in Arnold Rose's "Voluntary Associations in France" in which forty-one percent of the French said they belonged to at least one voluntary association (p. 145).

33. Arnold Rose ("Voluntary Associations in France") and Jesse Pitts ("The Family and Peer Groups") have suggested that there are numerous informal groups (e.g., *café* life and "delinquent peer groups") but few formally organized ones. Yet other students of group life in France have not discussed this conception. Rather, they have developed typologies of organized groups and compared these types according to their density and comprehensiveness. (See, for example, René Rémond, "Participation électorale et participation organisée," and Jean Meynaud, *Nouvelles études sur les groupes de pression en France.*)

34. This point is made in greater depth by Jean Meynaud in *Nouvelles études sur les groupes de pression en France* (p. 47). He also notes that similar types of statistics are not available for other societies, thereby making it impossible to reliably determine the *relative* density and comprehensiveness of group life in France.

35. For example, the following general expectations can be derived from the second proposition. If we begin with the notion that the most pragmatic goal which can be sought is a means of subsistence—i.e., a salary and money—then people who work should (1) seek whenever possible "independent" occupations and the most prestigious professions in the society should be of this type, (2) highly value holidays and vacations, and (3) highly value early retirement. In addition, citizens who do not work—e.g., tramps and the independently wealthy—are likely to be regarded with some jealousy. All of these characteristics seem, on impressionistic grounds, to be present in France.

36. Duncan MacRae, *Parliament, Parties, and Society in France 1946-1958* (New York: St. Martin's Press, 1967), p. 30. The French data are from Arnold Rose, "Voluntary Associations in France," pp. 84-85; and the American data are from Murray Hausknecht, *The Joiners* (Totowa, N.J.: Bedminster, 1962), p. 84.

37. These figures were calculated from the total percentages of members and the percentages belonging to trade unions, business, professional, and farm organizations presented in Table 2, p. 302 of Almond and Verba, *The Civic Culture* (Princeton, N.J.: Princeton University Press, 1963).

38. *Sondages,* No. 2 (1956), p. 66.

39. Gérard Adam et al., *L'Ouvrier français en 1970,* Travaux et recherches de science politique (Paris: Armand Colin, 1970), p. 23.

40. Sidney Tarrow, "The Urban-Rural Cleavage in Political Involvement: The Case of France," *American Political Science Review* 65 (June 1971), p. 354.

41. Michel Crozier, *Le Monde des employées de bureau* (Paris: Editions Seuil, 1965), p. 149.

EPILOGUE ON AUTHORITY

In this book, the findings from two case studies were synthesized into a set of interconnected hypotheses capable of describing, in non-unit specific terms, the various kinds of behavior toward authority and explaining when one or the other type of interaction would occur. Each descriptive concept was positively and empirically defined, as well as clearly distinguished from other phenomena which have attracted the attention of social scientists and historians: The differences between "authority-ladenness" and authoritarianism, "forcefulness" and the use of force, "chahut" and (anarchic or spontaneous) rebellion, and "assumed coverage" and internalized behavior were stressed. In addition, discrete explanatory variables were provided to explain the conditions giving rise to changes in the modal form of authority interaction. The independent and dependent variables combine to posit that if, and only if, certain conditions prevail (e.g., subordinates do highly value the goal sought by membership in the social unit and perceive it and its superordinates [who issue virtually no face-to-face directives] as acting effectively to achieve this goal for them), a *specific* outcome must necessarily follow (e.g., assumed coverage). Unfortunately, there has been little empirical study of authority relations per se and even less of how people *behave* toward authority. Therefore it is impossible to even superficially determine to what extent and in what combinations the modes of authority behavior observed in France also exist in other societies. But it is possible to sketch out the implications of my research for our understanding of authority.

Existing conceptualizations of authority tend, almost exclusively, to delimit a dyadic relationship in which each member —whether it be an individual or a group—seeks to exert control over the other.[1] The labels devised to define the relationship refer to the amount of actual control lodged in the hands of each member. One member of the dyad is in a nominal position of hierarchical superiority; the other is his subordinate. The first issues "directives"; the second "influences" the decisions made by the first. Whether the term be "directives" or "influence," the issue is always one of the amount of control each side has over the other. The total amount of maximum control is viewed as a constant.[2]

An analogy may help to clarify this conceptualization: The authority relationship appears as two channels—each capable of expansion or contraction as a function of the volume of "material" it is transmitting—encased within a rigid tunnel linking hierarchical superiors and subordinates. One channel carries superordinates' directives downward to subordinates; the other carries subordinate influence up to superordinates. Either or both channels may be empty and, hence, totally contracted. As the volume of flow through one channel increases, it expands; since the tunnel within which the channels are located is rigid, there is a reduction in the available space for any potential increase in the flow of the other channel. "Authoritarianism" refers to that case in which the downward channel tends toward occupying all available space in the tunnel—i.e., it is characterized by a large amount of superordinate control over subordinates' activities and a corresponding lack of subordinate influence on superordinates' decisions. "Democracy" is alternatively conceptualized as either a relatively equal level of flow through channels, or a large volume of upward flow of influence and a correspondingly low level of superordinate control over subordinates. The former notion seems to be shared by most political scientists, as well as such social psychologists as White and Lippitt.[3] The latter (or "radical") view of democracy has often been adopted by "post-behavioral" political scientists, but it is regarded as a relatively anarchic or insubordinate form of interaction by "the mainstream." A final possible combination of channels is one in which there is little volume flowing either upward or downward; this corresponds to White and Lippitt's notion of "laissez faire" (see Figure E.1 for a pictorial representation of these different combinations).

Conceptualizing authority as a dyadic relationship, varying

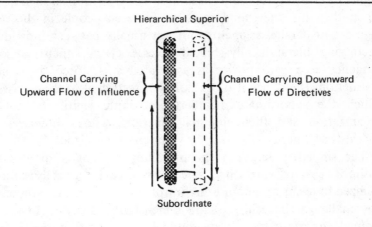

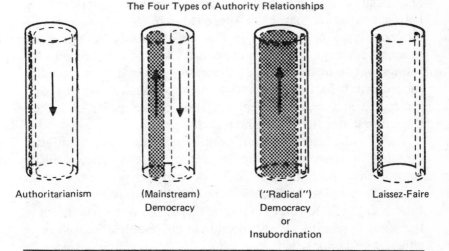

FIGURE E.1: The Prevailing View of Authority: A Pictorial Representation

according to the amount of control within each member's hands, bears a strong resemblance to the notion of "power." The two concepts are, however, distinct. First, authority relations necessarily occur within the confines of ongoing social units and refer to interactions between role occupants in hierarchically distinct segments. Power relations need not occur within a social unit; when they do, they tend to occur between people in the same segment or parallel segments, but not usually between individuals occupying hierarchically linked roles. Second, there is some tendency to regard power as associated with force. In contradistinction, the concept of authority is restricted to those cases in which the subordinate member(s) attribute legitimacy to the organization and their nominal superiors, whose directives are regarded as binding—i.e., there is voluntary compliance.

The similarity between the prevailing notions of power and authority is not surprising, since authority is basically conceptualized in terms of amount of control. The French case studies do not challenge the utility of this dimension of analysis. In fact, it seemed important to indicate the high amount of control French superordinates tended to have over subordinate behavior. But my findings do raise the possibility that the amount-of-control dimension may not be adequate in its present role as the key factor employed to distinguish between authority relations. Specifically, this dimension does not permit discrimination between what, it has been suggested, are two fundamentally different types of authority interaction—authority-ladenness and assumed coverage. The distinction stems from a difference in the form or mode of control—i.e., the source of the direction guiding subordinate behavior. This notion might be used to help provide a richer and more accurate representation of the reality of authority, without sacrificing parsimony in the process.

The French case did not exhibit meaningful or significant variation in reference to the amount of effective superordinate control over subordinates' activities—everywhere it was rather high. The simplest explanation for this finding is the nature of French culture. However, France is one of the very few nations in the world—presently or historically—to be "credited" with having either a "democratic" system or a "democratic" tradition. Consequently, it may be that distinguishing between national authority systems on the basis of the amount-of-control dimension, will result in a rather nondiscriminating typology—i.e., all regimes, with the exception of a dozen or so, would fall into the category of "authoritarian." In any case, there is no doubt that the overwhelming majority of contemporary and historical regimes have been considered "authoritarian."

The research reported in this volume may provide some clues about how to refine the notion of "authoritarian" and make it more discriminating. In particular, it might be useful to distinguish the amount of control exerted within different domains of coverage. For example, among younger secondary school students, alongside the very high level of task, instrumental, and comportmental coverage, virtually no control was exerted over the expression of ideas. This absence of ideological coverage led to labeling the mode of interaction "authority-laden" rather than authoritarian. If we simply conceive of coverage in each of the four domains as dichotomous—i.e., it may be either high or low—there are sixteen discrete, theoretically possible combinations running the gamut from high levels of control in all domains to low levels of control in all domains. Since the notion of authoritarianism seems to require, minimally, a high degree of control exercised over what subordinates do in the unit, attention may usefully be restricted to the eight cases meeting this condition.

Table E.1 lists and provides tentative labels for these eight combinations. The labels stay within the confines of the existing basic vocabulary of political science and seek to capture in words the essence of the authority relationship being delimited. (This

TABLE E.1: Theoretical Types of Authoritarianism

	Levels of Control			
	Task Coverage	Instrumental Coverage	Comportmental Coverage	Ideological Coverage
Totalitarianism	High	High	High	High
Limited Totalitarianism	High	High	Low	High
Inefficient Totalitarianism	High	Low	High	High
Authority-Laden Authoritarianism	High	High	High	Low
Instrumental Authoritarianism	High	High	Low	Low
Comportmental Authoritarianism	High	Low	High	Low
Ideological Authoritarianism	High	Low	Low	High
Liberal Authoritarianism	High	Low	Low	Low

effort is not entirely successful, but then a nomenclature is not important in and of itself, and at least a verbal shorthand has been devised.) The eight theoretical types refer to distinct kinds of "authoritarian" systems, all of which seem likely to have empirical referents.

The term "totalitarianism" has been associated only with those combinations involving high levels of control in three or four domains (including both task and ideological coverage). This labeling decision was based on the impression that the term "totalitarian" entered the vocabulary of political science, in large part, to distinguish modern, highly authoritarian regimes which sought to effectively control not only the behavior but also the ideas expressed by their citizens, from their traditional counterparts. Three theoretical types satisfy this criterion: "Totalitarianism" denotes an authority relationship in which a high level of effective control is exerted over all four domains; under "limited totalitarianism," there is a high level of explicit control over everything except comportment; and "inefficient totalitarianism" refers to those cases in which everything except instrumentalities is highly controlled. (The adjective "inefficient" was used because if there is no control over how to do the tasks which have been precisely defined, the "totalitarian" system seems unlikely to perform well.)

The remaining five combinations are all variants of "authoritarianism." The referent of "authority-laden" is clear. "Instrumental," "comportmental," and "ideological authoritarianism" denote relationships in which there is a high level of control within the domain referred to by the adjective, as well as over tasks. "Liberal (or limited) authoritarianism" simply meets the minimal condition for inclusion in the general category of "authoritarian" —i.e., there is a high level of task coverage.

This eightfold typology of "authoritarian" authority relations clearly provides an operational method for distinguishing between authority relations which are habitually lumped together under the general rubrics of "authoritarian" or "totalitarian." It provides both a means for making finer distinctions and a classificatory scheme applicable to all kinds of social units, and not limited to governmental systems. Finally, it seems likely that further empirical research in other contexts would increase its theoretical richness. Specifically, in the French case, the differential amounts of control exerted over the four domains had a distinct consequence—authority-ladenness led to the development of dual guides to action. It may be hypothesized that other types of authoritarianism will have distinct consequences.

At the risk of offending scholarly sensibilities, I would like to discuss another possible extrapolation from the French findings. Specifically, a two-dimensional scheme for categorizing authority systems, not including the amount-of-control criterion, will be presented. In this exercise, I am clearly treading on extremely shaky ground. Space limitations prevent anything more than a brief sketching of ideas. The lack of empirical data from a variety of contexts reduces the argument to little more than speculation. Finally, the failure to include the amount-of-control dimension, given its wide adoption, seems both immoderate and indicative of a lack of sufficient caution. However, there is, I believe, a justification for throwing caution to the winds. The goal of an epilogue may be construed as providing extremely provisional answers to significant questions posed by the research reported in the body of the book. This may be a somewhat imprudent procedure, but it has the value of being provocative, which usually means simple rejection but which occasionally leads to stimulating thought. I proceed with the hope that at least a few readers may be led to reflect on the problem.

On the basis of the French study, how might we go about conceptualizing and classifying authority systems? Two major dimensions of analysis are suggested. First, what is the source of behavioral direction for subordinates? In other words, what types of cues evoke the behavior of subordinates within a given social unit? Since it seems reasonable to assume that most activities within organized life are routinized, the problem is to locate the sources which lead either to "kicking-off" an established routine or creating new routines. Such sources may be dichotomously conceptualized as face-to-face directives from superordinates or material cues within the environment. Generalized, written instructions are of an intermediate nature, but closer to the environment as a cue—because something in the individual's environment must lead him to read, consult, and follow such rules.

This distinction overlaps Rousseau's notion of the difference between "dependence on men" and "dependence on things."

The second dimension is concerned with the subordinate's perception of the source of his own behavioral direction. Or, more specifically, to what extent does he attribute his behavior to internal factors, "doing what comes naturally"—i.e., what he wants and voluntarily chooses to do—as compared to external factors—i.e., his behavioral decisions are based on acts, requests, and/or commands of his nominal superiors?

These two dichotomously conceived dimensions combine into a simple, fourfold table (see Table E.2). The first type, "direct coverage," includes the authority-laden mode of interaction in French schools, the various kinds of "authoritarianism" which have been discussed (assuming that subordinates' perceive the face-to-face directives as the source of their behavioral decisions), and what seems often to be denoted by the terms "democracy" or "limited government." The second type is "assumed coverage," whether high (as in the French case) or low degrees of regimentation are involved. The third type, "manipulated coverage," is exemplified by the relationship between Rousseau and Emile, in which the "tutor" controls the environment and is thus able to get the "tutee" to do whatever he wants him to do, but the latter perceives himself as being totally "free." The final type, "internalized coverage," represents the "ideal" of "democracy," a government of laws, not of men, in which the "citizens" regard themselves as having complete freedom.

These four ideal types of authority systems result in a method for classifying regimes which disregards the amount of control

TABLE E.2: A Provisional Typology of Authority Relations

		Source of Direction	
		Dependence on Men	Dependence on Things
Perceived Source of Direction	External	(1) "Direct Coverage"	(2) "Assumed Coverage"
	Internal	(3) "Manipulated Coverage"	(4) "Internalized Coverage"

exerted by superordinates over the activities of subordinates. First, it might be noted, the failure to make this distinction need not necessarily be considered significant, given the problems which exist in attempting to apply the amount-of-control dimension, despite prolonged usage and widespread acceptance. On the one hand, scholars seem unable to agree how to classify given cases. For example, some have viewed Gaullist France as a dictatorship, while others regard it as a type of democracy. Similarly, many political scientists question whether any existing governments are really totalitarian or rather simply authoritarian regimes; other students of politics place contemporary empirical examples in both categories. On the other hand, scholars seem totally incapable of arriving at a common ordering of regimes habitually placed within a single category—i.e., segment of the continuum. Thus, there is no single answer to the question of which polity is more democratic, the French, the British, the American, or the Swedish. Rather, there are almost as many answers as there are observers.[4]

Second, and more importantly, the traditional distinction based on the amount of control can easily be incorporated within the proposed fourfold typology. Specifically, direct coverage systems can be distinguished according to the extent of control exerted over each of the four domains. The same is true for assumed coverage and manipulated coverage regimes, but such a method of discrimination seems inapplicable to internalized authority relations.

The proposed basic typology does seem to have two important theoretical advantages. First, it is not social-unit-specific. Rather, it can be applied with identical ease and reasonableness to such distinct kinds of organizations as families, schools, work places, asylums, and nation-states. This seems to be a necessary condition for theorizing. Clearly, theory must be problem-oriented, and to the extent that a problem may occur in a set of different contexts, initial and basic formulations should not artificially restrict the environments within which the pehnomenon may be studied. Naturally, a sophisticated theory supported by extensive empirical research might locate and explain variations in the nature of authority according to the scale of the social unit.

This argument may disturb some political scientists, who

consider government and political authority to be a special subset of authority relations, requiring its own theoretical apparatus. However, such an assumption is only tenable to the extent that it is derived from an application of general theory to empirical cases, which results in governments clustering in certain distinct ways separating them from other types of social units. While such an assumption may be "correct," at present it is simply an outgrowth of the nontheoretically informed development of the study of government as a separate, institutionally based field of inquiry. Thus, until the application of general theory creates subcategories of analysis for special theoretical concern—one of these being governments—there is no justification for isolating political authority relations for special or exclusive concern.

A second advantage of the proposed typology is that it takes into explicit consideration subordinates' perceptions. People behave in the real world not on the basis of how it *is,* but rather according to how they perceive it. To the extent that we are seeking theories which can provide accurate forecasts about future behavior, this distinction must be kept in mind. The typology of authority systems based on the mode of control recognizes this factor and presents the possibility of deducing psychological and group consequences from the categorization of a given social unit. For example, to the extent that a subordinate's activities, even if they are very precisely circumscribed, are guided by cues perceived to be internal, he has the feeling of being totally free. However, if direct coverage is the source of cues, the individual will feel that his behavior is controlled by others—that he is not free—and he may develop hostile feelings toward his superiors. A person who lives under assumed coverage is even more likely to feel constrained; he does not perceive himself as being a free agent, and yet since he cannot isolate specific superordinates who are "forcing" him to do things, he is unable to direct his hostility toward discrete and, hence, "conquerable" objects. Forecasts can also be made about such group consequences as stability and change. Manipulative and internalized regimes seem most likely to endure and function effectively. Assumed-coverage units are likely to be must less effective and to be characterized by more frequent serious "rebellions"—e.g., chahuts. Direct coverage regimes are the least stable, but only they and manipulative systems seem capable of significant change.

Other questions, calling for perhaps less grandiose and intimidating responses than a typology of authority systems, are also posed by the French case study. Most importantly, what is the meaning of rebellion? Typically, there is a tendency to regard people as either being obedient or disobedient in their organized life. Under the latter condition, they do what they want to do and do not follow anyone's orders. France, a society whose citizens are reputed to be "rebellious," "nonconformist," and "individualistic," does not seem to provide systematic examples of this kind of disobedience within organized life. Rather, even insubordination—i.e., the chahut—is characterized by a high degree of external control over behavior. Consequently, "rebellion" does not appear as pure disobedience but rather as a *transference* of obedience from one set of individuals to another. Subordinates continue to "obey," but not the same people. Obviously, France may be very special in this respect. However, given the prevailing view of the French, there seems to be some logic behind the suggestion to reconsider empirically the meaning of "rebellion" and "disobedience." To the extent that French conditions are widespread, we might want to ask: Under what conditions will subordinates switch loyalties from one set of directive-issuers to another? This is a fundamentally different question than why men rebel. And, to the extent that my observations in France are atypical, we would want to ask: Why don't Frenchmen rebel?

NOTES

1. Amitai Etzioni (*A Comparative Analysis of Complex Organizations: On Power, Involvement and Their Correlates* [New York: The Free Press, 1961]) is one of the rare scholars to consider factors other than the amount of control. However, even in his work, this dimension is central.

2. This last condition is inferred from the tendency to assume that, as the amount of authority exerted over subordinates increases, the amount of influence they have decreases, and vice versa.

3. See Ralph K. White and Ronald O. Lippitt, *Authority and Democracy: An Experimental Inquiry* (New York: Harper, 1960).

4. It is instructive to compare the rankings developed by Deane Neubauer and Robert A. Dahl. The differences are rather significant despite the usage of a common conception of "polyarchy." See Deane E. Neubauer, "Some Conditions of Democracy," *American Political Science Review* 61 (December 1967), pp. 1002-1009; and Robert A. Dahl, *Polyarchy: Participation and Opposition* (New Haven: Yale University Press, 1971), esp. Appendix A, pp. 231 ff.

APPENDICES

APPENDIX A

FRENCH SECONDARY SCHOOLS: THE SETTING

*

The Structure of French Education

The French educational system is normally characterized as being highly centralized.[1] All public educational institutions are subordinated to the Ministry of National Education in Paris, which makes all major decisions. To apply these decisions throughout the country, France has been divided into twenty-three *académies*,[2] each of which supervises the educational institutions located within its geographical sphere of influence. The académie's administrative head is the *recteur:* He is the agent of the Minister within each region. To implement the ministerial decisions on a departmental level,[3] each académie has inspectors (inspecteurs d'académie) who keep in relatively continuous contact with the heads of the individual schools.

This organizational arrangement is traced back to Napoléon I. By the law of May 10, 1806, and the decree of March 17, 1808, the emperor created a public monopoly of the secondary educational function. The "grand master" (Grand Maître) sat at the apex of the pyramidal structure, divided into a series of académies, each governed by a recteur. The Napoleonic system

Author's Note: This appendix describes the structure of secondary education at the time of my fieldwork (1967-1968); its purpose is to place my case study in context, not to provide an extensive analytical history of the French educational system. Those who seek an in-depth treatment should consult: Paul Gerbod, *La vie quotidienne dans les lycées et collèges au XIXᵉ siècle* (Paris: Hachette, 1968); Viviane Isambert-Jamati, *Crises de la société, crises de l'enseignement: Sociologie de l'enseignement secondaire français* (Paris: Presses Universitaires de France, 1970); Antoine Prost, *L'enseignement en France, 1800-1967* (Paris: Armand Colin, 1968); and Georges Snyder, *La pédagogie en France aux XVIIᵉ et XVIIIᵉ siècle* (Paris: Presses Universitaires de France, 1965).

was developed to train an elite; it was restricted to institutions of secondary and higher education and did not include either primary or vocational schools. On these two grounds, at least, the contemporary public educational system differs from the original structure.[4]

The great emphasis on the centralized nature of the system, and its tracing to Napoleonic origins, are in some respects misleading. First, not all public educational facilities are equally under the control of the Ministry of National Education and its local representatives. Some schools are run by other governmental agencies—e.g., most of the *Grands Écoles,* the elite institutions of higher education, as well as those secondary schools which have an agricultural program of study.[5] More significantly, depending on the type of institution of secondary education, powers other than the Ministry may play a role in the operation, especially the financing, of the school. For instance, the municipal lycées and the Colleges of General Education receive a substantial portion of their operating funds from the *communes* in which they are located.[6] Finally, a striking aspect of this centralized system is that the hierarchical superiors have only a very limited effective sanctioning power over their subordinates, although these subordinates consistently comply with the rules and orders given to them. While in no way diluting the hierarchical and pyramidal features of the educational system, this facet is of significance in trying to understand the way in which the structure functions. (This aspect of the system was more fully discussed in Chapter 4.)

Another factor which complicates the organization of education in France is the existence of a large network of private—both nonsectarian and Catholic—schools. The great majority of these are run by different religious orders, but that does not mean that the state has no control over their operation. Since private school students have to take the same national examinations as public school pupils, their programs of study are based on those used in the state schools. This factor has traditionally limited the autonomy of the private school system and, more recently, the degree of separation between the two systems has been further reduced by the law of December 31, 1959. Now any private school may enter into a contractual arrangement with the state. Schools that sign such a contract agree to follow certain rules and regulations set down by the public authorities and accept being inspected by them. As a counterpart to giving up some control over their own institutions, the private schools receive important financial aid from the state. As early as 1964-1965, almost all the private elementary schools and sixty percent of the secondary schools had completed contracts with the state.[7]

The Secondary School System

In theory, a child leaves elementary school and enters the classe de sixième of high school at eleven. A complete secondary education requires at least seven years of study, divided into two parts, each called a cycle. The first cycle is completed at the end of troisième after four years of study. Then the student enters the second cycle, which lasts three years; the grades are seconde, première, and terminale. Table A.1 presents a complete break-down of the French secondary school system according to grade and theoretical age at each level.

The age associated with each grade represents the *normal* age; in fact, there are very great divergences from this normal age within each grade. For instance, only 50.5 percent of the pupils in sixiéme are eleven years of age or less and only 30.6 percent of those in terminale are seventeen or less. Table A.2 shows the percentages of students at each grade level who: (1) have the normal age, (2) are younger than the normal age, (3) are one year older than the normal age, and (4) are more than one year older than the normal age.

The disparities between the theoretically normal age of the pupils and their actual age are due to the large number of students who must repeat one or more years of their secondary education. That each year so many must follow the same courses they have just completed is often less a sign of their scholastic ineptitude than a reflection of the educational system. Pupils who fail a single course may be required to repeat that entire year's program of study, including those subjects in which they did passing or even excellent work. One of the factors responsible for this situation is the absence of summer schools.

French secondary education is dispensed in a wide variety of institutions. Some are concerned only with the first cycle, others only with the second, and still others with both. Some seek to transmit a general cultural framework to the students, others to prepare then for the university, and still others to teach them specific occupations—from primary school teacher to garage mechanic. To facilitate comprehension of the complex institutional variety of French secondary education, we had best begin by oversimplifying the system and then build back some of its complexity. (As a preface to this discussion, consult Table A.3 for a list of the major types of French secondary schools and the number of pupils enrolled in each institution during the 1967-1968 academic year.)

At the highest level of generalization, there are two basic types of French secondary schools: the academic and the vocationally oriented. There are three distinct kinds of academic secondary schools in France, the lycée; the C.E.G. (Collège d'enseignement général—College of General Education); and the C.E.S. (Collège d'enseignement secondaire—College of Secondary Education).

The lycée is the most traditional and prestigious of all French institutions of secondary education. Created by Napoléon as the bulwark of his system, the lycée of contemporary France is the educator of the elite—i.e., of those who will pursue higher education. The academic credentials of lycée teachers tend to be rather high. The largest proportion of permanent teachers are *certifié*—i.e., they have a *license,* a university degree approximately equivalent to the American M.A., and have been among the few to pass an extremely difficult and competitive national examination.[8] A much smaller proportion are *agrégé.*[9] They possess a *Diplôme d'études superieures* (Diploma of Higher Education), which is obtained by writing a thesis after having been awarded the license. In addition, they have passed a national competitive examination which is even more difficult and selective than the one taken to become certifié.[10]

In recent years, much less qualified personnel—e.g., those only with a license or with even less of a university education—have had to be recruited to meet the needs caused by the very sudden increase in the lycée student population: Between the academic year 1958-1959 and 1967-1968, the number of public lycée students rose from 688,440 to 957,211.[11] Rarely are these less qualified people given tenured positions, but a large proportion of the students are being taught by educators who do not have the qualifications traditionally considered necessary to teach in a lycée.

A lycée always has the second cycle and often both cycles. During the first cycle, there are two basic curriculum-centered options: the classical and the modern. The classical section is more intellectually demanding than the modern. During the first two years of their secondary education, pupils in both groups study almost the same subjects: The only overt difference is that those in *classique* study Latin five hours per week, while those in *moderne* spend this time on increased work in a modern foreign language, French, and science. In quatrième, the students following the classical option are divided into two sections, one starting the study of Greek and the other beginning a second modern language.[12] In reality, there is more difference between these groups than studying or not studying any of the dead languages. The students who are regarded as the most gifted tend to be in the classical sections. In addition, while the subject headings of the courses studied by the different groups of pupils are identical, the content and depth of treatment is usually different, with pupils in classique being submitted to a more rigorous course of study.

While the major curriculum-centered criterion dividing pupils during the first cycle is the presence or absence of Latin, this is no longer the case during the second cycle. Lycée pupils in the seconde follow one of two basic options: literary studies or scientific studies. Within each of these sections there are further subdivisions, which, for instance, separate those who are studying the dead languages. After completing seconde, the pupils have another curriculum choice to make, which is influenced by the option followed in seconde. There are four basic programs available, each of which has a number of subdivisions: a literary, linguistic, and philosophical program; the study of economy and the social sciences (a new option, which only a few lycées offer); a program oriented toward mathematics and physics; and the physics and natural sciences program. Each of these options leads to a particular *baccalauréat*.[13] The baccalauréat is a national examination, which has both written and oral components. Passing this exam is the only way to complete one's secondary education, and thus is, in a sense, the functional equivalent of the American high school diploma. For the students who have the *bac*,[14] entrance to the university is automatic.

The C.E.G. is, nominally, a new institution, having only been in existence since 1959.[15] However, they are little more than a revised form of the *cours complémentaires* (complementary courses) which date from 1856.[16] The C.E.G., as its precursor, is largely a continuation of the primary school type of education. Usually it occupies part of the same building in which a primary school is located. Most of the teachers—normally, all except those who teach foreign languages, gym, music, and art—are primary school teachers (instituteurs or institutrices) with five or more years of pedagogical experience. Often, the school's principal (directeur) is also in charge of a primary school.

While some C.E.G.s offer a classical and a modern as well as a short-modern program, the great majority only offer this last option. The short-modern program (moderne courte) is a simplified and elementary form of the moderne. There is much similarity between the titles of the subject matters which are treated: The major exceptions are that those following the short-modern program take only one and not two foreign languages and study physics and chemistry while those in the moderne do not do so during the first cycle. The real difference between the two programs lies in the depth with which the same subjects are treated. Those in the short-modern program are taught only a small portion of what those in the moderne program learn when both are following a course with the same title.

The C.E.G. only offers a first-cycle education. Before leaving the C.E.G., pupils take a national competitive examination called the B.E.P.C. (Brevet d'études du premier cycle du second degré), the passage of which signifies the completion of the first cycle of secondary education. Few lycée students take this exam, because its only value is to permit one to take other competitive examinations for entrance into the lower levels of the civil service or special vocational schools, and they anticipate entering higher-status occupations. But, for the C.E.G. pupil who must, at the end of troisième, either go to another type of educational institution (and they go only very rarely to an academic lycée) or stop his schooling, the passage of this examination may be very important for his career.[17]

The third type of academic secondary school is the C.E.S. It is the newest of French institutions of secondary education, having only been created in 1963. In the future, the C.E.S. is to be the only school within which there will be instruction on the level of the first cycle. They are to absorb the C.E.G.s and the lower grades of the lycée, thus becoming a *polyvalent* (multifunctional) establishment having a monopoly on the early years of secondary education.[18]

The major motivating force for the creation of this new institution was the perennially expressed desire in France for a "democratic" system of secondary education. By democracy in this case, and most often in France, is meant equality of conditions and opportunities among individuals from different social class backgrounds. Under the C.E.G.-lycée system, there was a strong tendency for students from the lower socioeconomic classes to go to the C.E.G. (or stay in the primary school itself and never go on to secondary education)[19] and for those from the upper echelons of society to go to the lycée.

An explanation of this tendency toward social class segregation is found in the process by which a French primary school pupil is placed in a lycée, C.E.G., or continues studying in the primary school. During the last year of primary school, parents are sent information on the various options for further education open to their children and the careers for which each of these options prepares the pupil. On the basis of this information, they make a decision as to what course of study they want their children to follow. There is a very strong tendency for the lower-class parents to request that their child continue in the primary school or go to a C.E.G., while the upper-class parents tend to choose a lycée program, especially the classical one (see Table A.4). In eighty percent to ninety percent of the cases the pupil, in fact, ends up following the program his parents chose for him.[20] That the parents' desires tend to correlate very strongly with their social class results from their perception of the type of education their child should have and the value they place on education. French lower-class parents, when looking at the curricula offered in the C.E.G. and lycée sections, are impressed by the number of science courses offered in the former program that are absent in the lycées. Realizing that in the modern world scientific knowledge is of great value, they are attracted to the C.E.G. program, even though, in fact, the physics and chemistry courses offered there are extremely superficial. In addition, French lower-class parents tend to place little value in their children aspiring to a university education. The professions for which they think their children might be prepared are those which at most require a C.E.G. education.[2] [1]

Another element which strongly contributes to the social class stratification of the system is the style and content of a French education. French schools place an important premium on one's rhetorical ability and cultural background, thereby severely disadvantaging children from the lower classes. Table A.5 shows that, as one mounts the social hierarchy, there is an increasing tendency to do good or excellent work in school. Thus, only eight percent of all pupils, compared with more than fifteen percent of the children of professionals and executives, do excellent work in their last year of primary school.

The theory behind the C.E.S. is that every primary school pupil will go into the sixième. During the first trimester of that grade, the students will be "observed" and placed in either a classical section or in one of the two modern sections. Those children who in the past would have stayed in the primary school also go to the C.E.S., but they are placed in *sections de transition.* The first year in this transitional section is devoted to trying to help those who could follow a normal course of study to catch up. Those who cannot be helped will continue on with a terminal course of study until they reach sixteen and can leave school.

Serious doubts can be raised whether the C.E.S. will really remove social inequities from the French system of education. First, as these institutions now function, they do little more than regroup within a single complex of buildings schooling that previously was provided in separate edifices. There are different types of teachers for the lycée sections and for the C.E.G. section. The students following different courses of study have virtually no contact with one another. Second, the major reasons for social inequality within the schools remain: The desires of the parents and the fact that the French educational system puts a very high value on oral communication techniques and other factors likely to be learned from one's domestic environment.

The three types of schools so far discussed—i.e., lycée, C.E.G., and C.E.S.—are the only institutions to which a child completing primary education may go. Most students stay in one of them through the first cycle of their studies or until leaving school. At the end of troisième, those who do not go to a lycée may continue their schooling at a *lycée technique,* a vocational school, or an *école normale.*

The lycée technique prepares students over a three-year period for a technical baccalauréat or for the *Brevet d'agent technique,* which qualifies the individual to be a "technician" with one of four specializations: industrial, commercial, social, or hotel. As is the case with an academic lycée, the pupils take one of a series of possible programs, each of which prepares them for a slightly different technical bac—e.g., a mathematical and technical program. Those who pass this examination have the right to enter the university.[22]

The lycée technique's program has strong doses of mathematics and science, and its student population is rather selective. Such is not the case with the vocational schools (Collèges d'enseignement technique—C.E.T.). Each C.E.T. trains pupils for a specific occupation. Pupils learn how to become secretaries or cooks, mechanics or industrial designers, and so on. In gist, the C.E.T. is an educational institution which performs a role traditionally served by the apprentice relationship. As the completion of an academic or technical education is sanctioned by a national competitive examination, so is the completion of a vocational education. The degree is called either a *Brevet d'Etudes Professionnelles* (B.E.P.—Diploma of Professional Studies) or a *Certificat d'Aptitude Professionnelle* (C.A.P.—Certificate of Professional Aptitude). Normally, a pupil studies two years in a vocational school before taking one of these examinations.[23]

In the Colleges of General Education, there is a tendency to place the best students in special classes which prepare them to take an examination, the passage of which allows them to go to a normal school for elementary school teachers (Ecole Normale Primaire d'Instituteurs et d'Institutrices). A normal school education begins after the first cycle of studies has been completed and lasts for four years—the first three of which are devoted to preparing for the baccalauréat exam and the last for studying pedagogical methods. In general, there are two normal schools in each of Frances's ninety-five départements, one to train men and the other, women.

In this discussion of the institutional framework of the public system of education, many different types of secondary schools have been discussed, yet I have greatly simplified reality. A few of the many factors which would have to be included to complete the description can be mentioned. There are three different types of academic (and technical) lycées: lycée (technique) *d'état,* lycée (technique) *municipal,* and lycée (technique) *nationalisée.* These institutions are distinguished by the presence or absence of various local governmental agencies within the administrative structure of control. In addition, the idea that the lycées techniques are completely separated from the lycées is misleading: In many cases, an academic lycée also offers a technical course of study. Finally, I have not even mentioned a particular type of secondary school —the agricultural institution—which is distinct from any of the types discussed, although its programs and structure parallel closely those of the lycée technique and the C.E.T. Nonetheless, for the purposes of explaining the sampling procedure which was used and for placing the study of authority patterns in French secondary schools in context, the information presented suffices.

Alongside the public system of secondary education, there is a large private system, mostly under the control of the Catholic Church. It is not necessary to discuss the institutional setup of this system, because it parallels the public system. This parallelism results from the fact that the private school students must take the same national examinations that the public school pupils take and that they must be prepared to seek the same careers.

The Sampling Procedure

A stratified sample of secondary schools with the particular institutions in each stratum being randomly chosen forms the basis of the case study. Limitations of time and money restricted the sample to no more than about a dozen schools. Given this factor, plus the institutional complexity of secondary education in France, a purely random sample might well have been completely nonrepresentative. In the end, thirteen schools were studied, all of

them part of the public system and each of them either a lycée, a
C.E.G., or a C.E.S. Before giving a detailed description of the
sample, the criteria used to determine the kinds of institutions to
be examined must be made explicit.

First, the sample was stratified so as to include only public
schools. While it would have been desirable to cover both the
private and public sectors, the result would have been a rather
superficial sample of both types. The major reason for opting in
favor of the public secondary school system is that less than
twenty-five percent of the secondary school population is in the
private sector. Of the 3,515,838 pupils in secondary schools in
1967-1968, 2,719,775 went to public and 796, 063 to private
institutions (see Table A.3). Even this national figure is a bit
misleading because private schools tend to be strongly concentrated in particular regions; in the academies of Nantes and
Rennes, for example, almost as many pupils attend the private as
the public secondary schools.[24]

Some might object to overlooking the private, especially the
Catholic, institutions of secondary education on the grounds that
through their doors pass the French elite of tomorrow.[25] This
argument is not convincing because my purpose in examining
secondary schools was to understand the authority patterns which
have developed out of the general, mass socialization process and
not those characteristic of the "elite" as such. In addition, the
empirical evidence to support the view of the Church-run schools
as *currently* performing the crucial role as elite socializers is not
clear-cut. The research at E.N.A. suggests that, at least for the
administrative elite, parochial education is proportionately no
more common than in the rest of the population.[26] However, a
national study conducted under the auspices of the French
National Institute of Population Studies (L'Institut national
d'études démographiques) in 1962[27] concludes that "private
education recruits from a higher-level social stratum than public
education."[28] This argument is based on the fact that a larger
percentage of the private than of the public secondary school
population is composed of the children of high-level executives
and professionals (see Table A.6 for a complete breakdown of the
social composition of the private and public schools). From the
evidence presented, the accuracy of such a conclusion can be

seriously questioned. First, staying within the confines of the data presented in Table A.6, one must conclude that private education recruits from not only a higher-level social stratum but also a more rural one (i.e., farmers) than the public secondary school system. Second, the statistics presented in Table A.6 are misleading because the secondary school population is not evenly divided between public and private institutions. Since approximately seventy-five percent of all pupils pursuing a secondary education go to public institutions, a larger proportion of the upper classes' offspring receive their instruction in the public schools than in the private schools (see Table A.7). Third, the statistics in Table A.6 are misleading because they do not compare the social class composition of the different types of secondary schools in the public and private systems.[29] A much larger proportion of children from higher-class homes and a much lower proportion of children from lower-class homes go to the lycée than go to the C.E.G. (see Table A.4). But while fifty-five percent of the first-cycle pupils in private schools follow a lycée-style education, only thirty-one percent of those in the public system are in lycées (see Table A.3). Thus, the general measure of the social composition of public versus private secondary schools exaggerates the role played by the private schools in the process of elite recruitment.

Having decided to restrict attention to the public secondary school system did not end the problem of sampling but rather focused it. All types of institutions could not be examined. Since everyone must go through the first part of secondary education in either the lycée, C.E.G., or C.E.S., I decided to limit research to these three types of institutions. The universe from which the sample was drawn thus included all institutions offering a first cycle of studies, the only cycle with which everyone has to have some experience.

Consequently, the empirical basis for assessing authority behavior during the second cycle was limited to the lycées. The lycée technique and C.E.T. were not studied; although neither gives instruction to as many pupils as the lycée does, both deal with a large proportion of those students who continue their education beyond troisième (see Table A.3). Such a restriction, although inconvenient, was compelled simply by the resources available to me. There is, however, reason to believe that since most of the students from the C.E.G. who continue their education go to a C.E.T. or a lycée technique, the relationship between the C.E.G. and the technical-vocational schools is not significantly different from that between the first and second cycles of an academic lycée.

The actual sample of schools studied is described in Part I. All together, fieldwork was conducted in two lycées and two C.E.G.s in Paris; one lycée and one C.E.G. in the Parisian suburbs; one urban lycée, two rural C.E.G.s and one slightly urban C.E.S. in the northern region; and one urban lycée-C.E.S., one urban C.E.G., and one rural lycée in the southern region. These institutions were randomly selected from the Ministry's comprehensive listing of secondary schools.[30]

Since all the teachers, students, and classes in these thirteen schools could not be studied, research was arbitrarily limited to cinquième, troisième, seconde, and terminale.[31] Among the classes of cinquième and troisième existing in each school, a random selection was made to include at least one group following each of the options offered in the particular institution—i.e., classical, modern, and/or short-modern. The same tactic was used among classes of seconde and terminale to ensure the inclusion of groups following the literary, mathematics, and natural science options. All chosen classes were given questionnaires, and at least one at each grade level in each school was intensively observed. (Table A.8 breaks down the student sample according to grade and program of study.) From among the teachers assigned to the classes which were observed, a sample was chosen for interviews; this sample was stratified in favor of those who taught the pupils for the largest number of hours per week. (Table A.9 describes this sample according to the type of school in which they teach and their subject matter.)

A Note on Questionnaire Administration

The final student questionnaire is a revised version of one developed and then employed during a three-month pretest in a Parisian private school. The pretest questionnaire was, in part, derived from fieldwork manuals prepared by members of Princeton University's Workshop in Comparative Politics (including myself) under the guidance and direction of Harry Eckstein and Ted Robert Gurr. Approximately two hundred students took the pretest questionnaire. About five weeks after they had done so, twenty were selected randomly and given interviews using the same questionnaire. On the basis of this procedure, the questions which elicited the least reliable responses were changed, and the instrument was revised into a final form.

The reliability test suggested a new method for administering questionnaires which was, in fact, used during the actual survey. Specifically, each question was read aloud to the pupils. Before beginning, besides the normal introduction, the students were told to raise their hands whenever the meaning of an item was not perfectly clear. After the questionnaire was given to three classes, a small number of questions stood out as posing comprehension problems. As a result, we developed set ways of verbally supplementing these questions so as to make their meaning clear. For example, after reading aloud "To what extent are you able to determine by yourself the form of your school work? " the pupils were immediately told (as if it were part of the written question), "That is, how to do it. For example, how to present your homework? "

This procedure turned the written questionnaire into what might be called a "group interview." The reading of the questions aloud, in and of itself, helped to make their meaning clearer to many of the youngest pupils. In addition, we were able to define any words which a student did not fully understand. The end product, on the basis of casual testing, seems to be a set of responses which are much more reliable than if the questionnaire had been administered in the normal fashion.[32]

NOTES

1. See, for example: Henry W. Ehrmann, *Politics in France* (Boston: Little, Brown, 1968), pp. 65-66; W. D. Halls, *Society, Schools and Progress in France* (London: Pergamon Press, 1965), pp. 74 ff.; Georges A. Male, *Education in France* (Washington, D.C.: U.S. Department of Health, Education and Welfare, 1963), p. 29; and J. Minot, "Le ministère et sa mouvance," in *L'Education nationale*, ed. Jean-Louis Crémieux-Brilhac (Paris: Presses Universitaires de France, 1965), p. 345.

2. The académies are Aix, Amiens, Besançon, Bordeaux, Caen, Clermont-Ferrand, Dijon, Grenoble, Lille, Limoges, Lyon, Montpellier, Nancy, Nantes, Nice, Orléans, Paris, Poitiers, Reims, Rennes, Rouen, Strasbourg, and Toulouse.

3. At present, France is divided into ninety-five *départements* or states–i.e., the principal local governmental units. Each académie usually consists of three or four départements.

4. For a discussion of the Napoleonic origins of the system and its transformations, see L. François, "Le ministre et le grand maître de l'Université," and J. Minot, "Le ministère et sa mouvance," in *L'Education nationale*, pp. 307-318, 327-349.

5. For a detailed listing of the public educational institutions not under the control of the Ministry of National Education, see J. Minot, ibid., pp. 342-345.

6. For a full discussion of the relationships between various types of public educational institutions and their differing administrative bodies, see G. Bourjac, "L'administration locale," in *L'Education nationale*, pp. 505-528.

7. For a detailed discussion of the relationship between the private and public sectors of education, see B. Vacheret, "L'enseignement privé et ses rapports avec l'enseignement public," in *L'Education nationale*, pp. 607-615.

8. In 1968, of the 13,232 men and women who took the written and oral examinations required to be certifié, only 2,463 (18.6 percent) passed (*Statistiques des enseignement: Tableaux et informations,* Chapter 3 "Le personnel enseignant," Fascicule 2 "Le principaux concours de recrutement, Année 1968," [1967-1968], p. 24).

9. Of the 64,578 lycée teachers in the 1967-1968 academic year, 9,675 (15 percent) were agrégé and 33,045 (51 percent) were certifié (ibid.; Chapter 3, Fascicule 1 "Nombre et répartition du personnel de l'enseignement public, Année scolaire 1967-68," [1967-1968], p. 20).

10. In 1968, 8,153 people took the examination for agrégation. Of these, only 1,332 (16 percent) passed (ibid., Fascicule 2, p. 21).

11. *Tableaux de l'éducation nationale, statistiques rétrospectives 1958-68: édition 1969* (Paris: Ministère de l'éducation nationale, n.d.), pp. 34-37. If other academic years were selected for comparison, the increase in the secondary school population is even more dramatic. See, for example, Dominique Maison and Elisabeth Millet, "Niveau d'instruction et enseignement," *Population,* special issue (June 1974), p. 164.

12. For the complete curriculum and the number of class hours spent on each course, see *Horaires et Programmes de l'enseignement du second degré* (Paris: Librairie Vuibert, 1967), pp. 11-12 (hereafter cited as Horaires).

13. For a full listing of the options available in the second cycle, see *Horaires,* pp. 379-380; and Ministère de l'Education Nationale–Direction de la Pédagogie, des Enseignements Scolaires et de l'Orientation, *Orientation après la classe de 3e* (Paris: Bureau universitaire de statistique et de documentation scolaires et professionnelles, 1967), pp. 4-12 (hereafter cited as Orientation).

14. In general, only a little more than a half the students who take the baccalauréat examinations actually receive the diploma. For instance, at the 1966 session, only 51.5 percent of those trying for the philosophical bac, 53.5 percent of those trying for the scientific bac, and 43.2 percent of those trying for the mathematical bac received it (Institut National de la statistique et des études économiques, *Annuaire statistique de la France 1967: Résultats de 1965 et de 1966,* 73 vol. [Paris, 1968], p. 130). However, since 1968 and the May crisis, the percentage of students passing the baccalauréat examinations has risen sharply, and now approximately 70 percent pass.

15. See André Jacotin, "Enseignement du second degré," in *Encyclopédie pratique de l'éducation en France* (Paris: L'Institut Pédagogique National, 1960), pp. 130-131 (hereafter cited as Encyclopédie).

16. For details on the cours complémentaires, see Pierre Mayeur and René Guillemoteau, "Enseignement du premier degré," in Encyclopédie, p. 106.

17. For additional information on the C.E.G.s, see "Lycées et Collèges d'enseignement général," *Cahiers pédagogiques*, no. 43 (September 1963), pp. 32-76.

18. For a detailed discussion of the C.E.S.s, see "Les Collèges d'enseignement secondaire," special issue of *Cahiers pédagogiques*, no. 75 (May 1968), throughout.

19. At the time of my study, the *classes de fin d'études* (the end of studies classes) in the primary schools were already well on the way toward disappearing. Previously, a large proportion of pupils stayed in these classes until they reached the age when they could legally stop their education—i.e., fourteen or sixteen.

20. Alain Girard and Henri Bastide, "La stratification sociale et la démocratisation de l'enseignement," *Population* 18, no. 3 (July-September 1963), p. 444.

21. The complete process by which a child is oriented at the end of primary school is as follows: After the parents have expressed their wishes, a commission composed largely of teachers and school administrators examines the pupil's record and decides if the orientation choice of the parents is reasonable. If the commission feels that the child cannot intellectually cope with the type of education proposed by the parents and if the parents are unwilling to change their request, the child must take a special examination to enter into the section chosen by his parents. If, on the other hand, the commission believes the child is capable of following a more difficult program than the one which has been selected, the commission tries to convince the parents to change their request (Horaires, pp. 346-360).

22. For more details on the lycée technique, see *Orientation*, pp. 9-12; and Halls, pp. 132-137.

23. For further details on the vocational schools, see *Orientation*, p. 13; and Male, pp. 131 ff.

24. *Tableaux de l'éducation nationale: édition 1968* (Paris: Ministère de l'éducation nationale, 1969), pp. 504-505.

25. For instance, see Jesse R. Pitts, "Change in Bourgeois France," in *In Search of France*, eds. Stanley Hoffmann et al. (Cambridge, Mass.: Harvard University Press, 1963), p. 288.

26. Only 24 percent of the members of the class at E.N.A. which was studied went to a religious school for the first cycle of their secondary education and 17 percent for the second cycle.

27. The results of this study are presented in a series of five articles: Alain Girard, Henri Bastide, and Guy Poucher, "Enquête nationale sur l'entrée en sixième et la démocratisation de l'enseignement," *Population* 18, no. 1 (January-March 1963); Alan Girard and Henri Bastide, "La stratification sociale et la démocratisation de l'enseignement," *Population* 18, no. 3 (July-September 1963); Paul Clerc, "La famille et l'orientation scolaire au niveau de la sixième. Enquête de juin 1963 dans l'agglomération parisienne," *Population* 19, no. 4 (August-September 1964); Alain Girard and Paul Clerc, "Nouvelles données sur l'orientation scolaire au moment de l'entreé en sixième," *Population* 19, no 5 (October-December 1964); and Alain Sauvy and Alain Girard, "Les diverses classes sociales devant l'enseignement. Mise au point générale des résultats," *Population* 20, no. 2 (March-April 1965).

28. Girard, Bastide, and Poucher, p. 34.

29. Such a comparison does not exist in any of the published articles based on the results of the survey made on the orientation and democratization of French education by the Institut national d'études démographiques.

30. In France, it has been the rule to select schools for study on the basis of personal contacts and relationships (see, for example, Annick Percheron, *L'univers politique des*

enfants, p. 47). This procedure has been followed because of the difficulties of obtaining official access to educational institutions for the purposes of research; ministry and/or académie approval is required. I was most fortunate to obtain this approval through the help of François Bourricaud and the cooperativeness of Alain Peyrefitte, Minister of Education at the time of the case study.

31. The logic behind this choice of grade levels was to include grades common to all institutions (cinquième and troisième), to catch anyone having any experience with secondary education (cinquième), to view pupils' last stage of secondary education (troisième and terminale), and to appreciate the passage from the first to the second cycle (troisième and seconde).

32. Because of length constraints, I have been unable to include a complete copy of student questionnaire in this book. I will, however, be happy to provide a mimeographed version for anyone who desires one.

TABLES

TABLE A.1: Grade Levels and Age in French Secondary Schools

Cycles	Grades	Age
First Cycle	Sixième (sixth grade)	11
	Cinquième (fifth grade)	12
	Quatrième (fourth grade)	13
	Troisième (third grade)	14
Second Cycle	Seconde (second grade)	15
	Première (first grade)	16
	Terminale (last grade)	17

TABLE A.2: Ages of Pupils at Each Grade Level in French Secondary Schools

	% with Normal Age	% Younger	% 1 Year Older	% More than 1 Year Older
Sixième	42.1	8.4	39.7	9.8
Cinquième	36.3	7.8	41.1	14.8
Quatrième	33.7	7.5	40.9	17.9
Troisième	31.1	7.1	39.2	22.6
Seconde	28.3	7.0	39.1	25.6
Première	26.1	6.4	37.9	29.6
Terminale	24.4	6.2	35.2	34.2

SOURCE: *Tableaux de l'éducation nationale: édition 1968* (Paris: Ministére de l'éducation nationale, 1969), p. 241.

TABLE A.3: The Number of Students Attending the Major Types of French Secondary Schools: 1967-1968 Academic Year

	Public Schools	Private Schools	TOTAL
Institutions of the First Cycle:			
Colleges of General Education (C.E.G.)	678,052	203,788	881,840
Lycées (sixième to troisième)	539,691	249,986	789,677
Colleges of Secondary Education (C.E.S.)	516,583		516,583
Total, First Cycle:	1,734,326	453,774	2,188,100
Institutions of the Second Cycle:			
Lycées (seconde to terminale)	417,520	142,433	559,953
Colleges of Technical Education (C.E.T.)	377,497	166,301	543,798
Lycées Technique	170,616	33,555	204,171
Ecoles Normales	19,816		19,816
Total, Second Cycle:	985,449	342,289	1,327,738
TOTAL, First and Second Cycles:	2,719,775	796,063	3,515,838

SOURCE: *Tableaux de l'éducation nationale, statistiques rétrospectives 1958-68: édition 1969* (Paris: Ministére de l'éducation nationale, no date), pp. 29, 31, 33, 35, 37, 39, 53, 55, 57, and 59.

TABLE A.4: The Choices Parents Make for the Type of Secondary Education to be Followed by Their Children—According to Social Class (in percentages)

	TOTAL	Farm Workers	Farmers	Workers	Artisans, Small Businessmen	Employees	Middle-level Executives	Liberal Professions	High-level Executives
Lycée									
Classical	16	8	8	6	19	17	37	55	61
Modern	11	5	7	9	14	17	18	16	16
C.E.G.	29	23	25	31	33	33	27	17	12
Sixième (without specifying which section)	6	2	4	5	7	7	8	6	6
Stay in primary school	38	62	56	49	27	26	10	6	5
TOTAL:	100	100	100	100	100	100	100	100	100

SOURCE: Alain Girard and Henri Bastide, "La stratification sociale et la démocratisation de l'enseignement," Population 18, no. 3 (July-September 1963), p. 443. (The results presented in this table are based on the official school records of a representative sample of 1,176 pupils.)

TABLE A.5: Student Success in Primary School—According to Social Class of Parents (in percentages)

	TOTAL	Farm Workers	Farmers	Workers	Artisans, Small Businessmen	Employees	Middle-level Executives	Liberal Professions	High-level Executives
Excellent	8	4	8	5	8	9	17	15	19
Good	27	25	28	23	29	29	39	35	36
Average	33	33	33	34	34	34	27	34	29
Mediocre	22	25	21	25	20	21	12	13	13
Bad	10	13	10	13	9	7	5	3	3
TOTAL:	100	100	100	100	100	100	100	100	100

SOURCE: Alain Girard and Henri Bastide, "La stratification sociale et la démocratization de l'enseignement," *Population* 18, no. 3 (July-September 1963), p. 438. (The results in this table are based on the grades which a representative sample of 1,176 pupils received in primary school. These grades were taken from the official school records of the pupils in the sample.)

TABLE A.6: The Social Class Composition of Public and Private Secondary Schools (in percentages)

Fathers' Profession	Public School Population	Private School Population
Farm workers	4	2
Farmers	13	26
Workers	44	23
Artisans and small businessmen	9	14
Employees	17	15
Middle-level executives	4	4
Liberal professions	2	7
High-level executives	4	7
No profession, others	3	2
TOTAL:	100	100

SOURCE: Alain Girard, Henri Bastide and Guy Pourcher, "Enquête nationale sur l'entrée en sixième et la démocratisation de l'enseignement," *Population* 18, no. 1 (January-March 1963), p. 35. (The results presented in this table are based on the official records of a representative sample of 1,176 French pupils.)

TABLE A.7: Type of Secondary Education (Public or Private) Received by Children from Different Social Classes

Fathers' Profession	Percentage in the Public Schools	Percentage in the Private Schools
Farm workers	86	14
Farmers	60	40
Workers	85	15
Artisans and small businessmen	66	34
Employees	77	23
Middle-level executives	75	25
Liberal professions	46	54
High-level executives	63	37
No profession, others	82	18

SOURCE: The statistics presented in Table A.6 were adjusted on the assumption that exactly 75% of all secondary school pupils were in the public schools and 25% in the private schools. In fact, 77.4% are in public and 22.6% in private schools (based on the statistics in Table A.3).

TABLE A.8: Student Questionnaires: According to Grade and Program of Study

	Classique[a]		Moderne[a]		Moderne[a] Courte		A[b]		C[b]		D[b]		TOTAL	
	%	N	%	N	%	N	%	N	%	N	%	N	%	N
Cinquième	9	166	8	153	11	212							28	531
Troisième	9	174	11	215	14	272							34	661
Seconde							7	130	9	174			16	304
Terminale							7	136	7	125	8	144	22	405
TOTAL:	18	340	19	368	25	484	14	266	16	299	8	144	100	1901

a. These sections only exist within the first cycle of studies. Classique and moderne are the lycée sections, and moderne courte is the C.E.G. section.

b. These sections only exist within the second cycle of lycées. "A" identifies the literary program; "C," the mathematics program; and "D," the program in experimental sciences.

TABLE A.9: Teacher Interviews: According to Type of School and
Subject Matter of Respondents

	C.E.G. N	C.E.S. N	C.E.S.-Lycée N	Lycée N	TOTAL N
Literary subjects: French, history, geography, philosophy, Latin, Greek, and civics	7	3	10	21	41
Scientific subjects: physics, chemistry, mathematics, and natural sciences	9	1	4	13	27
Modern foreign languages: English and German	4	2	2	5	13
Physical Education:				1	1
TOTAL:	20	6	16	40	82

APPENDIX B
ECOLE NATIONALE D'ADMINISTRATION: THE SETTING

The Importance of the School

The *Ecole Nationale d'Administration* (National School of Administration—E.N.A.) was created in 1945 by an "ordinance"[1] of the provisional government which sought to reform the upper grades of the civil service. The motivating force behind the reform was a desire to modernize the French administration. Prior to the establishment of E.N.A., each service recruited its own top level personnel. The result was an overspecialized and compartmentalized civil service. In addition, the training necessary for passing the entrance exams could best be obtained at the *Ecole Libre des Sciences Politiques,* which catered largely to members of the upper social classes living in Paris. Hence, recruitment into the highest levels of the civil service was not "democratic." Another disadvantage of the pre-World War II system which the reform sought to correct was the absence of a period of apprenticeship for young civil servants before they were actually given a position of responsibility. Finally, within the existing system, there was a tendency to stifle individual initiative and creativity, because highly trained and capable individuals often spent many years doing little more than menial jobs as a result of an insufficient division of labor.[2]

While many of the goals sought through the creation of E.N.A. have not been totally achieved, the reform did centralize recruitment to the upper echelons of the civil service. Two factors prevent the alumni of the National School of Administration from monopolizing the positions of control in the French administrative structure. First of all, many of the senior members of the civil service were recruited prior to the creation of the school. These men, however, will be retiring within the next ten to twenty years, and they will be replaced by E.N.A. graduates. Second, in those ministries dealing with technical problems which demand a specialized form of expertise, E.N.A.s have had to and will continue to have to share power with technical experts. For example, doctors play an important role in the Ministry of Public Health, and engineers who graduated from the very prestigious *Ecole Polytechnique* tend to occupy as many, if not more, important positions than the alumni of E.N.A. in the Ministry of Industry.

Given these caveats, E.N.A. remains an agency of administrative elite recruitment par excellence. Already graduates of the school dominate the Grands Corps[3] (Conseil d'état—Council of State; Cour des Comptes—Court of Accounts; and Inspection des Finances—Inspectorate of Finances).[4] For example, in 1974, 138 of the 262 members of the Conseil d'état (52.7 percent) were E.N.A. graduates. More importantly, since the Conseil has four ranks through which a member virtually automatically climbs with increasing age and seniority, it is significant that at the highest echelon (Conseillers d'état), in 1969 there were no E.N.A.s, but five years later there were 11 (out of 108), 10.2 percent; the percentage of E.N.A. alumni at the next highest rank (Maîtres des requêtes) progressed from 64 percent (87 out of 135) in 1969 to 78 percent (95 out of 122) in 1974.[5]

The Grands Corps provides a pool from which the directors in the various ministries as well as the ministerial cabinets tend to be selected.[6] Graduates of E.N.A., including but not limited to members of the Council of State, the Court of Accounts, and the Inspectorate of Finances, are gradually rising to positions of high prestige and power in the administration. From 1960 to 1967, the percentage of directeurs (heads of the major divisions of a ministry) who graduated from E.N.A. increased from 7.2 percent to 14.5 percent.[7] And, in 1974, for example, two of the six (33 percent) directeurs in the Ministry of Cultural Affairs, six of the twelve (50 percent) directeurs in the Ministry of the Interior, and nine of the thirteen (69 percent) directeurs in the Ministry of the Economy and Finance were E.N.A. alumni.[8] A similar trend is apparent among the members of the ministerial cabinets; in 1958, 11 percent were E.N.A.s; in 1960, 17.6 percent; and in 1968, 32.6 percent.[9] Moreover, in the first government formed under the presidency of Georges Pompidou, nineteen of the thirty-nine *directeurs de cabinet*[10] (49 percent) had attended the National School of Administration.[11]

E.N.A. alumni do not simply play a key role in the administrative world. Increasingly, they are moving into important political positions. Graduates of the school are being elected to the National Assembly. They are also entering the government. For example, three of the nineteen ministers (15.8 percent) in President Pompidou's first cabinet (1968) and eight of the sixteen ministers (50 percent) in his last government (1974) were E.N.A.s. Finally (and certainly one of the most striking indicators of the role played by the school in French political life), the three most important and powerful individuals in the actual government (President Valéry Giscard d'Estaing, Prime Minister Jacques Chirac, and Minister of State, Minister of the Interior Michel Poniatowski) are all E.N.A.s. Moreover, key people in the left opposition—such as Michel Rocard and Jacques Attali—are also graduates of the school. One might conclude that as long as France continues to place a high value on expertise and efficiency, many E.N.A.s will probably continue to move from the administrative to the political world.

The Structure and Organization of the E.N.A. System[12]

THE "MANAGEMENT" OF E.N.A.

The National School of Administration is an educational institution with no hierarchical relationship with the Ministry of National Education. Rather, E.N.A. is subordinated to the office of the Prime Minister. A lengthy and detailed series of legislative and governmental decrees and "ordinances" determine the way the school functions.[13] The daily management of E.N.A. is carried on by a director selected by the Council of Ministers.[14] The director is "assisted" in his work by a *Conseil d'administration* (Administrative Council).[15] This council has eighteen members and meets once a month. By law, the compositions of the council is as follows: the vice president of the Conseil d'état, the general director of the administration and the public service, five university professors or administrators, five civil servants, three people not in the public service, two individuals nominated by the civil servants' unions, and an alumnus of E.N.A.[16] In fact, the council oversees the activities of the director and often decides how to resolve a particular problem.

Besides the director of E.N.A., there are three other important members of the school administration who handle problems of daily operation. The *Secrétaire général* is in charge of all matters pertaining to finances and the physical operation of the school. The *Directeur des études* handles all curriculum-centered matters. The *Directeur des stages* (director of the in-service training periods) controls those aspects of the school's program in which the pupil is not pursuing academic studies but is rather working in a préfecture or embassy.

Thus, the basic elements of the E.N.A. program have been determined by governmental laws and "ordinances." The application of these rules is largely in the hands of the directors of study and in-service training. The major role played by the director of E.N.A. is to coordinate and supervise the school's functioning. The Administrative Council seeks to ensure that the rules are being properly applied and aids the administration in resolving problems not foreseen by the governmental regulations.

ADMISSIONS PROCEDURES

There are two distinct but parallel channels of entrance to E.N.A.: The first is open to students less than twenty-five years old, with a university degree (e.g., a license); the other is reserved for civil servants, less than thirty years old,[17] who have worked for the state for at least five years.[18] The minister (or secretary of state) of the public service decides how many people will be admitted to the school each year (recently, the figure has been approximately 100). Normally, two-thirds of the places go to individuals trying to gain access through the students' channel and one-third to those using the civil servants' channel.

A student who wishes to enter E.N.A. must first take a series of long and difficult written examinations which seek to test his knowledge of modern history, economics, political science, and a foreign language. The examinations in the social sciences give the student between four and six hours to write an essay in response to a given question—e.g., "Is the search for security compatible with progress in contemporary societies?"[19] The applicant's competence in a foreign language is measured by the accuracy with which he translates a passage in that language into French. These essays are anonymously examined and appraised by a panel of judges. Only about twenty-five percent of the students pass the competitive examinations.[20]

The successful students are called *admissible;* they are allowed to take a second series of examinations, all of which are oral and, as in the case of the first group of tests, are graded by a panel of judges. Even if all the students who took both sets of examinations were considered by the judges as capable of doing good work at E.N.A., only a limited percentage could be admitted, the actual number being determined by the minister or secretary of state in charge of the public service. To decide which of the candidates are to be chosen, the judges develop a rank ordering of students who passed the written exams and a second ordering based on the oral examinations. Then, if, say, sixty-six students can be admitted to E.N.A., those who were classified one through sixty-six (based upon an average of their positions on the two sets of exams) are admitted. Finally, a list of the students admitted along with their precise position in the rank ordering is published. This list with class rank is called the *classement.*

As in the case of the students, the civil servants must first pass a series of written examinations before they are allowed to take the oral exams. Their exams are quite similar in style and content to those taken by the students but are easier to pass. As a result, there are a certain number of *faux fonctionnaires* (false civil servants). The faux fonctionnaires are usually students who, desiring to enter E.N.A. but lacking self-confidence, take a job in an educational institution (as, for instance, surveillant or primary school teacher) and after the required years of service take the school's entrance exams.

In fact, few of the civil servants present themselves directly for the entrance examinations. Most of them first take a preliminary examination, the passage of which permits them to follow a course of study designed as preparation for the entrance examinations. These studies take either a year or two years to complete, during which time the civil servant is on leave with pay from his agency. Since the entrance examinations to the school basically measure academic knowledge, and since most civil servants have been out of contact with the university for quite a few years, a civil servant who has not followed the preparatory cycle of studies has little chance of gaining admittance to E.N.A.

So far a summary of the official procedure for entering the National School of Administration has been presented.[21] However, a series of factors that are not part of the official procedures play an important role in determining which of the student candidates will have the best chances of being admitted. First, those who have studied at Paris' Institut d'Etudes Politiques (Institute of Political Studies, popularly known as Sciences Po) have a tremendous advantage over the other candidates. The subject matter of Sciences Po, as well as the intellectual and rhetorical training received there, give one an excellent preparation for E.N.A.'s entrance examinations. Second, those students who have followed the year-long preparation for the E.N.A. exams which is given at Sciences Po to those who have a diploma from an Institute of Political Studies[22] are particularly well equipped for passing the exams. The instructors in this section are civil servants who graduated from the school and thus are prepared, on the basis of personal experience, to teach their students how to pass the entrance examinations. Third, some students participate in the infamous *écuries* system—i.e., a small group of students from wealthy families hire a young, brilliant civil servant who has recently graduated from E.N.A. to tutor them for the entrance examinations. Finally, and by no means least, students from the lower strata of French society who have managed to pass over the hurdles placed in their way by the secondary and higher educational system are at a distinct disadvantage when taking the E.N.A. exams which place a premium on culturally transmitted knowledge and rhetorical style. A combination of these four factors helps to explain why the overwhelming proportion of the students admitted to the school reside in the Parisian region (90 percent), have studied at Science Po (70 percent), and come from the higher strata of French society (82 percent).[23]

THE PROGRAM OF STUDIES: THE ADMINISTRATIVE STAGE

Students and civil servants who pass the written entrance examinations in September and the orals in December are notified at the end of December that they are admitted to E.N.A. The former students are now *fonctionnaires stagiaires* (individuals being trained to be civil servants), and the distinction between those who entered the school by the different channels of access, officially at least, ceases. In January, the new E.N.A.s attend a series of meetings with the school's directors to receive further information on their forthcoming program of studies. In addition, each has a short, private meeting with the director of stages and the director of the school.

Then, in mid-February the student-civil servants begin a year's on-the-job training period (i.e., stage) in an important French administrative agency. Most are sent to various préfectures to work with the préfet and his colleagues, who represent the central government in the provinces and implement its decisions. About a half-dozen of the new E.N.A.s will go to a French embassy for the major portion of their stage and will spend only the last three months in a préfecture. Others will be sent to work with the governors of French territories.[24] Another group (about ten or twelve), whose studies inadequately prepared them for the courses they will be taking, is sent to Grenoble for a few months of intensive study before beginning the stage.[25]

The director of stages decides where each new E.N.A. is to be sent.[26] The student-civil servant is called into the director of stages' office for a short conversation in which he is asked where he would like to spend his stage. In theory, the student's placement is determined by three criteria. He will not be placed in a region which he knows. An attempt will be made to satisfy the student's expressed desire, especially in the sense that he will not be sent to a large préfecture if he has requested a small one. Finally, given that the director of stages knows the préfets relatively well, he tries to place the student with the type of préfet with whom he should be able to get along and have a successful stage. These theoretical guides are followed rather closely in practice, although a small number of students complain that they were sent to a préfecture which was totally different from the type they requested. In addition, given that the criteria used by the director of stages to determine whether there is good psychological fit between préfet and E.N.A. student are personal, intuitive, and with no reliable basis (i.e., the director hardly knows the students and they have not been given a battery of tests), it naturally follows that there are some cases in which incompatible personality types are thrown together.

During the year-long stage, the student-civil servants are placed in direct and close contact with the men who literally run France. For the former "students," who are normally well-versed in the theory of French administration but largely ignorant of its practice, as well as for the "civil servants," who have rarely been exposed to the high-level coordinating functions of the administration, this is an extremely novel and often trying experience. They work with a group of important decision makers (the préfet, the director of his cabinet, the secretary general of the préfecture, etc.) and often participate in or contribute to the decision-making process.[27] To the outside world, they have suddenly become important people. Occupying this new role, especially for those who have come directly from the university, often has an immense psychological effect.

Normally, the stagiaire is not given a particular position in the préfecture. Through a combined process of being asked to do certain tasks by the highest-level superordinates in the unit and soliciting work from them, the new E.N.A. gradually carves out a domain of competence in which he will do most of his work. During the summer vacation, the stagiaire may assume the post of Directeur du Cabinet (the préfet's staff director) for a few weeks.[28] Some E.N.A. students occupy this position (or a similar one) for a longer period of time, sometimes for a few months or even during their entire stage. This occurs when the post is vacant because the former occupant has left and a replacement has not yet been chosen.

Throughout the stage, contact is maintained with the school in four tangential ways. First, the student must write two short (approximately eight-page, single-spaced typed) *compte-rendus* which are sent to the school administration. These papers summarize the student's activities during the stage. One is written after being in the field for about four months and the other after eight months' experience. Before these can be sent to E.N.A., they must be seen, approved, and signed by the head of the stage (e.g., the préfet). Second, once during the year, either the director of stages or his assistant comes to visit each student and discusses with him as well as with the other members of the préfecture the work he has been doing. This "inspection" normally lasts only a day or two. The third form of contact occurs through a series of conferences where about a dozen stagiaires from the same geographical region are brought together for a few days of discussion. The director of the school usually attends these conferences. Finally, the last month or so of the student's stage is absorbed by writing his *mémoire de stage*. This is a twenty-five-page, single-spaced, typewritten paper examining an issue of importance to the geographical area within which the stagiaire worked. Theoretically, it should be closely associated with the work the student has been doing. In reality, it sometimes tends to be a research project on a particular local problem. Guidelines for what can be done are established by the school administration, and the actual topic must be approved by the préfet.

Grades play a fundamental role in determining the behavior of E.N.A. students. One general grade is given for performance during the stage and a second for the mémoire. The former represents thirteen percent of the student's final grade used for determining his classement, and the mémoire represents five percent. Thus, these two grades significantly affect how the student will be ranked at the end of his course of study, and it is this ranking which will determine the type of job he will obtain.

Since the stagiaire is assigned to a préfet who is considered his boss—i.e., his instructor and judge—it might be assumed that this man's appreciation of the student's performance during the year should play a very important role in determining how the stage will be graded. In fact, it is the director of stages at E.N.A. who determines what grade each individual will receive. His decision is based on three criteria: (1) the compte-rendus written by the stagiaire; (2) his or his assistant's perception of the student's performance during the past year, as gleaned from their inspection; and (3) a questionnaire sent by E.N.A. to each préfet in which a series of relatively precise questions is asked and a general estimate of the character and ability of the stagiaire is sought.[29]

The justification for not allowing each préfet to have grading power over his stagiaire is that certain préfets have a tendency to see all their stagiaires as excellent while others would judge all as mediocre. By using the questionnaire technique which prevents the préfet from simply giving a vague appraisal of the student and forces him to concentrate on certain aspects of the stagiaire's experience–considered the most important ones by the school's administration–and by adjusting the results obtained from the questionnaire in light of the director of stages' personal estimate as gathered from the compte-rendus and the inspection, it is claimed that a certain equality on the level of the bases which determine the grade is created. Unfortunately, this system has a certain number of unintended and inequitable results. The stagiaire, working on a daily basis with his préfet and not with the director of stages, attempts to please and satisfy the préfet. If he is successful in this endeavor, he continues to behave in the same manner and assumes he is doing well. But, in certain cases, to satisfy the préfet is not equal or even close to satisfying the director of stages; and since the stagiaire has personal contact with the former and not with the latter, he tends to assume that it is of greatest importance to win the praise of the people who are close to him. Even if the stagiaire perceives an incompatibility in trying to live up to the expectations of his two judges, either he will have psychological difficulties in rejecting the need to win the approbation of the préfet, or, if he does not, he will be caught on the horns of a dilemma because the préfet, if antagonized by the stagiaire's activity, can easily place a large number of stumbling blocks in his way which will make it very difficult for the stagiaire to satisfy the director of stages.

As has been mentioned, the school administration gives the stagiaires instructions as to what subjects can form the basis of their mémoires.[30] Then the student selects a precise topic which must be approved by both his préfet and the school administration. Once completed, this document is examined and graded by a jury of three people.[31] In theory, the grade given for the mémoire is not at all affected by the stage itself. In fact, since the jury interviews both the student and the director of stages to learn about "the conditions in which the students have chosen their subject and written their mémoire,"[32] it is inevitable that the appraisal of the stagiaire formed by the director of stages will affect, even if only slightly, the grade given on the mémoire.

THE PROGRAM OF STUDIES: THE ACADEMIC PROGRAM

After completing their stages, in December, all the students in the *promotion* (i.e., the class) are brought together for a short ski holiday in the Alps. The purpose of this vacation is to provide an opportunity for the E.N.A.s to get to know each other and to develop an esprit de corps. However, since skiing in France is a bourgeois sport, a form of class cleavage tends to develop between those who can and cannot ski. The former civil servants tend to develop a certain group solidarity based on their common inability to ski and their similar life experiences, which are different from those of the former students. (They are normally six or seven years older, married, have children, come from relatively modest social backgrounds,[33] and have been employed for the past few years of their life.)

Besides crystallizing a cleavage between the E.N.A.s who were admitted to the school through different channels, the ski holiday serves as a terrain on which political campaigning begins. Each promotion at E.N.A. elects members of a *délégation*. This group (composed of almost ten percent of the class) serves as a transmission belt between the students and the administration, passing information down and complaints and difficulties up. During the ski holiday, individuals who wish to get elected to the délégation try to win support for their candidacy.

Once the ski holiday is over, everyone goes to Paris and a seventeen-month period of course work begins. The curriculum is divided into four parts. The first trimester, which starts in January and is completed just before the Easter vacation, is composed of a series of seminars on administrative and judicial affairs. From after the Easter recess until July, when summer vacation begins, there are seminars on economic and financial affairs. From September to December, the topic of study is international affairs. Finally, from January to March of the second year of classes, there are seminars on social problems.[34] The actual content of these courses is not new for many of the students, especially for those who have been at Sciences Po.

In addition to these regular courses, there are classes in foreign languages (each individual must study two), a series of nongraded, nonrequired courses on such subjects as statistics and communication theory, and physical education classes. To round out their program of study, students have a short, one-month stage in a private enterprise. During this stage, they might occupy such diverse functions as reporter or coal miner.

E.N.A.'s seminar method of study requires a small number of students in each class. The director of studies creates a series of groups of ten to twelve students for all of the courses offered in a given trimester.[35] The criteria used for organizing these groups vary only slightly from trimester to trimester and are constantly characterized by an attempt to create equally heterogeneous groups. The goal is to establish a series of seminars each having students with equally good and poor records of past academic performance.[36]

The grading system used for seminar work at E.N.A. explains why this goal of equally heterogeneous groups is sought. Students receive two grades for each trimester's work: one based on an anonymously corrected examination taken at the end of each trimester to test knowledge of the subject matter studied in the various seminars, and the other based on a combination of the grades given by each teacher in each seminar. Since grades are the only real sanction or reward which exist at E.N.A. and since each small seminar group has a different teacher, the school administration felt it necessary to establish a system which would equalize the opportunity of students in different groups and would eliminate the difference between a hard and an easy marker. The system chosen requires that the average of the grades given in each seminar be thirteen.[37] Given this system, if students were placed in different groups on a random basis, some seminars would have more good students than other seminars, and these good students would have a more difficult time obtaining a high grade than good students who were in seminars composed largely of mediocre people. As a result, the director of studies tries to create a series of equally heterogeneous groups.

Putting this theory into practice is relatively successful. The enforced average of thirteen is the aspect of the system which can be most seriously questioned, because the idea that an equality among the tendencies of the various teachers is thereby established is not really valid. Certain instructors may cluster their grades around the magical number thirteen because they underestimate the performances of their better students and see everyone within the same mediocre mass; others who may see "stars" among their pupils will be forced by the system to give lower grades than really deserved to the less brilliant members of the class.

The grading system for the written examinations is also characterized by an extreme concern for equality. The paper used by the students has a small box in the upper righthand corner of the top page. There are matching numbers in this box and on the paper. The student writes his name in the box. Once the paper is handed in, this box is cut out, leaving only a numbered paper which is judged by a panel of three people who decide what grade it deserves. Once all the grades are determined, the director of studies is informed and reassigns the grade to a name.

One striking feature of E.N.A. is the lack of a permanent teaching staff. The regular seminars are led by men who generally occupy civil service positions of a rather high level.[38] They are recruited by the school to teach two hours per week for a single trimester. The rest of their time is spent fulfilling their official functions. A large proportion of these instructors are graduates of E.N.A. All who accept teaching positions do so more for the honor than for the "honoraria," which are quite modest. The same system applies to the language teachers, except that, rather than being civil servants, they are university professors.

CLASSEMENT

Prior to the time when the 1967 promotion[39] entered E.N.A., the students were periodically informed of their rank in class—i.e., once the grades for the stage had been determined, a classement of the promotion was put up on the bulletin board, and this was constantly revised each time a new set of grades had been handed out. This practice was done away with in an attempt to reduce the very high level of competitiveness which has traditionally characterized the atmosphere at E.N.A. There is some question as to how successful and durable the new system will be. Within a couple of months after the end of their stage, the students were given their grades. Then, through a network of private discussions, students learned what most of their classmates had received. Thus, the basis on which competitiveness was built continues to exist, albeit with a lower degree of precision. Since classement at the end of one's studies (classement de sortie) determines what civil service position, career, and prestige the student will obtain, the uncertainty under the present system about how well one is doing might press the students to request a return to periodic public classements so as to reduce the problem of psychological adjustment to their forthcoming career.

Much of the E.N.A. system cannot be clearly understood without reference to this all-important classement de sortie. In April-May of the last year at E.N.A., the school administration, using a weighted average of the grades received by each student during the past two and one-half years, makes a rank-ordering of the members of the promotion.[40] This is then made public and serves as the base on which the various posts offered by the ministries and public agencies are distributed—i.e., among the available jobs, the students choose whichever position they want with the first person in the class having first choice, the second person, second choice, etc. Since the status, interest, and career possibilities vary significantly from post to post, being as well *classé* as possible has crucial importance for each student. The first fifteen to twenty will usually choose one of the three Grands Corps (the traditionally accepted order of preference being Inspection des finances, Conseil d'état, and Cour des comptes). Membership in one of these three bodies carries with it the highest status, a promise that ten years henceforth one will have the highest of salaries, and the greatest potential for becoming an administrative head of one of the ministries. The next twenty or so students on the list of classement tend to choose the Ministry of Foreign Affairs or the Ministry of the Interior. Some of these, as well as the next fifteen or so, will go to the Ministry of Economic Affairs and Finance and the Agency of Economic Expansion Abroad. For those students not among the first fifty-five, a choice will be made among the remaining posts with an attempt to choose the one which personally seems to be the least undesirable, with the lowest-ranked members of the promotion recently going to the Ministries of Social Affairs, Cultural Affairs, or National Education.

Under this system, the last person in the class could go to the Inspection des finances if no one in front of him had chosen one of the offered posts. In fact, this possibility remains purely theoretical.[41]

The Sources

The major portion of my research at E.N.A. took place from May through July 1968. Besides observing the students' activities during the period of crisis at the school, fifty percent of the members of the 1967 promotion (i.e., the only class in attendance at E.N.A. during this time) were randomly selected for nondirective interviews. These interviews took between thirty-five and sixty minutes to administer. They sought to tap the students' behavior and attitudes toward four distinct groups of people: their superordinates during the stage, their teachers at E.N.A., the members of the school's administration, and their classmates. In addition, at attempt was made to determine what the students' attitudes toward E.N.A. had been prior to the crisis, and what effect the crisis had had on these attitudes.

In a nondirective interview, the interviewer poses a very general and neutral question to the interviewee (e.g., "Would you tell me a bit about the contacts you had during the stage? "). Then the interviewer interjects, from time to time, a brief remark (e.g., "How? " or "More precisely? ") so as to guide the respondent toward particular problems and questions. The goal of this technique is to replicate a "confessional" atmosphere. A nondirective interview can only be successful if the interviewee trusts the interviewer and perceives him to be a peer or, at most, mildly superior, but not in any way threatening.

A combination of reasons led to the use of nondirective rather than structured (either open- or close-ended) interviews. E.N.A. students tend to have highly developed rhetorical skills and often speak about the environment in which they live in totally impersonal terms. In a "normal" interview, many students might have analyzed what, for instance, a stage or a préfet is like without ever describing the particularities of *their* stage or *their* attitudes toward it. The nondirective interview served to curb these impersonal tendencies. In addition, the students at the National

School of Administration are hesitant to express their own opinions. Most tend to guard their views and to express for public consumption views which they perceive as acceptable to their audience. A "normal" interview might have helped the respondent to keep up his guard, but a nondirective interview had the potential of penetrating to the level of his personally felt opinions and actual, lived experiences.

Before any interviewing was done, I spent approximately one month with the students, observing their committee meetings and discussions. This gave them an opportunity to know me and to learn to trust me.

In order for the interview results to be analyzed, they had to be tape-recorded. Thus, before each interview began, the respondent was asked if he objected to having our session recorded (none did).[42] During the interview, the microphone was put in an inconspicuous place so that after the respondent had spoken for a few moments, he would no longer be acutely aware of its presence.

May through July 1968 was hardly a normal period in the history of the National School of Administration. The students, with the hesitant approval of the school's administration, were working on a reform project for E.N.A. and the French civil service; the normal program of courses had been suspended; and the relations between the students and their superordinates ranged from tolerance to outright hostility and conflict. To observe the school during a more routine period of time and to permit an analysis of the differences and similarities between normal and crisis periods, I returned to E.N.A. for a few weeks in February-March 1969 (this being the latest time I could return and still observe the same students who had gone through the crisis). At the time of my return, a new cohort of students (the 1968 promotion) had just begun their academic program of studies. Since they had not participated in the crisis, and since there was some reason to believe that the crisis may have left a durable imprint on those who had participated in it, I also studied these students during my second research visit to the school.

In February-March 1969, I randomly chose forty percent of those students whom I had interviewed in 1968 and gave them another nondirective interview, going over the same terrain which had been covered previously. (Table B.1 indicates the representativeness of my sample, in at least one sense: It breaks down the 1967 promotion, as well as the students who were interviewed in 1968 and 1969, according to the channel of access through which they were admitted to E.N.A.) In addition, I observed the classes followed by the two promotions. Finally, each group was asked to respond to a questionnaire. (Table B.2 shows the number and percentage of students in the two promotions who filled out the questionnaire. A much higher percentage of the students in the 1967 promotion—ninety percent compared to fifty-six percent—responded to the questionnaire. This difference, I believe, is largely attributable to the fact that they knew me well and, therefore, trusted me more than the students in the 1968 promotion.)

NOTES

1. An *ordonnance* is quite different from an American ordinance or an executive order. Rather, the French parliament may authorize the Government to make rules having the force of law in a domain which is normally under the legislature's competence. Such rules are called ordonnances.

2. That these were, in fact, the motivating forces for the administrative reform is clearly expressed in the law enacted by the provisional government (see "Ordonnance No. 45-2283 du octobre 1945," *Journal Officiel* [October 1945]).

3. The term Grand Corps is a customary rather than a legal concept. Sometimes included in this category are the major technical corps (e.g., mines and ponts et chaussées) and the major nontechnical corps (Conseil d'état, Cours des comptes, Inspection des finances, the prefectoral and diplomatic corps). E.N.A. is *the* recruitment agency for all these nontechnical corps. My restricted usage of the term "Grands Corps" follows the practice employed by E.N.A. students.

4. For a discussion of the role played by these three agencies, as well as for a description of the functions they perform, see Pierre Escoube, *Les Grands Corps de l'état* (Paris: Presses Universitaires de France, 1971); Charles E. Freedeman, *The Conseil d'Etat in Modern France* (New York: Columbia University Press, 1960); Pierre Lalumière, *L'Inspection des finances* (Paris: Presses Universitaires de France, 1959); Marie-Christine Kessler, *Le Conseil d'état* (Paris: Armand Colin, Cahiers de la Fondation nationale des sciences politiques, 1968); Margherita Rendel, *The Administrative Functions of the French Conseil d'Etat* (London: Weidenfeld & Nicholson, 1970); and Pierrette Rongère, *La Cour des comptes,* Thèse de doctorat de recherche (Paris: Fondation nationale des sciences politiques, 1963).

5. These statistics are based on the list of the highest civil servants contained in the *Répertoire permanent de l'administration française: Année 1969* (Paris: La Documentation Française, 1969), *Répertoire permanent de l'administration française, 1974* (Paris: La Documentation Française, 1974), and the names of E.N.A. alumni as given in the school's *Anciens élèves de l'Ecole National d'Administration.*

6. For further details, see especially Ezra N. Suleiman, *Politics, Power and Bureaucracy in France: The Administrative Elite*, pp. 239-281.

7. Jeanne Siwek-Pouydesseau, *Le personnel de direction des ministères: Cabinets ministériels et directeurs d'administrations centrales* (Paris: Armand Colin, 1969), p. 59.

8. These statistics were calculated on the basis of the information presented in *Répertoire permanent de l'administration française, 1974* and *Anciens élèves de l'Ecole Nationale d'Administration.*

9. Siwek-Pouydesseau, *Le personnel de direction des ministères*, p. 41.

10. Each minister and secretary of state in the Government chooses a civil servant to head his personal staff and oversee the administration of the ministry; this civil servant is called a *directeur de cabinet.*

11. Data on the characteristics of E.N.A. graduates who have served in ministerial cabinets are presented in Jean-Luc Bodiguel, "Les anciens élèves de l'ENA et les cabinets ministériels," *Annuaire International de la Fonction Publique, 1973-1974* (Paris: I.I.A.P., 1974), pp. 359-381.

12. The information given in this section describes the E.N.A. system as it was during the time of the case study. The system of admissions and program of studies is being revised; the first group of students to whom the reform will fully apply will graduate in 1976. The altered system is not described because the students who were studied never had contact with it.

13. These "ordinances" and decrees can be found in Ecole Nationale d'Administration, *Concours et scolarité* (Paris: Imprimerie Nationale, 1964), pp. 145-197.

14. Since the founding of the school, there have been three directors, all of whom were members of the Conseil d'état.

15. "Ordonnance du 9 octobre 1945," Art. 6 in *Concours et scolarité*, p. 149.

16. "Décret No 58-1249 du 13 decembre 1958," Titre III, Article 41, ibid., pp. 164-165.

17. This age limit is increased by one year for each child the candidate has.

18. In addition to these channels, two graduates from among the top 100 of the 300 students at the prestigious Ecole Polytechnique are automatically admitted each year simply on request.

19. This question was on the 1967 examinations. (Ecole Nationale d'Administration, *Epreuves et statistiques des concours de 1967* [Paris: Imprimerie nationale, 1968], p. 66).

20. In 1967, 726 signed up to take the exams, 629 actually did, and only 138 passed (ibid., p. 104).

21. For a complete description of the official procedure, see "Décret No 65-986 du 24 novembre 1965," *Journal officiel* (November 25, 1965).

22. There are seven Institutes of Political Studies in France: Paris, Aix, Bordeaux, Grenoble, Lyon, Strasbourg, and Toulouse.

23. These statistics describe the students who took the entrance examinations in 1967. Students who have passed the examinations in other years have similar characteristics. Of the sixty-six students accepted in 1967, fifty-nine were residents of Paris or the surrounding regions, forty-six had received a diploma from the Institute of Political Studies in Paris, and fifty-four had fathers who were high-level civil servants, industrialists, executives, or professional people (see *Epreuves et statistiques des concours de 1967*, pp. 116-117, 108-111, 115). For a brief discussion of the social and geographical homogeneity of E.N.A. students, see Jean-François Kesler, "Les anciens élèves de l'Ecole Nationale d'Administration," *Revue française de science politique* 14, no. 2 (April 1964), pp. 250-253. For a more detailed and sophisticated analysis of the background of E.N.A. students, see Ezra N. Suleiman, *Politics, Power and Bureaucracy*

in France, pp. 52-63. For a polemical, but well-argued attack against this system, see Jacques Mandrin [pseud.], *L'Enarchie* (Paris: Editions de la Table Ronde, 1967). The social origins of E.N.A. students, it must be emphasized, are similar to those of students in all French institutions of higher learning (see Pierre Bourdieu and Jean-Claude Passeron, *Les Héritiers* [Paris: Editions de minuit, 1964], pp. 136-137).

24. France is composed of ninety-five départements and a series of territories–e.g., Martinique, Polynesia. The departments are administered by a préfet, while a governor is the national government's representative in a territory.

25. In fact, those men who pass the entrance examinations but have not yet fulfilled their military obligations do not start their stage right away. Rather they first enter the army or *Coopération* (the French Peace Corps) and begin the stage the following year.

26. To simplify the following discussion, I will only refer to stages in a préfecture. Of course, much of my description also applies to stages in embassies or with a governor.

27. The préfet is a decision maker at the level of applying the laws passed by parliament and the measures having the force of law issued by the Government. In this task, he is controlled by a *décrêt d'application* (i.e., rules as to how the law should be applied) issued by the Council of Ministers, as well as by certain regulations established by the Ministry of the Interior. As a result, the decision-making power of the préfecture is restricted. (For a discussion of the historical role of the préfecture, see Jeanne Siwek-Pouydesseau, *Le corps préfectoral sous la Troisième et la Quatrième République: Travaux et recherches de science politique* [Paris: Armand Colin, 1969]. For an analysis of the organization of a préfecture and the style of authority relations existing within it, see Jean-Pierre Worms, *Une préfecture comme organisation* [Paris: Copédith, 1968].)

28. This is referred to as serving an *interim* as Directeur du Cabinet. In most, but not all, cases, the stagiaire does serve an interim. Sometimes this may be in a position of responsibility other than that of director of the cabinet–e.g., as a *sous-préfet* (assistant préfet).

29. There are six general headings under which the specific questions fall: exterior elements (e.g., physical appearance), intellectual qualities, personal character, moral and psychological qualities, administrative ability, and particular qualifications for specific administrative functions.

30. These instructions are presented in Direction des Stages, Ecole Nationale d'Administration, "Thèmes de Mémoires de Stage 1968," D.S. no. 194, mimeo.

31. This procedure is used to guarantee equal treatment to all stagiaires and to eliminate the idiosyncratic corrections of a single grader.

32. Direction des stages, Ecole Nationale d'Administration, "Instruction sur le mémoire de stage," no. 195, mimeo, p. 14.

33. It has already been pointed out that about 82 percent of those who pass the entrance examinations for students come from the higher strata of French society. But only fourteen of the thirty-three men and women who passed the exams in 1967 which were reserved for practicing civil servants (i.e., 42 percent) came from similar social backgrounds (*Epreuves et statistiques des concours de 1967*, p. 115).

34. In each trimester there are usually three or four seminars for each subject matter studied. For instance, there were three seminars in the first trimester of study for the 1967 promotion: the public service; the adaptation of administrative structures to the changes in regional government; and the public law.

35. Prior to the time of my case study, these seminar groups were created just after the stage and remained the same throughout the entire course of study.

36. To illustrate this argument, let me note the specific criteria used to divide up the students for their seminars in the first and second trimesters of 1968. The nine groups

which functioned during the first trimester were created on the basis of the following three criteria. In each group, there should be three individuals who passed the examinations reserved for practicing civil servants. In addition, those former students who possessed a juridical diploma were to be dispersed so that one or two would be in each seminar. Finally, and most importantly, those who had entered through the examinations reserved for students were to be distributed according to their classement –i.e., each group was to have a similar mix of those who had done very well, moderately well, and relatively poorly. (Distribution of the former civil servants was not based on their ranking on the entrance exams.)

Three different criteria were used to create the groups of the second trimester. Those who had special competence in economic matters, as demonstrated by the possession of a license in economics or by having been in the economics' section at Sciences Po, were dispersed. Second, students were distributed according to the grades they had received during the first trimester of study. Finally, all the groups of the first trimester were to be broken down in such a manner that no one was to find the people of his first trimester seminars in his second trimester seminars. (It was very difficult and not always possible to satisfy this final criterion.) Thus, neither the channel of access through which the individual had been admitted to E.N.A. nor how well he had done on his entrance examinations played a role in determining seminar assignments after the end of the first trimester.

37. The French marking system works on a zero to twenty basis, with ten generally considered as passing and anything above fifteen as quite good.

38. Many of those who teach economic affairs as well as some other instructors occupy important positions in private enterprise.

39. The 1967 promotion is the class of students who began their stage in January 1967. They completed their studies in May 1969. They adopted the name "Jean Juarès."

40. Each grade is multiplied by a particular coefficient; the higher the coefficient, the greater the importance of the grade. The classement is made according to the number of points the student has accumulated, 2,000 being the highest possible number of points and signifying that all of the student's grades were twenty. The coefficients are as follows: administrative stage, thirteen; mémoire de stage, five; stage in a private enterprise, two; professors' grades for each group of seminars, five (since there are four groups of seminars, the total coefficient is twenty); written examinations on each of the four general subject matters covered, nine (making a total of thirty-six); two oral examinations, each having a coefficient of nine (making a total of eighteen); and examinations in the two foreign languages which have been studied, six (the examination taken in the student's first [i.e., strongest]language has a coefficient of four while the exam in the second language only has a coefficient of two).

41. The classement de sortie of each E.N.A. promotion along with the post chosen can be found in the "Chronique de l'E.N.A." which appears in *La Revue Administrative.* A list of civil service positions chosen, according to class rank, for the 1961-1965 promotions is presented in an appendix to *L'Enarchie,* pp. 156-157. The lowest-ranked person ever to go to the Inspection des finances was twenty-second, and this occurred with the "Charles de Gaulle" promotion and its "refusal" to follow the system of classement (for further details, see above, Chapter 3).

42. Some readers might wonder if there is not a contradiction between this readiness to be tape-recorded and my assertion that the E.N.A. students are guarded and hesitant to express their personal views. This would be the case, if the interviewee knew precisely what the interview was going to be about before it began. In fact, in my introduction to the interview as well as during my discussions with the students before beginning the interviewing stage, I only gave them the most general notion of what my research interests were.

TABLES

TABLE B.1: E.N.A. Interviews

	Interviewed May-July 1968		Interviewed February-March 1969		1967 Promotion[a]	
	%	N	%	N	%	N
Former students	69	31	66	12	70	63
Former civil servants	31	14	33	6	30	27
TOTAL	100	45	100	18	100	90

a. These are the statistics for the 1967 promotion as of May 1968.

TABLE B.2: E.N.A. Questionnaires: Return Rates

	1967 Promotion[a]		1968 Promotion	
	%	N	%	N
Filled out questionnaire	90	85	56	59
Did not fill out questionnaire	10	9	44	46
TOTAL	100	94	100	105

a. These are the statistics for the 1967 promotion as of February 1969.

INDEX

ABOUT THE AUTHOR

WILLIAM R. SCHONFELD received his Ph.D. from Princeton University. He is presently Associate Professor of Political Science at the School of Social Sciences, University of California–Irvine. In 1973-1974, he was a senior Fulbright Lecturer (at the Fondation Nationale des Sciences Politiques, Paris). The author of a sage Professional Paper in Comparative Politics *(Youth and Authority in France: A Study of Secondary Schools)*, he is the contributor of scholarly articles to such journals as the *Revue Française de Science Politique* and *World Politics*.